ACTIVE TECHNIQUES
AND
GROUP PSYCHOTHERAPY

ACTIVE TECHNIQUES
AND
GROUP PSYCHOTHERAPY

by

TED SARETSKY, Ph.D.

JASON ARONSON, INC.
New York, N.Y.

Copyright © 1977 by Jason Aronson, Inc.

Library of Congress Cataloging in Publication Data
Saretsky, Ted, 1932-
    Active techniques & group psychotherapy.
    Bibliography: pp. 5
    Includes index.
    1. Group psychotherapy. 2. Group relations
training. I. Title.
    RC488.S18   616.8'915   77-87149
    ISBN 0-87668-272-7

Manufactured in the United States of America

Acknowledgments

I would like to convey my warmest personal thanks to a number of people who contributed their time and effort in helping me to put this book together. Drs. Lawrence Epstein, Donald Milman, and Lorelle Saretsky read different sections of the book and offered me constructive criticism, conceptual clarification, and positive feedback which sustained my level of motivation in facing such an ambitious challenge. Drs. Elizabeth Mintz, Zanvel Liff, and George Goldman were all very generous and considerate in volunteering to be interviewed regarding their attitudes toward the theoretical and technical problems inherent in integrating new techniques in ongoing group therapy. The students in my group therapy course at the Adelphi University Postdoctoral Institute were very encouraging in their positive feedback regarding the practical application and therapeutic value of the various theoretical constructs that I was trying to formulate. Secretarial assistance was provided by Corrine Boni and Sandra Messinger, both of whom helped to shape this book into readable form.

Finally, I want to mention my psychoanalyst, the late Dr. William Menaker, whose wisdom, earthiness, and patience provided a very special model of the human being functioning as a therapist.

Epigraph: Rules of the Bands

The design of our meeting is to obey that command of God, "Confess your faults one to another, and pray one for another, that ye may be healed" (Jas. 5:16).

To this end, we intend:

1. To meet once a week, i.e. at the least.
2. To come punctually at the hour appointed, without some extraordinary reason.
3. To begin (those of us who are present) exactly at the hour, with singing or prayer.
4. To speak each of us in order, freely and plainly, the true state of our souls, with the faults we have committed in thought, word, deed, and the temptations we have felt since our last meeting.
5. To end every meeting with prayer suited to the state of each person present.
6. To desire some person among us to speak his own state first, and then to ask the rest, in order, as many and as searching questions as may be, concerning their state, sins and temptations.

Some of the questions proposed to everyone before he is admitted among us may be to this effect:

1. Have you the forgiveness of your sins?
2. Have you peace with God through our Lord Jesus Christ?
3. Have you the witness of God's Spirit with your spirit that you are a child of God?
4. Is the love of God shed abroad in your heart?
5. Has no sin, inward or outward, dominion over you?
6. Do you desire to be told of your faults?
7. Do you desire to be told of all your faults, and that plain and home?
8. Do you desire that every one of us should tell you, from time to time, whatsoever is in his heart concerning you?
9. Consider! Do you desire we should tell you whatsoever we think, whatsoever we fear, whatsoever we hear concerning you?
10. Do you desire that, in doing this we should come as close as possible; that we should cut to the quick, and search your heart to the bottom?
11. Is it your desire and design to be, on this and all other occasions, entirely open, so as to speak everything that is in your heart without exception, without disguise, and without reserve?

Any of the preceding questions may be asked as often as occasion offers; the five following at every meeting:

1. What known sins have you committed since our last meeting?
2. What temptations have you met with?
3. How were you delivered?
4. What have you thought, said, or done, of which you doubt whether it be sin or not?
5. Have you nothing you desire to keep secret?

John Wesley (1744)

Contents

Introduction

In recent years, there has been a remarkable proliferation of interest in the more active forms of group intervention. A wide variety of innovative techniques have been developed for use in such diverse settings as Synanon, "haircut" sessions with drug addicts, NTL meetings with business executives, Esalen workshops open to the general public, and community-building programs for theological students. Many of the approaches (e.g., Gestalt, nonverbal, and encounter) have come to occupy a prominent place in the methods arsenal of a growing number of psychoanalytically oriented group therapists. Unfortunately, in the profusion and tumult of today's activities with groups, the theoretical underpinnings and the contextual framework necessary for applying these new methodologies properly to ongoing group therapy are only spottily provided for in the literature (Yalom 1970).

Moreover, practically no attention has been paid to such relevant issues as: how to evaluate when it would be appropriate to introduce some of the new techniques; how the nature of resistance and the process of change are effected by these attempts to accelerate group movement rather than by slowly working through within the framework of a more traditional resistance-analysis approach; how transference is contaminated as a result of the therapist's new leadership dimension; how to assess and deal with patient refusal to cooperate with individual or group tasks; how to avoid manipulation or brainwashing and still enthusiastically encourage participation in new, potentially threatening experimental procedures.

More and more group therapists seem to agree that familiarity with many of these specialized formats and procedural aids can serve as useful additions to our repertoire of treatment interventions, but there is growing concern that they should be used systematically, for specific preconceived purposes, and not as a matter of whim or fad. I myself have practiced group therapy for the past fifteen years. My professional training, individual analysis, group therapy experience, and inner orientation have all been closely related to psychoanalytic theory. In the past five years, however, my involvement in sensitivity groups, NTL laboratories, gestalt awareness workshops, in training paraprofessionals, sitting in on Daniel Casriel's New Identity Groups, working with Jim Sachs in psychodrama, and attending several marathons with Betsy Mintz have drastically changed my perspective. I am now firmly convinced that a whole range of exciting new possibilities exists for helping group members to experience their problems more directly and to gain fresh impetus for change. At the same time, I have also become aware of the pitfalls that can be met in a blind, indiscriminate application of these new group technologies unless we are sensitive to the needs of the individual patient. My major intention in writing this book is

1. To provide a comprehensive guide to the new techniques and concepts that I have found particularly effective in facilitating group movement
2. To relate these approaches to what I consider the core of traditional group psychoanalytic theory (such concepts as the unconscious, resistance, defenses, the part the toxic introject plays in pathology)
3. To carefully examine the dangers, limitations, and precautions that should be taken into account to avoid psychiatric casualties in groups, and in addition
4. To introduce the reader to a special interest of mine, namely, the use of countertransference reactions in group for the members' benefit

The group exercises presented here are designed to add flexibility to the leadership role and supplement the spontaneous reactions of the leader and the group members. When applied they should fit into a coherent design which meets the needs of the participants. These techniques must be creatively employed, with special emphasis on proper timing, in order to further group goals and to avoid imposing inappropriate structure upon the groups. The therapist shouldn't feel called upon to use techniques as pieces of a patchwork quilt with a little bit of this and a little bit of that thrown in. Patients flourish best when the therapist can successfully help them to integrate cognition with feeling. At the same time, the therapist has to honestly assess his own motivations and counter-needs when he introduces these methods. Skilled therapists frequently see them as helpful in gaining physical release of emotions, demonstrating and giving overt expression of feelings, reducing inhibitions, and undermining defenses against a greater participation and involvement. In the hands of a self-appointed, untrained leader, with many unresolved problems himself, the lack of in-depth understanding of the powerful nature of human emotional process can prove very destructive.

After three months of group treatment, a patient was behaving very withdrawn, frightened, and passive. The therapist suggested she approach each member and tell them what she didn't like about them. In the middle of this go-around, another patient came out with a flood of abuse directed at the shy woman. The therapist became impatient with her resistance to continue in the exercise and urged her on. The woman became hysterical, ran out of the room, and subsequently dropped out of treatment.

The therapist must constantly make careful judgments of readiness and foster the climate for voluntary, rather than coercive, participation. In this case, the therapist manifested a countertransferential need to express frustrated anger toward a patient who was thwarting his wish for a confronting, verbal group. This prompted him to displace his anger by precipitously encouraging the patient to act out her feelings, eliciting a hostile response that unconsciously served the purpose of punishing her for her uncooperative attitude vis-a-vis the therapist.

On the other hand, when a love-in celebration solely is promoted, there is no opportunity for the proper working through of repressed rage. As Liff (1970) has pointed out, the bad introject figure remains repressed and is unlikely to be resolved by tokens of unconditional, indiscriminate acceptance. There is an illusion of reconstructive change which in reality is only transitory, palliative relief. I think that it is extremely important to be aware when a confrontation is therapeutic and when it operates only to prevent the individual from working through unpleasant experiences that he or she really needs to go through. The expression, "Red Cross nurse," has been coined for the person who immediately comforts anyone who is upset. It is the technical responsibility of the leader to stop such a person, because experiencing one's own basic pain, facing it, and coming out at the other end of the tunnel, has to be gone through alone. Premature solicitousness smothers such opportunities. Moreover, there does not seem to be any carry-over from the bubble of compassion and too earnest motherliness. The unconscious drive toward regressive fusion experiences prompts patients to want to chuck the pesky details of everyday living, transcend their ingrained suspiciousness and distrust, break through loneliness barriers, and satisfy their craving for instantaneous contact and connection. The movie, *Bob and Carol, and Ted and Alice* savagely caricatured this love–love tendency and suggested that it is difficult to reconcile communal emotional celebrations with the realities of every day life.

> One therapist suggested that an impotent man and a frigid woman play-act sexual intercourse in front of the group by asking the woman to cup her hands in the shape of a vagina with the man using his forefinger as a penis. Supervision revealed the therapist's negative identification with the male patient's passivity. While pressuring him to embarrass himself in front of the group, the therapist was artificially elevating his own ambivalent masculinity by pushing for a task that would show him as freethinking and liberated.

The clinician who has been exposed to those techniques and concepts at workshops and seminars has found them meaningful, and through careful experimentation discovers that they fit in with his personal style, is not an issue here. Unfortunately, many inexperienced marginal professionals have learned that sensory awareness exercises and nonverbal techniques yield very dramatic results. Consequently, they employ a buckshot approach, offering a smorgasbord of intervention possibilities, straining to put on a good show, and most often turn the session into a therapy charade, where these entertaining games become ends in themselves. Moreover, group leaders must resist pressure from participants who consider them squares if they aren't hip to the new wave. Patients have often heard sensational accounts of Esalen-type weekends, and want to experience them for themselves. Popularization soon becomes vulgarization of technique. Out of context, and in the absence of a sound rationale, nonverbal techniques take on the aspect of a cult and at the very least, reflect a lack of professionalism.

Five years ago, it was the very rare therapist who did not have to prepare his patients carefully for group therapy. Many journal articles were written on how long a patient should be in individual psychotherapy before he went into a group, how to broach the idea of group to the patient, how to deal with his resistance to the suggestion, etc. The recent upsurge of popularity in group experiences apart from psychotherapy proper (e.g., weekend marathons, sensitivity groups in college) has meant that many patients are referring themselves to us with the wish to go immediately into a group. Once in the group, these members, who have picked up quite a bit of dilettantish sophistication in the various methodologies, will try to establish a group norm for instantaneous acting-out of any blocked feelings. Since traditional group psychotherapy, with its emphasis on resistance and transference analysis, can be a slow and tedious process, other group members may join in with any suggestion that offers a jazzier, more immediately gratifying payoff. A contagious conformity begins to take place in which the only price of group membership is tears, the open expression of rage, or a loving embrace. The resulting fake intimacy leads to a sort of "as if" behavior; meaningless, perfunctory, nonfeeling substitutes for genuine experiencing. Any approach, of course, if misused, can soon become a caricature of itself (e.g., the Gestalt empty-chair technique).

Overpopularity carries with it another unfortunate possibility. The greatest value of any intervention is its novelty. A first exposure in a meaningless context can bring about a significant reduction in emotional impact at some future time when it might really be appropriate.

No fine line can be drawn to define who should be using these techniques and when they should be used. Research studies have yielded mixed results concerning the relationship between the level of the therapist's experience and the psychological gains made by group members. Perhaps a more satisfactory approach is to expect the leader to use prudent initiative and to provide well-thought-out answers to the following questions:

1. How does your selection and use of the various new techniques fit into your understanding of the way people change?
2. What position does each specific technique hold in regard to the therapy goals toward which you are working?
3. What immediate and observable needs does this technique meet at this time with these participants? (Mill and Ritvo 1969)

The greatest mistake a leader can make is to be unwilling to analyze the basis of any action he takes and what the outcome will be. Games, structured exercises, sensory awakening, nonverbal communication, body movement, the T-group method, and encounter techniques all offer traditional psychotherapy some imaginative means for challenging ego-syntonic, self-defeating character defenses. It is imperative, however, that these approaches be subjected to careful scrutiny, and that clear guidelines be provided for the most effective application to our profession of these new modalities. What we most need at this juncture is more hard data on the necessary conditions for change and on the depth, direction, and duration of change that is specifically facilitated by the use of new group techniques.

This book is an attempt to provide a framework for organizing and comprehending these various approaches, along with a detailed description of the new methods used. It will concentrate primarily upon techniques and concepts that I have personally employed and found effective. I will try to explain, along the way, why I have chosen to use a particular exercise at this moment in the life of the group, how successful it has been, which techniques have backfired and why, and what exercises I have tended to avoid or have not yet tried out. In addition, I would like to share with the reader some of the imaginative ways that we can capitalize on countertransference reactions, to the advantage of group members. The subject of countertransference is often treated in the literature somewhat as is a child of whom the parents are ashamed. In the various discussions on countertransference I will try to demonstrate how the analyst's own subjective reactions can be strategically employed and disclosed as part of a highly sensitive instrument, to work through resistances.

Before I finish this introduction, let me reiterate my belief that these methods are all interesting but they're definitely not the be-all and the end-all for salvaging bad groups (and poorly trained group leaders) nor should they be seen as a territorial threat to more conventional group therapy practice. If you are looking for a magical emotional filler—something to keep your group occupied when things seem to be dead or at an impasse, recognize that cop-out now. If you are more realistically inclined, however, and are seriously disposed toward discovering how some of these procedures may accelerate the process of involvement for members of your group, then come along! It is my impression that the deliberate performance of many of these tasks at the appropriate time may bring preconscious or unconscious thoughts or feelings into consciousness. This phenomenon, in itself, offers a rich potential. But the sheer emergence of previously little-understood feelings without some cognitive integration and considerable working through is of little value and is definitely not corrective. And so, while the major thrust of this book is not the experience, the concentrated effort, and the length of time that is required for lasting change to take place, I want to remind the reader that Max Rosenbaum was right when he suggested that there is more to the practice of psychotherapy than excitement.

ACTIVE TECHNIQUES
AND
GROUP PSYCHOTHERAPY

Countertransference
and Patient Selection

A survey of the extensive literature covering the procedure for the proper selection of patients for group therapy is bound to confuse the reader. The only assumptions that hold true for almost every worker in the field are that patients cannot be thrown together haphazardly without consideration of mutual suitability, and that not every patient is necessarily going to benefit from group treatment (Mullan and Rosenbaum 1962). Even this moderate consensus is confounded by the fact that there are continuing differences between therapists regarding the specific criteria for inclusion. Moreover, all the kinds of patients about whom certain workers are most pessimistic (addicts, severe character disorders, alcoholics, border-line psychotics) have been successfully treated in a group setting by other therapists (Joel and Shapiro 1950). Nevertheless, there does seem to be a recent trend toward greater individualization and less concern for screening out a patient on the basis of his formal diagnostic classification (Leopold 1957). Instead, compatability, willingness to expose weakness before a peer group, tolerance for tensions aroused by hostile expressions of others toward himself, and desire for mutuality of experience are all seen as of more paramount importance than diagnostic labels. Along these lines, many workers have written about getting a good interaction going with regard to such variables as age and educational spread, homogeneous versus heterogeneous personality combinations, the mixing of sexes, the placement of new patients into ongoing groups, and the putting together of people from different socioeconomic, racial, or religious backgrounds (Ziferstein and Grotjahn 1956).

In view of the amount of attention that is devoted to selection procedures at symposia, in introductory texts and in the various journals of group psychotherapy, it is quite remarkable that the countertransference aspects of this process are rarely recognized— just a few paragraphs in two articles have appeared in the past twenty years (Neto 1970, Foulkes 1969). In my opinion, this neglect is only partially related to the lack of reliable criteria for the most effective grouping. Under the present ambiguous circumstances almost any selection procedure can be easily rationalized in terms of current theory and practice. More important, whatever neurotic expectations and distorted values the therapist's philosophy of life may contain are obscured and camouflaged by these rationalizations. Thus, my main interest here is to help clarify the following issue: to what extent the criteria for selection are subject to the therapist's personal needs and countertransferential problems; and how placement in a particular group meets the real needs of the individual patient and the rest of the group.

To start with, is it possible that referral to group therapy can sometimes itself represent countertransferential acting out? A therapist struggling with a difficult case, feeling himself particularly exasperated, frustrated, and at an impasse, wondering what dynamics he might be overlooking, could understandably see group as the solution. The Kleinians, for example, have described in considerable detail the power dynamics of the transference-countertransference situation in individual therapy, whereby depressive, masochistic patients render the analyst impotent and gain the upper hand by repeatedly rejecting his interpretations (Guntrip 1968). Under these circumstances, sending the patient to group could represent a wish for vindication on the part of the analyst. His own set of internalized accusing objects, put into motion by the patient's resistance to change, could be appeased by exorcising the bad, unyielding traits of the patient. Thus, therapists sometimes unconsciously orchestrate their groups like Greek choruses, pressuring the patients to shape up and surrender their stubborn defenses to salve the therapist's own bruised ego.

A shy quiet woman who was prematurely pushed into group and then shamed into participating, spoke for many other exploited patients when she wrote the following poem:

When I first entered therapy, my problems
    there to solve,
I did not know what would become or what
    would soon evolve.
All was pleasant—my transference grew and
    things were going well.
But who could know that in so short a time,
    I'd enter the bowels of hell.

The silence came, the silence went and
    progress seemed in sight,
And things were looking up for me, when
    suddenly—came night (Wed.).
The judge appeared in robes of black,
    a smile upon his face,
His eyes were icy, his words were harsh,
    his aim was to disgrace.

The provocateur did set the mood,
    the tragedy did start,
Then one by one his players spoke and
    pierced the victim's heart.
Their words spewed forth with venemous force
    and range of prophetic doom,
And then from twinkletoes arose—
    "Dona, please leave the room."

Another patient who had not been properly prepared for group and was therefore bewildered by the goings-on, painfully captured the acute sense of dislocation that she suffered, in the lines:

The stranger has no face
He is of stone when he surrounds

I'll ride with you
May I please
Shall I please
I do command

I ride the inner surface
Of a cold and crusty sphere
Heading back against its orbit
Since no point in space is dear

You are headed for a place
That is apart from my direction
Though you've occupied my space
And you claim you're my reflection

Make no claims and wander further
On this surface nothing lingers
Though I travel on a mirror
I must always be a stranger

There is also the policy of systematically excluding patients who are markedly different from the rest of the group. In this context we could take note that there are many clinics that are beginning to get a substantial number of black referrals and are systematically forming segregated, all-black groups, most often serviced by black leaders. Many therapists in private practice have reservations about putting blue-collar factory workers in work clothes, ghetto blacks, and even gentiles in with their middle-class Jewish patients. While there may be some validity to arguments that protect the rights of the individual ("He'd feel uncomfortable"; "He'd be ostracized"; "His problems would be different—he wouldn't get the kind of understanding he needs"; "They'd feel more at home with a black leader"). Kadis (1962) has pointed out that this attitude can be rationalized and used against decisions that might be beneficial to the patients but threatening to the therapist. While we are on this topic, I could also list a number of other culturally tabooed types of patient who are often arbitrarily refused admission into ongoing groups (drug addicts, psychopaths, homosexuals, borderline psychotics). There is however considerable research evidence to suggest that these patients can be helped in nonhomogeneous groups. Moreover, heterogeneous grouping can significantly improve the breadth of discussion, make for less programmed interaction, and circumvent denial mechanisms by generating less predictable reactions and ones that are more difficult for patients to ward off.

I think that the countertransferential reaction that keeps people with differences out, has to do with a general fear and suspiciousness of strangers. At bottom, this infantile paranoia is related to the primitive tendency to disassociate ourselves from and declare as not "part of me" any feeling or experience that isn't consonant with the self-image. Hence the presence of patients who are different is seen by the fellow members as a return of the repressed, as a disturbance and a threat that must be externalized and dispensed with rather than properly dealt with and integrated.

If the therapist's unconscious wish is to establish the kind of relationship with the group that gratifies his narcissistic exhibition-istic needs, then he may unwittingly screen out potential sources of group displeasure. Attacks on and ostracism of the new member may be experienced by the therapist as reflections of his own poor judgment and sensitivity. The therapist's overidentification with his choice of members for a group may cause him to overprotect and be overresponsible, which soon leads to irritation and resentment. Group members quickly pick up the therapist's ambivalence, leaving him annoyed at the new patient for not showing appreciation of the therapist's martyrdom by acting like the others and rescuing the therapist from his predicament.

I have also noticed the inhibition that many therapists have about mixing young adults (14-23-year olds) with older adults (45-50-year olds). Many texts rationalize this separation in terms of a lack of overlapping interests and an inability to easily identify with each others' age-specific problems. Early in my practice, I began to question my own resistance to the obvious advantages that crossfertilization might offer. It then occurred to me that the insecurity that I felt in the adult professional role, accompanied by the nagging feeling that I was still a relative beginner and incompletely trained, made me vulnerable to anticipated criticism by the older patients. I tried to deny the very existence of a younger group to guard against the possibility that I might be associated with the "kids" and thereby lose the adults' respect. The other side of the coin was that I shielded the younger patients from the older patients in order to keep their youthful allegiance. I imagined that the younger patients would feel awkward and tongue-tied in the presence of people their parents' age. Being forced into such an unpromising situation they might turn against me as no longer their pal, the good older brother.

In more classical terms, the anxious need to keep the two groups apart reflected a lack of integration between my own impulses and controls. With the adult group, my whole manner encouraged a sense of freedom and expansiveness, youthful enthusiasm, "act, don't think," unbridled sexuality, and a "what the hell" attitude, much of which was really a disguised way of tweeking my own uptight superego. On the other hand, with the youthful group, I fulfilled their transference expectations by acting as a restraining force, simultaneously identifying with their youthful carousing, cynical, antiestablishment attitudes, and general irresponsibility while at the same time preaching a more realistic, practical accommodation to the power structure. The phony joining in their adolescent acting-out tendencies while really "spying" on them and undercutting by trying to tame the impetus of these impulses was a roundabout way of punishing my own wayward needs and drives.

The acting out of a positive countertransference can also be a problem here. A therapist may have a very favorable impression of a patient. The patient may make good progress, be very receptive to the therapist's interpretations, and characterize that constellation of personality features which the therapist would prize as a catalytic force in the group. In exchange for introducing this special patient into the group, the therapist may expect the patient to live out the role of the therapist's ego ideal, and perform well. This complementary fit may actually make for considerable patient progress so long as the patient operates according to the therapist's wishes. If the patient disappoints either through active rebellion, growth and development, or simply by behaving differently than the therapist would have predicted, the latter may repudiate and deny this piece of behavior and the honeymoon will be over. This often leads to escalating regressive behavior on the part of the patient and to perplexity for the leader. The analyst finds himself in the strange position of being irrationally irritated and impatient, wishes the patient would behave in a way that would stop himself from feeling like this, wonders whether he is doing anything to elicit such disappointing behavior, and generally winds up thoroughly confused.

In one of the writer's groups, there was a vivacious, attractive, intelligent young woman. She was aware, seemingly well motivated, insightful, and open. My earliest impressions were that she was a rare patient—hard-working, responsive, cooperative—and besides everything else we seemed to understand one another. She received my interpretations regarding her masochism thoughtfully and her associations were most helpful in clarifying the underlying dynamics. The halo effect that I projected on to this woman made it difficult to accept her unchanging behavior. If she saw everything so clearly and if she had all the positive qualities that therapists prize in their patients, then why does she continue to conduct her life so foolishly? The positive countertransference distorted my whole sense of proper timing, kind patience, realistic expectations, and the ways of growth. In the midst of this disillusionment, the patient was encouraged to enter into combined treatment.

Six months passed, during which time the patient became increasingly defensive, withdrawn, and resistive (broken appointments, coming late). In group, she would anticipate attack for what she was about to relate. Then, sure enough, she would reveal a flagrant bit of masochism and provoke utter exasperation at her lack of self-respect, or barely controlled tolerance to appease her fear of retaliation. In the individual sessions, her resistance took the form of self-blame or manipulative rationalizing: "If I could only give you a clear picture of my relationship with M, then you'd understand that what I'm doing isn't so foolish."

Statements such as this aroused strong feelings of impotence and annoyance. These feelings were difficult to openly express because the patient would quickly blackmail the group by acting contrite, defensive, and bewildered. Her apparent fragility created a climate of guilt-motivated carefulness.

Around this time, I began to act on the proposition that these induced reactions were designed to recreate the ways in which the parents probably behaved toward the patient. While I was pursuing this point, the patient began to produce material revealing how cheap her parents were and how guilty this made her feel. On the one hand, for example, the parents, who were well-off, were pretending to be generous and giving by sending her off to college, while in fact they were sending her only to a state college (brother went to Ivy League school), not giving her any spending money, forcing her to work twenty-five hours a week, and making her donate all of her summer earnings toward the tuition, etc. In the midst of this story, the patient made a slip and called the therapist "Father." When asked whether she ever felt that I had cheated her, she replied, "Sure. I didn't want to go into that group. You acted as though you were doing it for my benefit and I'm sure that was part of it. I went in without balking because I knew you were already disgusted with me. I was afraid if I fought with you, you'd drop me. I'm so busy pleasing, I can't deal with what I need. Do you think I didn't know that you felt that I let you down?"

The patient was right. I was discouraged when she fell short of being a "model patient." In subsequent sessions, it became more clearly apparent that the introjected parent punished her whenever she took anything for herself. By hooking me into a rigid transference-counter-transference bind, whereby she would get approval and help so long as she was my good little girl, she was trying to avoid the wrath and rejection that follows upon gross disobedient behavior. Her "stubborn" masochistic defenses were now revealed as compromise formations. These rebellious acts of assertion (e.g. remaining with a destructive boyfriend) were designed to protect a fragile sense of identity and individuality. Part of her ego wanted to appease but another part wanted to prevail as a separate entity free from my influence, even if the conditions necessary to insure this separateness turned out to be self-defeating. By taking the blame onto herself, the patient was trying to retain the therapist as a source of nurturance and protect him against the rage she must have experienced by having to submit to his "plans" for her. The blanket resistance and defensiveness manifested in both group and individual sessions could now be seen in a new light. The patient resented being transferred to the group in the midst of the therapist's trying to work through his surprising shift from a positive to a negative countertransference position. A good part of the patient's supposed "resistance" in the group was a composite of hurt and anger at the therapist's rejection and the wish to please, which kept her attending group despite her reservations.

One could see how the group posed an insoluble dilemma for the patient, the only solution being resistance. If taking in necessarily involves submission, being controlled, and producing for others, it is no wonder that the quality of what could be accepted had to be thinned down. The group undoubtedly picked up the therapist's impatient, unrealistic expectations and in an unconsciously collusive manner pressed the patient to swing with group norms. When the patient's reaction to this pressure was falsely labeled as "resistance," her approach was to consciously try to appease these unjust accusations but secretly rebel against our efforts by a compulsive insistence on continuing faulty behavior patterns.

With this understanding, I removed the patient from the group and saw her only in individual treatment. After I explained to her my role in some of her problems in therapy, the patient relaxed, became significantly less defensive, and made much better use of the sessions. A good deal of time was spent exploring what had happened between the two of us with specific reference to how the transference-countertransference interaction clearly paralleled prototypical neurotic interactions of the past. Several months later, I placed the patient in a new group with very positive results. There was a steady improvement in her outside life and substantial participation in the group life.

Finally, I would like to describe a group phenomenon that has received very little notice in the literature. About five years ago in a supervisory session I was describing a problem I was having with one of my groups. The people in the group seemed in a state of chronic resistance. They were passive, inhibited, not interactive enough, and rarely expressed feeling openly. I was presenting the impasse in terms of what group dynamics might be operating and what techniques might help to break through the heaviness. I came to realize that unconsciously I had gathered an extremely difficult assortment of people to work with. While I was trying to bring them out, I was unconsciously blaming them for not being more free. Very self-righteously I said to myself, "Here I am doing everything I can to get them to relate and they're still sitting there withdrawn and unresponsive. Boy, if I were a patient in that group, I'd know how to provoke them and get things rolling." I contrasted this group with another that was so much more verbal, vibrant, and alive. After considerable exploration, it became clear to me that I was referring to my "better patients" (those who were more outspoken, confronting, and spontaneous) as the "good group." Unwittingly, I had polarized the two groups into good and bad by collecting my most difficult cases and channeling them to the bad group. This group consisted of people referred to me by other therapists who couldn't make progress or people whom I placed in group with the hope that the group could reach them in ways that I couldn't. This insight was interesting but I was still intrigued by my resolute resistance to the supervisor's suggestion that I mix the "good group" and the "bad group."

Further investigation revealed that the "good group" was my showpiece. They represented living proof that I could be respected and accepted. They were like children one could be proud of, or parents one needn't be ashamed of. With regard to the "bad group" it would appear that I had consciously constructed this inhibited, unassertive group out of impatience with my own short-comings. While sitting sympathetically with these patients, I could gain a sense of mastery and vicariously escape more honest self-examination   by exhorting them to be more open and direct, take responsibility for their actions, trust people, risk taking a chance, and all the little platitudes that therapists enjoy telling their patients. So long as my masochistic identification with their passivity and sense of failure continued, this group was bound to resist my "sincere" overtures by stubborn withholding, quiet hostility, and general self-defeating negativism. When I finally worked through my problems about switching patients more freely from one group to another and changing the original composition of a group, many significant changes took place. The group became more resourceful, constructive and goal-directed, the climate became more flexible, and many individuals began to show strengths that they hadn't previously demonstrated.

In conclusion, let me say that there are an infinite number of countertransferential acting-out possibilities in the selection and combination of patients for a therapy group. Many of the inexplicable dead spots and impasses experienced throughout the different stages of group treatment are probably related to the unconscious and preconscious attitudes and expectations of the therapist, of each participant, and of the group as a whole. I think that it would be particularly helpful for group therapists to stop disguising their ambivalences with the stale guidelines of the traditional literature, and to look for illumination in the special personal meaning to them of the selection procedures that they seem to follow so matter-of-factly. A starting point for the therapist would be to tap his preconscious fantasies about his patients. What role do you expect each patient in the group to play for you? What function does he play in your own feeling of well-being? Which patient have you gossiped to colleagues about or day-dreamed about? If a particular patient is late or absent do you sometimes fail to notice this? List the patients in your groups. Whose name was first and whose was last; why? In what way would you like your troublesome patients to change? Why would that please you? Draw a picture of a therapy group and write a story about it. Do your associations to these productions clue you in to recent conflicts regarding one of your ongoing groups?

By clarifying for himself just how his values influence his procedures and their impact on his patients, the therapist can systematically integrate this insight with his understanding of the way in which the patient's evoked "resistances" relate to the preexisting transference potentials. In this way we will have gone a long way toward resolving seemingly intractable treatment impasses.

Laying the Groundwork

The most crucial period for determining whether or not a patient will continue in group is the first three months. Despite this, many therapists with high turnover rates fail to carefully examine the cause for this. They dismiss it in terms of resistance and low tolerance for anxiety on the part of the patients. Research studies have consistently suggested, however, that the patients' anxiety from being placed in a group situation in which his expected behavior, the group goals, and the relevance to his personal goals are exceedingly unclear, is closely related to premature termination. In the face of this evidence, therapists who follow the psychoanalytic model continue to maintain that if the development and eventual resolution of patient-therapist distortions are the key curative factors in therapy, then it follows that one should seek in all respects to enhance the emergence of transference. From this point of view, enigma, ambiguity, absence of cognitive anchoring, and frustration of conscious and unconscious wishes all facilitate a regressive reaction to the therapist and are deliberately regulated to create an atmosphere favorable to the development of transference. Therapists who identify with this orientation are strenuously opposed to any intervention that threatens to dilute or distort the emerging group transferences. In their eyes, excessive interference explicitly includes "structure by suggesting procedures, providing definitions, and offering reassurances" (Whitaker and Lieberman 1964).

While this line of thinking seems to have a sound theoretical rationale behind it, some therapists hold to it inflexibly even in the face of clinical experience that suggests that for many patients, particularly in the early stages of treatment, there is a realistic need for greater support and a manageable level of anxiety. Since crippling amounts of tension prevent patients from easing into the kind of introspection, interpersonal exploration, and risk taking that are necessary for the later stages of therapy, it seems reasonable to expect that the thoughtful clinician would use the early sessions to relax his patients, help them to feel less defensive, and provide them with useful concepts that would assist them in a better understanding of the hard work ahead. The forging of this therapeutic alliance is best achieved by appealing to the healthy part of the patient's ego, treating him like an adult who is entitled to a collaborative role in planning for his future, and consciously toning down magical images of ourselves by not being secretive and mysterious. By clarifying group goals, providing a cognitive structure which will enable them to participate more effectively (how to give help, how to accept help), and by conveying an accurate formation of typical group processes, the leader can greatly reduce the possibility of the disenchantment which leads to flight, and at the same time can draw nearer to the goal of group cohesiveness.

The following chapter offers a variety of preliminary technical procedures developed by different workers in order to harmonize a new patient's absorption into the group. In the course of presenting this survey, the author will attempt to critically examine these approaches in terms of their practical effectiveness.

SYSTEMATIC GROUP PREPARATION

Yalom (1970) has described a comprehensive procedure of systematic preparation which is designed to "resolve misconceptions, erroneous expectations, and initial problems of group therapy." He indicates that the therapist should anticipate and predict common problems and unrealistic fears that arise in early sessions, and that these potential sources of resistance should be dealt with by detailed discussions in preparatory sessions. In addition, he feels that a conceptual framework and clear guidelines to effective behavior should also be presented to the patient.

Although each patient's introduction to group must be individualized according to the concerns expressed and the amount of prior knowledge and sophistication about the therapy process, Yalom covers certain basic points with every patient in an orientation session.

He has obviously given a great deal of thought to the rationale for the preparatory process. He suggests that the therapist must walk a thin line between overstructured, didactic group therapy (which he believes leads to ritualistic behavior) and the unproductive high level of anxiety that results from a lack of clarity as to group goals and preferred modes of behavior. But, since by verbal and nonverbal reinforcement, even the most nondirective therapist structures his group so that eventually they adopt his values as to what is important in group process, why not make this explicit?

Since the formation of a freely interacting, autonomous group is crucial to the operation of effective therapy, Yalom believes that the first step in getting the group moving in the right direction is a carefully designed preparatory interview.

Patients are presented with a brief explanation of the interpersonal theory of psychiatry, beginning with the statement that although each manifests his problems differently, all who seek help from psychotherapy have in common the basic problem of difficulty in establishing and maintaining close and gratifying relationships with others. They are reminded of the many times in their lives that they have undoubtedly wished to clarify a relationship, to be really honest about their positive and negative feelings with someone and get reciprocally honest feedback. The general structure of society, however, does not often permit totally open communication. The therapy group is described as a special microcosm in which this type of honest interpersonal exploration vis-a-vis the other members is not only permitted but encouraged. If people are conflicted in their methods of relating to others, then obviously a social situation which encourages honest interpersonal explorations can provide them with a clear opportunity to learn many valuable things about themselves. It is emphasized that working on their relationships directly with other group members will not be easy, in fact, it may be very stressful, but it is crucial because if one can completely understand and work out one's relationships with the other group members, there will be an enormous carry-over. They will then find pathways to more rewarding relationships with significant people in their lives now and with people they have yet to meet.

The patients are advised that the way in which they can help themselves most of all is to be honest and direct with their feelings in the group at that moment, especially their feelings toward the other group members and the therapist. This point is emphasized many times and is referred to as the "core of group therapy." They are told that they may, as they develop trust in the group, reveal intimate aspects of themselves; but the group is not a forced confessional and people have different rates of developing trust and revealing themselves. It is suggested that the group be seen as a forum for risk taking and that, as learning progresses, new types of behavior may be tried in the group setting.

Certain stumbling blocks are predicted. Patients are forewarned about a feeling of puzzlement and discouragement in the early meetings. It will, at times, not be apparent how working in group problems and intragroup relationships can be of value in solving the problems which brought them to therapy. It is almost impossible to evaluate the eventual usefulness of the group during the first dozen meetings and they are asked to make a commitment of at least twelve meetings before even attempting to evaluate the group. They are told that many patients find it painfully difficult to reveal themselves or to express directly positive or negative feelings. The tendencies of some to withdraw emotionally, to hide their feelings, to let others express feelings for them, to form concealing alliances with others, are discussed. The therapeutic goals of group therapy are ambitious because we desire to change behavior and attitudes many years in the making; treatment is therefore, gradual and long. I discuss with them the likely development of feelings of frustration or annoyance with the therapist, and how they will expect answers from him, but in vain. The source of help will be primarily the other patients, although it is difficult for them to accept this fact. (Yalom, p. 222)

The obvious value of Yalom's approach is that it anticipates practically every possible apprehension that a new patient is likely to experience. By short-circuiting the "surprise" aspect of common group anxieties, Yalom makes the patient feel less isolated and better understood. If the therapist conveys a feeling of understanding and acceptance of early group anxieties, this would seem to encóurage the patient to more readily reveal the special problems with the group that he is encountering.

I find myself taking issue with Yalom on a number of counts:

1. There is a very obsessive, intellectualized quality to his explanations. While Yalom's writing style may not accurately reflect what he does in face to face contact, I do get the impression that the patient is given too much to digest. It may have a boomerang effect ("If the therapist is forewarning me of so many dangers, maybe I really should be scared! I wonder if group is the right place for me"). An even greater possibility is that the relatively unsophisticated group therapist may not be sufficiently aware of how much patients try to comply. There is a likelihood that if patients took the "instructions" too seriously, they would be trying to be good patients instead of being themselves. The therapist has to be sensitive to the patient's need to live up to the therapist's expectations. What was originally intended as anxiety-reducing reassurance can easily be interpreted as indirectly pointing out therapeutically desirable behavior. The patient may come to feel that since his anxiety feelings are already understood and anticipated, he mustn't act unduly upset because he's already been told he's understood. When the therapist unwittingly joins the patient's resistance in this manner, he may be helping to shape the patient who can be characterized as "someone who does everything right in treatment but never gets better."

2. Perhaps I can illustrate this paradox in a clearer way if I talk about something specific. A careful reading of Yalom's instructions suggests that he places a premium on the group as an intimacy-enhancing experience. This emphasis might put many patients off in the sense that they might be frightened by a "pressure" to relate. I would rather stress the stimulus value of the group situation for creating a wide range of feelings and thoughts in an interpersonal setting. Relating does not only involve warmth, closeness, openness, and sharing of self. The chief difficulty that patients have early in treatment involves learning how to handle negative rejecting reactions in a constructive way. This skill is especially important to master since a majority of patients fear the consequences of expressing their own hostility and anger ("it means I'm not a good

person") as well as dealing with the destructiveness of others directed toward them ("they don't think I'm good either"). I generally will explain that when people don't like things in other people, they tend to dissociate themselves from the noxious situation. I suggest that these cut-off feelings get turned inward and do bad things to our heads and bodies. I don't advocate people dumping things on one another capriciously or expressing their capacity for destructiveness in all kinds of outrageous ways as some encounter-group proponents suggest. No. The group is there to work these feelings out—to express the negative constructively.

To state this point a little differently, patients should be encouraged to feel free not to become intimate. If a resistance (e.g., withholding of negative feelings) is overcome during the course of treatment and this leads to greater intimacy, then at least it's the patient's choice that this is what he wants.

3. The greatest anxiety that patients seem to have regarding group therapy is fear of the unknown. They don't really know what they're getting into. The don't know what's going to happen to them, and they fear losing control. Yalom's preparatory practices go a long way toward providing a rich roadmap of what's up ahead, and it's probably helpful in allaying a certain amount of anxiety. However, I believe that we also need to let the patient know that he always retains control of the situation—that it's his decision about staying or leaving, participating or withholding, sharing or being more private, getting angry or not revealing his anger, etc.

In summary, my own experience has taught me that two main ingredients go into establishing a good mental state with which a patient can begin a group: (1) The patient must know that it's his own responsibility and his right alone to give or take as little or as much as he chooses, that nobody else can make that decision for him, and (2) Yalom's approach with a few modifications—presenting a broad overview with some specific detail, answering questions in an honest, direct way, providing a down-to-earth, friendly explanation (accompanied by a similar manner in the group)— allows the patient to relax and feel as off-the-cuff and homey as possible.

A survey of the literature suggests that there are many variations that go beyond Yalom's group preparatory practices. Bach (1954) has allowed prospective group patients to read typed protocols of group meetings or to listen to actual recordings. Others have used a written instructions format. A brief mimeographed paper entitled "Introduction to Group Psychotherapy" is given to each patient, with printed advice for greater participation. These instructions have many of the same benefits and limitations that were discussed in regard to Yalom's approach. They seem to be geared to highly sophisticated, intelligent, motivated patients. Their value lies in the fact that many important points are covered that could lead to confusion, anxiety, and resistance if not brought out in the open. For the therapist who sees some advantage in using this sort of model, I would suggest tailoring the content to your own style and to the level of the patient population that you are servicing.

Several authors offer anecdotal evidence supporting the efficacy of written instructions in fostering constructive patient activity, assisting the patient to understand his role, and reassuring him. The recent development of videotape techniques offers an exciting, innovative way to educate for group therapy by showing vignettes from an actual therapy group. With a certain kind of patient it is conceivable that by playing samples of "good" group communication as opposed to defensive verbal patterns, we might accelerate more meaningful interaction.

ORIENTATION GROUPS

Another approach which might be used in a busy institution or clinic is early and brief group experience. These groups, variously known as intake, vestibule, or orientation groups, provide early contact with the institution in a group setting with other patients and conducted by a leader. This group experience is usually preliminary to the primary therapy prescribed. Rabin (1970) indicates some of the value of this procedure: "The group is a diagnostic aid and it has a prognostic-dispositional helpfulness. It is supportive and anxiety reducing while patients are waiting for intake processing or treatment. Fewer patient drop out while waiting." Rubin et al (1963) found that those who had the intake experience often stayed in group somewhat longer. "Perhaps the explicit preparing of patients was one determinant with another possible facilitation being the method of transferring patients in pairs or larger groupings from the intake group to the regular therapy group."

Malamud and Machover (1965) operating within a self-confrontation workshop format, developed a large repertoire of ingeniuous experiments to increase the sensitivity and awareness of prospective patients on a clinic waiting list. Over a fifteen-week period, participants in their groups viewed topical movies and then discussed them (e.g., Feelings of Hostility), engaged in sensory awareness exercises and role playing, and participated in communication games. The rationale here was to encourage group members to better understand themselves by having personalized firsthand experiences with such psychodynamic concepts as (1) That all behavior is caused; (2) that all unconscious phenomena are real and meaningful; (3) that childhood experiences have a crucial bearing on personality development; (4) that the apparently trivial is often significant as self-revelations and as communications; (5) that a coherent and understandable style may often be discerned threading its way through the core of one's life; (6) and that the self is an active agent in its own development" (p. 5). Malamud and Machover attempted to facilitate these discoveries by arranging open-ended, novel, planned situations, tasks, and procedures that were then integrated with cognitive material. The real significance of their work is that it is an important advance in effective mental-health education because it stimulates intense personal-emotional involvement and positive motivation on the part of a large number of people who might need psychotherapy but are either unaware of their need or shrink from the acknowledgment, effort or expense.

In many instances, the therapist has a good deal of information available about a prospective group member. If he has been in individual therapy with a colleague or in the therapist's own practice, then a rich picture of the patient's dynamics, character defenses, typical patterns of resistance, transference, and possible objections to entering group therapy are known. This knowledge can be profitably used to educate the patient for entry into group and to avoid premature placement.

DRAW A PICTURE

If this data isn't available, then there are other ways of predicting a patient's functioning in a group setting. One of the most valuable principles in understanding a patient's anticipations of group therapy is derived from integrating the Adlerian concept of the family constellation with the Freudian theory of transference. "Prior to his entrance into the group, the actions and anticipations of the prospective group member tend to reflect the role he assumed in his own family unit; these anticipations also reflect the role the new member typically displays in all his group relationships" (Kadis 1962, p. 64). One projective method that has drawn some attention in this regard is to ask the patient to draw a picture of what he imagines a group therapy session would be like (see Figures 1 and 2). This drawing could be used to anticipate potential sources of anxiety and resistance and to integrate genetic role relationships with anticipated role experiences within the group. When this data is interpreted and predictions are made to the patients, he may deny their implications but they can often prove helpful at a later time. If the predictions are accurate they at least alert the healthy part of the ego to past destructive behavior and impulsive acting out.

Susan was in group for three sessions when she began complaining that it was a completely useless, stupid enterprise that she no longer wanted any part of. Her drawing and the accompanying story reveal the intense conflict that this woman is undergoing. On the one hand, the story begins and ends with loneliness—a terrible void, a bottomless pit. This basic position is covered over by a deep sense of suspiciousness, a conviction that the world is a phony place, and that the group offers false hope. People are seen as ungiving, unfeeling, denigrated creatures. The sense of despair and futility is pervasive.

With this knowledge at our disposal, we are in a much better position to deal with Susan's resistance than if we simply encourage her to stick with the group because it will ultimately be good for her. We could start off with the drawing. Does she notice how she puts herself above the drawing, looking down at the other "shmucks"? What does this spatial representation reflect? Superiority, contempt, condescension? Does this role seem familiar to her? What could she be defending against by this style of one-unmanship? Is she afraid that if she loses control people will gain the upper hand and become critical of her? If so, what is there to be judged harshly? What part of herself is she most ashamed of, most secretive about? If every section of a drawing represents a splinter aspect of the self-image, then the stones can furnish us with important clues. If she can

analysis   Well of lonliness, everyone
trying to make believe — it isn't there
but its just a mirage — there isn't any story just
stones — stones don't have stories or get analyzed

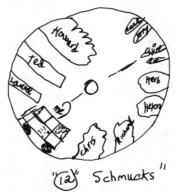

"12 Schmucks"

This is a story about 12 schmucks —
ridiculous schmucks trying so hard
not to be just plain old garden variety
everyday-loving lying phony non human
iron cased schmucks. Just aint any
damn use cause thats the way it goes
when your born a + alone —   a

FIGURE 1

identify with a stone, what does that make her feel? What's it like to be stone? Does she ever wish she weren't a stone? What's the effect on her when an occasional person touches her in a human (unstonelike) way? I could continue with these possibilities but the point is that if the therapist can make the patient aware that her resistance is not a simple matter of disliking the people and writing them and the group off, then some fruitful work can be accomplished in the group.

To get down to mechanics, if a patient is resistive but not really dealing with his resistance in the group, I request an individual consultation at which time I ask for the drawing. I discuss the implications of the story and the drawing with the patient privately, and encourage him to deal with his fears and reservations more openly in the group itself. Another tool that the reader might want to experiment with is to have the patient draw a picture of a family and to tell a story about it. The remarkable correspondence between the family drawing (symbolically representing the original family of childhood) and the group representation of the patient is apparent even to very resistive patients. It is the therapist's task to elucidate the transferential aspects of the patient's resistance to group and its historical meaning. If this is done skillfully the patient is made aware of repetitive behavior patterns. His negative therapeutic reaction is not felt solely in relation to this cluster of people—it has broader, deeper implications. This approach frequently results in a patient's developing renewed courage and an interest in returning to the group and trying to understand his reactions instead of acting them out by leaving.

Roberta was in a successful course of individual treatment over a three-year period. During this time, she worked out many problems regarding confused sexual identification, her tendency to cloister herself in the house and never go out, and her avoidance of anything approaching a close relationship. She was referred to group to focus on the interferences that she erected against the development of more sustained, satisfying relationships. Here was a situation where the patient saw the group as offering a potentially beneficial experience but requested an individual consultation because she wanted to know how to get more out of it. After five months in group, her level of relatedness remained relatively shallow, her participation was mostly on an advice-giving or -requested basis and she was unemotional and inhibited in her overall behavior.

Once upon a time there was a lovely garden where only two flowers grew. Both flowers bathed in the sun and drank the rain and grew up.

One day three butterflies discovered this special garden. The butterflies flew straight to one of the flowers and hovered, danced and fluttered around her. The other flower felt very sad, lonely and angry. She just couldn't understand why the butterflies didn't dance and hover around her. She tried to attract them by waving her petals, but alas they barely noticed her.

Once she thought that she was a happy flower, because she never really cared about butterflies, but now she had begun to care and that hurt the most. What should she do. Maybe she would dry up, wilt and return to the soft, warm earth. Maybe she would suffer in silence the hurt she felt or maybe even make believe the butterflies didn't exist at all or maybe she would keep on searching . . . .

FIGURE 2

The drawings, her story, and her associations to the story reveal a strong underlying ambivalence in everyday living, but more specifically within the group. To begin with, Roberta's story is told as if it were a fairy tale. The happy flower and the woebegone flower represent two opposing forces within her. The happy flower looks happy all right: she's winning the popularity contest and look at the big smile on her face! On closer examination, however, the smile looks rather fixed and forced. When questioned about this, Roberta suggested that she had been able to attract men in her life but only by putting herself in their hands, being what they wanted her to be, and losing her own sense of identity. The sad flower was unhappy but at least she was left alone. She didn't have to try so hard, she wasn't in danger of being controlled. It occurred to Roberta that she felt freer when she felt unhappy. "When I'm happy, it feels insincere. I'm putting on a happy front, but is it for me?"

This discussion was brought back into the group. Roberta started getting in touch with the idea that her withdrawn manner was a way of preserving her independence. Once she allowed herself to start feeling for others or needing something from other people, her own individuality would be lost. These insights were discussed in individual treatment before she entered the group. What the group setting offered, however, was a very graphic demonstration of the push-pull phenomenon. Roberta had often talked about but never really comprehended why she pulled people toward her up to a certain point and then turned something off by rejecting them and withdrawing. The discussion of the drawings afforded Roberta a task to focus on and seemed to make the group experience more meaningful.

THE GROUP THERAPY TEST

Another test that has recently been developed for use as a selection instrument for membership in group therapy is the GPT (Group Psychotherapy Test). The GPT consists of fifteen pictures, each portraying group members in a different interaction with the leader and one another. The prospective group member is instructed to write a story about each card. By evaluating stories with regard to the extent of good interpersonal relationships demonstrated, Kingsley (1968) demonstrates that the GPT has good predictive validity insofar as it forecasts minimal requirements for group therapy participation. Beyond this, a content analysis of the stories can provide important clues about major areas of conflict and anxiety that can be focused upon and attended to in the interest of short-term treatment plans.

A word of caution. A danger can arise from the misuse of these projective instruments in conjunction with group therapy. The sensitive clinician must be very aware that what he sees may be more than the patient is ready to accept and work with at a particular point in his development. The therapist who is made overanxious by a patient's resistance and compensates for this by grandiosity and the expression of power needs can do some very destructive things in the name of helpfulness. For example, a therapist may be prone to lapse into excessive intellectualizing, forecasting the likely course of events for the patient in the group, telling the patient how he should behave and what he should do. Under these circumstances, a patient could feel that now that his resistances are explained away, he shouldn't have them anymore. As with any powerful tool, the clinician has to be highly selective and discreet in his interpretations, always keeping in mind the patient's level of readiness to integrate the material.

EXPERIENTIAL FOCUSING

In order for treatment change to take place, Gendlin (1969a and b) suggests that something special must occur inside the patient during the session. He calls this "something" an "experiential effect," which he defines as the patient's awareness of his shifting feelings, bodily states, and imagery as they occur in the interview, with the words and concepts flowing from this deep kind of experiencing. Gendlin presents a wide range of experimental evidence that a high experiential level during an interview is significantly related to positive outcome in therapy. This data further suggests that if a patient does not reach an experiential level early, he and the therapist can spend many fruitless hours together with nothing of consequence happening. Gendlin concludes, "therapy as usually practiced does not teach the patient how to do therapy."

Operating within this framework, Gendlin has gone on to develop two new approaches that are designed to teach his patients how to work in therapy. One proposes that the therapist's responses be experiential. They should aim to deepen and broaden the patient's sense of what is going on within him by responding to and expanding the felt meaning in the patient's communications. In his paper "The Experiential Response," Gendlin (1969b) sets forth the procedures that he feels can be taught to therapists to make them more experientially responsive.

The second approach that Gendlin proposes is a technique called "experiential focusing" (1969a). This involves teaching the patient to relax and get in touch with what is going on inside him. It urges him to notice what he is experiencing in his feelings, his body sensations, his thoughts, and his imagery. Essentially, this represents a very direct attempt to teach him how to do therapy. An example of some of the instructions given to patients who are being taught to focus will illustrate the flavor of the method:

This is going to be just to yourself. What I will ask you to do will be silent, just to yourself. Take a moment just to relax . . . . . 5 seconds. All right—now, just to yourself, inside you, I would like you to pay attention to a very special part of you . . . . . Pay attention to *that part where* you usually feel sad, glad, or scared. 5 seconds. Pay attention to that area in you and see how you are now. See what comes to you when you ask yourself, "How am I now?" "How do I feel?" "What is the main thing for me right now?" Let it come, in whatever way it comes to you, and see how it is.

30 seconds or less

If, among the things that you have just thought of, there was a major personal problem which felt important, continue with it. Otherwise, select a meaningful personal problem to think about. Make sure you have chosen some personal problem of real importance in your life. Choose the thing which seems most meaningful to you.

10 seconds

Of course, there are many parts to that one thing you are thinking about—too many to *think* of each one alone. But, you can *feel* all of these things together. Pay attention there where you usually feel things, and in there you can get a sense of what *all of the problem* feels like. Let yourself feel *all of that.*

30 seconds or less

As you pay attention to the whole feeling of it, you may find that one special feeling comes up. Let yourself pay attention to that one feeling.

1 minute

Keep following one feeling. Don't let it be *just* words or picture—wait and let words or pictures come from the feeling.

1 minute

If this one feeling changes, or moves, let it do that. Whatever it does, follow the feeling and pay attention to it.

1 minute

Now, take what is fresh, or new, in the feel of it *now* . . . . . and go very easy. Just as you feel it, try to find some new words or pictures to capture what your present feeling is all about. There doesn't have to be anything that you didn't know before. New words are best but old words might fit just as well, as long as you now find words or pictures to express what is fresh to you now.

1 minute

If the words or pictures that you now have make some fresh difference, see what that is. Let the words or pictures change until they feel just right in capturing your feelings.

1 minute

Now I will give you a little while to use in any way you want to, and then we will stop.

Continuing with this type of instruction the client is directed to focus on a personal problem, get a sense of the total feeling of the problem, attend carefully to any changes in feelings, and notice and stay with whatever fresh and new emerges in his experience.

Gendlin notes that even after being successfully taught, patients encounter difficulty in focusing. The way to work on this block is, again, by focusing on it. There is a turning upon "that," which makes the inability itself the object of focusing. Gendlin's total push is to get into concretely felt versions of problems instead of simply talking about them. In this experiential approach, the therapist responds to what is directly felt even while it isn't yet conceptually clear.

The key phrase in focusing is "what's wrong," followed by shutting up and waiting for the mind to stop wandering. The deliberate, forced character of this orientation must be stressed. It is not letting oneself go, but very intently keeping quiet, zeroing one's attention in, and then letting come what comes.

The most appealing aspect of Gendlin's contribution is that it makes very efficient use of everything we know that accelerates working through. It directs patients to attend to the data that research findings indicate are most consistent with therapeutic movement. Gendlin makes no mention of the application of his techniques to ongoing group therapy, but I have occasionally introduced experiential focusing to patients who are awaiting admission to groups, with considerable success. During those sessions when I am orienting a patient to the whole concept of group participation, I describe the experiential focusing procedure, and advise a patient that it might prove helpful in improving the quality of his involvement in the group.

As with all new approaches, it is best to use experiential focusing with discrimination. Obviously in the case of hysterics, adolescents, and borderline patients who come to us overaware of what is going on inside them, to the point where the use of self-attending could become a resistance to *doing* anything differently, this procedure is contraindicated.

Finally Rabin (1970) has summarized the different rules that have been found most helpful in individualized preparation of patients for group psychotherapy:

1. The more frightened or resisting the patient is about joining a group, the more he needs careful preparatory analysis to reduce his fears and resistances.

2. Pay special attention to patient cues that suggest premature termination from the group or other destructive acting out. The basic technique is to alert the patient to the possibility by specific predictions.

3. Take the patient's conscious goals for being in therapy and link them explicitly to the group therapy situation. When the patient is in individual psychotherapy and group therapy is added to or substituted for individual treatment with the same therapist, a couple of additional guidelines have been found fruitful.

4. Establish a reasonably good working alliance in the individual situation before placement in the therapy groups.

5. Have a workable understanding of the transference and counter-transference in the dyadic therapy situation before placement in a therapy group with its powerful impact and complex transference-countertransference potentials. (p. 144)

Rabin's points seem simple enough and yet, as was indicated in Chapter I, too many therapists use group therapy as a dumping ground. Just as certain agencies refer patients to group therapy to reduce long waiting lists, some therapists suggest group therapy as a way of clarifying what's going on with their patients. The suggestion of group therapy should only be made when a good working alliance has already been established, when the patient is in a positive transference, and when there is mutual agreement as to what work remains to be done.

Cohesiveness

If a group is to be used effectively as a medium of change, those people who are to be changed and those who are to exert influence for change must have a strong sense of belonging to the same group (Cartwright 1951). It can be said that communication is not possible unless it takes place in the context of a common aim. In a group setting, only distorted communication occurs if it is conceived of as going from the I to the Thou. Communication only works from one member of us to another. The word "us" here indicates a true working group only if it implies a shared commitment, not just a feeling of togetherness. The transfer of a collection of people into an effective working group—an "us" instead of a collection of "me's" is possible given the right commitment. It does not happen of itself, just by sitting people in a circle and dealing with individual problems. A strong sense of mutual involvement is required.

This principle of cohesiveness (we-feeling) is particularly relevant to the therapy group, for much of the therapeutic process is mediated by all members. The most unique feature of group therapy, in fact, is the cotherapeutic influences of peers, not of the therapist alone. Research evidence documenting the importance of a sense of group "belongingness" in the therapeutic process is in a rudimentary stage. Nevertheless, there are a number of relevant studies which suggest that positive patient outcome is correlated with individual attraction to the group, total group cohesiveness, mutually satisfying intermember relationships, and number of significant member-to-member interactions (Dickoff and Lakin 1963). But if group acceptance, group support, intermember trust, and clear communication are of prime importance in producing change in group patients, then the group therapy literature has been sadly negligent in defining explicitly just how the therapist can actively promote a facilitating group climate.

There is a large body of concepts and methodologies that could be very helpful in this regard, but most therapists are only remotely aware of their relevance. I am referring, of course, to the laboratory approach known variously as sensitivity training, T-grouping and the National Training Laboratory workshops. In this chapter, I would like to describe some interesting developments in this area that could be very directly applied to ongoing group therapy.*

CRITICAL ASPECTS OF AN EFFECTIVE HELPING PROCESS

In a number of thoughtful papers, Gibb (1964a) has summarized the difficulties involved in trying to develop the constructively helpful attitudes necessary for a supportive learning climate. According to Gibbs, four factors, which he calls group norms, must be operating simultaneously for optimal growth to take place:

Exposure of Intrapersonal and Interpersonal Ideas and Feelings. "Interaction must occur and it has to be of a kind that allows the individual to look at himself and to see how his ideas and feelings are viewed by others." Learning is a social process. "In order to learn, one can't be a passive participant in the interactive process."

Feedback. Another essential norm is that which facilitates relaxed introspection and honest interpersonal feedback. Honest self-disclosure before others, in the here and now, is the genesis of feedback leading to greater intimacy. In reaction to this presenta-

*Readers who are interested in acquainting themselves better with the NTL literature are referred to the *Journal of Applied Behavioral Science* and an excellent collection of articles by Golembiewski and Blumberg, *Sensitivity Training and the Laboratory Approach,* Itasca, Ill.: F. E. Peacock, 1970.

tion, the other members respond to the speaker as a person, and not only to the verbal message he conveys. This in turn prompts a counterreaction—how I respond to you responding to me. Throughout this sequence, a participating member has an opportunity, through feedback, to appraise his self-image as well as to reevaluate the prediction of the others' perception of him.

Linda often became very defensive when the group inquired about her relationship with the man she was going with. She sent out signals that this made her quite irritated, and by her sour expressions and obvious annoyance she discouraged continued group focusing. When the analyst pointed this pattern out, she replied, "Every time you make an observation, you imply that I am always doing something wrong." Some group members indicated that this was inconsistent with their perceptions. One person suggested that perhaps her defensive behavior itself makes her feel under attack. Another member supported Linda and agreed that he was getting progressively annoyed at her but that "it wasn't coming out of the blue." Linda's tendency to exonerate herself from taking any responsibility for other people's reaction to her was seen as very provocative. Still another person said, "When you start speaking, I feel sympathetic; by the time you finish I feel like attacking. So maybe I am angry, maybe you're right. But you have to try to figure out how you manage to have that effect on me." By means of consensual validation and a gradual shift toward an independent taking of responsibility for her own feelings and actions, Linda was encouraged not to be so defensive.

The task of the "good group" is to progressively reduce mistaken beliefs, distorted perceptions, and self-defeating illusions by constant exposure, feedback, and working through. The essential issue that should always be kept in mind is, "Are our attitudes and feelings adequate for the achievement of our personal goals for growth?" Critical and supported self-examination favorably lends itself to interpersonal change.

The Supportive Atmosphere Norm. If feedback takes place in a judgmental, punitive, or defensive climate the result is loss of motivation, defensiveness, and refusal to look at the data. All significant feedback hurts or creates anxiety because it implies something about himself the listener does not realize, some kind of intellectual or emotional shortsightedness. It is easy to interpret this as an attack. If this feedback occurs with people we like and trust, in a warm, encouraging, supportive atmosphere, even the most critical and telling feedback is palatable.

Learning occurs best in group situations where the participants feel a climate of motivated sharing in a search for better answers to problems that the learner acknowledges as his problems. When one feels the necessity to defend or justify one's ideas and feelings in the presence of others, one is not open to risk taking and creative collaboration. The group member who is anxious, overconcerned with the adequacy of the image he is projecting, and too sensitive about the clarity or popularity of his own ideas, is not ready to pursue honest inquiry. If too much energy is consumed in defending his ego and maintaining security, then little is available for developing new perspectives. Help should constantly be shaped by the feedback from the target patient concerning what is most effective for him.*

> Jerry was reluctant to enter group because he felt ashamed to talk about his impotence problem. When he finally chose to discuss this topic, he turned to a very strong, highly respected group member whom he viewed as the least likely person in the room to know what he was feeling. When this other man acknowledged that he had streaks like this himself and talked about his own pain when it happened over a period of a year with someone he loved dearly, Jerry noticeably relaxed. The women in the group were warm and sympathetic, and conveyed the notion that caring and love were of primary importance to them, and the fact that he wanted to change should be encouragement for a woman to be patient with him. Other men in the group joined in a discussion of their own fear of not performing adequately if they couldn't give women regular orgasms, and altogether a natural, matter-of-fact climate was created.

*Gibb is making a very important point here but I think this concept could use further elaboration. A frequently observed group phenomenon is the tendency to attack a person for his defenses. This lends itself to a vicious cycle of attack-defend-attack with no constructive outcome. If somehow we could teach our patients to attend not only to their answers to feedback but also to how the feedback itself is making them feel, it would go a long way toward making them understand their subsequent behavior. For example, if you intend your comment to be helpful and sympathetic but I take it as covertly critical and demanding, my behavior, if it's defensive, will make no sense to you. At least if I tell you that you threaten me, we may disagree but we have a more solid basis for working toward an understanding.

The Provisional Behavior Norm. The group member must feel free to express tentative and poorly formulated ideas with the secure anticipation that others will try to help him test the adequacy of these ideas in action. If he senses that there is a good possibility that he will sound stupid and be vulnerable to contempt, impatience, or disinterest, he will tend to maintain his previous attitude and keep things to himself.

Gibb's strong emphasis on how a group atmosphere that is heavily saturated with defensive feelings interferes significantly with openness and productivity overlaps in many ways with my own thinking that it is of primary importance, if the group is to work at all, for every patient to be encouraged to have a task-oriented attitude and to take responsibility for what he wants to happen.

PROMOTING A GOOD GROUP CLIMATE

First of all, I try to establish a warm, generous introduction to group. I don't spring new patients on the group without discussing the move with the veteran members first. Groups in any case are usually competitive and resentful regarding new members. By forewarning them that a new person is coming and dealing with their reactions to this information beforehand, the therapist can lessen the brunt of the antagonistic feelings. In this way, hostility toward the therapist won't be displaced onto the new patient to such a destructive degree that the member will become too threatened to stay. Before the new patient speaks, I have the other patients go around giving five minute capsule versions of why they came and where they are. Some therapists run a looser ship. They spontaneously bring new patients into a group and let them find their own place in the scheme of things. I believe this lack of support asks too much of the newcomer and generates unnecessary anxiety and early resistance.*

---

*Another way that I try to make the new patient comfortable is by discreetly drawing him out, making him feel welcome, inquiring as to how he wants to be treated. For example, if a new patient was almost totally silent and looked frightened during his first session, I would ask how the group seems to him, how he's feeling about it, is there anything he would like to tell the group about himself, etc. If the patient appears disinclined to talk much, I would respect his own sense of readiness, and say something like, "Whenever you feel ready, please feel welcome to come in."

Secondly, I˙ try not to practice what Buber (1970) calls "Semblance," or "Seeming." This has to do with manipulating one's image and self-disclosures so as to shape the patient's perceptions, feelings, and attitudes.

During one session, the arriving group members reported spotting a disgruntled former member sitting in a parked car around the corner. A wave of anxiety and giddiness swept over the group with several members reporting an apprehension that this man was going to come in with a gun and shoot us. I entered into this mood for a short while but then tried to steer the members back to what I thought was more relevant group discussion. As a member present introduced some "more appropriate" material, I noticed myself getting depressed. I soon got in touch with my foolish feeling that as the leader, I had a responsibility to protect the group against irrational anxiety, but in the process I was denying my own anxiety. While I was sharing in the group fantasy about murder possibly being committed, I was also enjoying the experience of myself indulging undefended public anxiety, with no need for a cool professional pose. Once I mechanically shifted from this genuine state of being, my depression told me that I was becoming false and unreal.*

Finally, the enforced analytic position of only making reflections or interpretations is inappropriate for the development of an honest relationship. I tell my patients how they are making me feel. I try to use this part of myself constructively with full awareness of treatment goals, the patient's level of development, the nature of the resistance, and the potential impact on the patient of what I want to come out with. I find that the longer I practice, the more I trust and respect my own spontaneity and the appreciation patients have for straight talk. I am absolutely convinced that even if this approach is anxiety-provoking and controversial, at least it opens the way for all parties concerned to level with each other. I work from the assumption that the more authentic I am and the more I say what is

---

**I recognize that there is a very thin line between sharing of oneself in an honest, open way and acting out. Some therapists still hold to the extreme orthodox position that any expression of personal feelings contaminates the transference. Therapists at the other end of the continuum tend to come out with their inner feelings willy-nilly; in effect, temporarily regressing and becoming a fellow patient. My own position is that discretion, common sense, clinical judgement, and a consistent rationale can make the experienced therapist secure in the knowledge that he is not using the group in order to gratify his own needs. I would not recommend this style for the beginning therapist.

really on my mind, the more likely I am to up-end the patient's expectancies and bring something fresh and exciting into the interaction. As Jung says, "Be the man through whom you wish to influence others." Again, I have to emphasize that I use this style of revealing myself in a measured way. I don't overload new patients with more than I think they can profitably handle. As therapy proceeds, however, to the later stages, I find myself being more personal and self-disclosing. I laugh, I give advice, I get angry, I interpret, I ask questions, I tell my fantasies, I draw parallels and analogies from my own life and background, and altogether I try to sustain an earthy, informal, less role-bound atmosphere. The degree to which I succeed or fail is probably as important in the determination of patient progress as the extent of my technical knowledge and the accuracy of my interpretations. Widely divergent orientations in psychotherapy have always agreed upon the critical nature of the leader's empathic understanding and respect for his patients, his specificity in emphasizing emotional experiencing, his concreteness in problem solving, and his ability to strongly confront the patient when appropriate. Only lately has the therapist's personal integrity and genuineness in the therapeutic encounter been viewed as one of the most crucial variables in determining patient progress. Somebody said it very well with the statement, "In the end, the secret is always in the relationship!"

Personal Anecdotes Further Collaborative Exploration. Every patient worries about whether he will be able to convey to the therapist how things really are with him. At the same time, every therapist concerns himself with whether he can inwardly experience and then verbally communicate his discrete, affectively textured appreciation of the patient's inner reality. One way that I have had success in contributing leverage to a patient's reaching after the confusing feelings inside, is to share personal experiences and draw interesting analogies. This seems to reduce the possibility of resistance by offering a common bond with the patient. I invite him to join me instead of protecting himself against me.

If a group theme of self-blame as a defense against hostility toward one's parents is emerging, I sometimes tell the following story. Two people were hanging by their fingernails from a cliff. The first person (A) is at the mercy of someone who inalterably hates him. Nothing can be done to sway this victimizer from his wrath. The second person (B) is also at the mercy of someone but this person is only angry because B did something that disturbed him. Who is worse off, A or B? The discussion soon clarifies the dynamics of the "bad child" who takes the blame for his parent's crime in order to protect them against his anger, thereby ensuring his survival, but at a high emotional price.

If someone in the group begins to identify his role in the group as the assistant-therapist-favorite-child, I like to tell the following story: When I was nineteen, I worked the whole summer to earn $400. On my return, a family debate was going on about moving to a better neighborhood. My father was reluctant to pay $17 a month more rent. I volunteered to donate my salary and convinced him that the $400 would make up the difference for years. This sense of responsibility and sustained maturity was my contribution to the family equilibrium. When my mother and sister fought in the new apartment, I calmed them down so that the landlord wouldn't dispossess us. It wasn't until years later, that I realized that I was cheated. Who was taking care of me while I was taking care of everybody else? I was sending out signals that made everyone take me for granted. Nobody ever questioned whether I was happy or unhappy or needed something, because I always looked competent and effective and made a fetish of appearing relaxed. This story seems to stimulate discussion about the burdens of being the favorite child, the use of superiority and protectiveness as defenses, and it often succeeds in evoking more overt expressions of sibling rivalry.

If people in the group become plagued with self-doubt and reject positive feedback by claiming that they're fooling others, I often tell the story of Ingmar Bergman's *The Magician*. In twelfth-century Scandanavia there was a mind reader who would travel from town to town telling people their fortunes. He regarded himself as a charlatan because he had an advance man fill him in so that by the time he spoke to anyone he had their whole dossier memorized. There was only one catch—he was telling people more about themselves, far more, than the advance man ever told him. He really was a magician, except that he didn't know it.

If any unexpected metaphor comes to mind while I am dealing with a patient and I can sense how it relates to the on-going process,

I offer it for general discussion. I was once working with a forty-four-year-old man who was terribly unhappy in his marriage but resisted making any move because of what his relatives and business associates would think. The words that came to me were, "The dog with five legs has no tail." This proverb got the patient talking about his lack of guts, his inordinate need for security, and his awareness that he was castrating himself by staying resigned to a fruitless situation with few redeeming features except habit.

If the group is talking about anxiety over too much pleasure in their lives, I enliven things by telling this story about an old friend of mine. I was sitting with him in a restaurant one day and he was savoring his main course immensely. He motioned to the waiter, ordered another main course, took three lusty bites, and left the rest untouched. This incident flabbergasted me. I myself had never exercised such unbridled freedom. When I tell this story, groups immediately pick up threads that pertain either to their aversion to pleasure or their guilt when they've permitted themselves too much pleasure.

Another story in this same vein is one a patient related. A certain man would wait for the Flatbush Avenue bus at the same corner on his way home from work for seventeen years. Each night a frankfurter man was there, and from his wagon beautiful smells would waft down the block. Visions of onions and peppers blended together with a savory garlic smell. But the man would never treat himself to the hot dog because supper was waiting and after all, how would he explain his loss of appetite to his wife? After awhile he continued to notice the frankfurter man but he had lost any desire for his wares. Then one day the patient died. He still hadn't bought his first frankfurter.

This story brings forth discussion of how if you keep cutting your feelings off, you stop having them. It also elicits an exploration of what happens if the reality principle always takes precedence over pleasure. The concept of You only have one life, so why not enjoy it? also frequently comes up.

In order to prime the pump for earliest memories, I first tell one of my own. "I remember being a bear snuggly nestled next to my mother in a very dark cave. I felt very protected." At first, patients may be skeptical that I could ever have imagined being a bear. They may follow this with the thought that they really got hooked up with a crazy therapist, i.e. but then they realize that if the authority person can exercise his imagination in such an extravagant way, then so can they. As a result, I get very vivid early memories that are much richer and more useful than if I simply ask a patient cold, "What was your earliest memory?"

If I feel that a patient in the group is overintellectualizing to such a point that he is keeping himself from experiencing anything new, I'll share the following anecdote. In the first year of my psychology internship I thought I was expected to write sophisticated clinical reports about my patients. Since I had a knack for being very articulate, I was able to turn out reports that impressed my supervisors and made them think I understood more than I actually did. Most probably I had unreasonable expectations on what level I was supposed to be performing and felt the need for approval so much that I was very defensive about seeming naive. In actuality, I was scared silly, felt very insecure, and yet very ashamed to show any of this. My front was effective but inwardly I felt empty, bitterly resenting the extent to which I robbed myself and the envy I felt toward other interns who could be more appropriately dependent.

In order to ease the conversation into oedipal talk, I feel that it is first necessary to set the stage so that patients won't feel too threatened by such material. I occasionally share with the group an oedipal dream that I recollect from my fifth year. "I was the aide-de-camp and my mother was the empress of China—my father was nowhere in the picture." I also describe some of my fantasies, curiosities, and actual experiences that border on oedipal material.

Along similar lines, when I was an early adolescent I used to be fascinated by page 4 of the New York *Daily News*. The stories of beautiful Hollywood divorcees were of particular interest to me. I would fantasize that if I could be magically transported into the adult body of this man whom they were dissatisfied with, I could make them much happier. I would make up for everything that was missing in their lives. If patients are hung up about mixed sexual identifications, and fearful of revealing latent homosexual trends, I try to lead the discussion into a less threatening context by relating the following fantasy: "When I was fifteen I wished that I was Marilyn Monroe so that I could be close to Joe DiMaggio."

These stories are excellent catalysts for heated discussions of early family dynamics, the evolution of identification processes, recurring childhood fantasies, and the emergence of oedipal conflicts, in a matter of fact, nondefensive way. Again I have to emphasize that the purpose of this sort of sharing is to make group discussion less stilted, intellectualized, and guarded, and correspondingly, to further motivate introspection and enhance awareness and recognition of previously neglected personal experiences.

If a patient gets defensive when I focus on a significant slip of the tongue, I try to relax him for an understanding of unconscious motivation by telling him some stories such as the following: "During one session a patient was complaining that he was doing all the work, and that I was just sitting there not saying anything. At the end of the session, when it came time to pay, he made the check out to himself." Or, "When I first bought my house, I felt a lot of ambivalence because I thought it was too expensive. It was a long trip to work and I was afraid if something broke down I wasn't handy enough to repair it. For two months, until I started to feel better about the purchase, I kept forgetting the phone number and making the wrong turn going home."

We all have a rich reservoir of important memories, personal anecdotes, visual images, and striking metaphors. The creative use of this material demands appropriateness to the patients' needs at the moment. The therapist's sense of timing, his intuition, and his theoretical grasp of personality dynamics must be harmonized, carefully integrated, and effectively communicated to get the patient to take another step forward. Caution should be exercised by means of supervision and discussion with colleagues to avoid counterproductive self-revelation in the service of exhibitionism, self-aggrandizement, ingratiation, or the wish to become one of the group by status denial.

The therapist must also guard against using this method mechanically and compulsively. What was originally inventive can easily become shopworn if used too often. The most creative route in therapy steers a middle course between what Holt refers to as "the swamps of oversubjectivity and the deserts of overobjectivity." The therapist who is too undisciplined, impulsive, or loose with his "third ear" functions robs the patient as much as does the therapist who is too tightly guided by reason, plays thinking games with his patients, and functions as a mere technician.

Before I conclude this section, I'd like to address myself to the issue of transference distortion as a result of personal revelation on the part of the therapist. I've already commented on the possibility that this approach could be dismissed by some psychoanalysts on the grounds that it may be unconsciously satisfying the therapist's infantile needs and could conceivably foster intensified resistance patterns within the group. Analysts who might be sympathetic to my contention that it is sufficient for the leader to be aware that this might happen and guard against it, may still have misgivings on different grounds. "By coming through as such a real person, doesn't that limit the patient's fantasies about you? If you (the therapist) come across as such a human, regular, problem-ridden-like-everybody-else person, doesn't this undercut the patient's capacity to attack you? Isn't this seductive? If you're so nice and open, doesn't it arouse guilt for resenting such a paragon of virtue?"

Another line of criticism could take a somewhat different form. For those familiar with object-relations theory, the major works of Kernberg (1966), Fairbairn (1952), and Winnicott (1965) suggest that narcissistic patients need to work through an idealized transference onto the therapist. The theory contends that significant love objects disappointed, hurt, and destroyed them in a continuous way during the formative years. This leaves the developing person devoid of the experiences that would help to create an inner structure. In normal development, there is gradual disappointment in the omnipotence of father and mother regarding their power and goodness. This leads to a temporary feeling of disappointment, of upset, and a sense of loss. A kind of depressive reaction sets in. The recuperation process occurs when the other person is seen not so much as disappointing but as realistic, human. They are less idealized but more like the child himself. This leads to a more substantial sense of self and the internalization of a "good" superego introject. Normal growth takes place with a parent who disappoints in an optimal, relatively reliable way. Under these circumstances, normal children are able to separate more from the parent who disappoints them; they create an inner structure so that in effect they have their own parent within them. This process has to repeat itself over and over again—each time with each loss, more reality, more separation, more internal structure.

To get back to the therapy setting, narcissistic patients continuously search for this idealized parent. They tend to find him (or her), symbiotically attach themselves, get disappointed in a catastrophic way, and then start the whole process over again. This may be why narcissistic patients are so difficult to treat. They never seem to change, they never seem to grow. Kohut (1971) and others claim that the analyst, by providing a reliably disappointing person, a "constant" disappointment, will slowly help the person to mature. This is only possible if the analyst is skillful at negotiating the experience of disillusionment.

Followers of Kohut could criticize my self-revelation approach by arguing that I'm perpetuating the idealized transference by making it more difficult for patients to attack me. If I present myself as warm, decent, having the same frailties as everyone else, I could cheat patients of the opportunity of accusing me of being cold, not saying anything, not revealing very much about myself. This argument would continue that, contrary to seeing me as more human and available (as I seem to believe), patients would interpret this behavior in an idealized way and not be able to move on toward a more realistic perception (objective transference).

My own stance in this regard is that I try to carefully monitor what I choose to reveal. There is some compromise between my natural spontaneity and my clinical judgment. I try to stay abreast of the image that I am currently projecting—the transference object that I am offering to the group. I try not to shape their impression of me in a one-dimensional, self-aggrandizing way. But the important point here is that my mistakes, anxieties, and insecurities do come through, and not necessarily in noble ways. I can sound foolish and sometimes be a deep disappointment. Patients tend to see me in all different ways according to their mood and my mood at the time. If anything, I have found comfort in Kohut's writings because it lends theoretical support to something I've done in practice but had a difficult time conceptualizing. To put it very simply, this has to do with the belief that if you can see me (the therapist) as a substantial person even if my shortcomings are glaringly apparent, then maybe you (the patient) can relax, and not feel that you have to be perfect in order to be respected and loved.

EDUCATING THE PATIENT TO BE A BETTER PATIENT

Like Yalom, I have also found it beneficial to pay close attention to education of patients, before and after they come into group, about their role and the therapist's role in psychotherapy. In early group sessions, I sometimes "stop the action" to establish a conceptual point that can be reinforced and referred to later, as live illustrations emerge from the group process. Following Gibb's lead, I usually keep the following propositions in mind:

1. Because our attitudes toward others are frequently evaluative, statements which the defensive person will regard as nonjudgmental and not accusative are hard to articulate. Even the simplest question can make the listener uptight because there is often a hidden correct answer.

In the midst of a session where the therapist felt bogged down, he hopefully inquired whether the patient had had any dreams recently. She said no and then went on to apologize for not being able to remember her dreams. Later analysis revealed that the patient accurately felt that she was made to feel guilty for not producing what the therapist was anxiously pushing for. The therapist, on the other hand, became aware that by asking for something that the patient couldn't come up with, he was regaining control of the session and maintaining his one-up position.

2. Insecure, group members are quite likely to blame, see others as good or bad, make moral judgments, and question the value, motive, and affect loadings of speech which they hear. Since values imply a judgment of others, a belief that the standards of the speaker differ from his own often causes the listener to become defensive and hostile.

Descriptive speech, in contrast to that which is evaluative, tends to arouse a minimum of uneasiness. Speech acts, which the listener perceives as genuine requests for information, are descriptive. Specifically, presentations of feelings, events, perceptions, or processes which do not ask or imply that the receiver change behavior or attitudes are minimally defense producing. In other words, watch out for your overtones.

4. Speech which tries to control the listener evokes resistance. But methods of control are many and varied, and sometimes very subtle (gestures, facial expressions, conformity norms, etc.). Implicit in all attempts to change another person is the assumption that he is inadequate in some way. That the change agent secretly views the

listener as uninformed, indecisive, immature, unwise, or having the wrong attitude, is a subconscious perception which gives the latter a valid base for defensiveness.

5. Problem orientation, on the other hand, is the handmaiden of permission. When the sender communicates a desire to cooperate in defining a common problem and in seeking its solution, he tends to create the same problem orientation in the listener; and, more important, he implies that he has no predetermined solution, attitude, or method to impose. Such behavior is permissive in that it allows the receiver to set his own goals, make his own decisions, and evaluate his own progress. When the sender is perceived as engaged in strategy involving ambiguous motivations, the target patient becomes defensive.

6. Neutral speech, that is, speech with low affect that communicates little warmth or caring, is sometimes experienced as a form of rejection. Group members want to be perceived as valued persons, as individuals of special worth, and as objects of concern and affection. Communication that conveys empathy for feelings and respect for the uniqueness of the listener, however, is particularly supportive and defense-reductive.

Relaxation occurs when the listener becomes aware that the speaker identifies with his problems, shares his feelings, and accepts his emotional reactions at face value. Abortive efforts to deny the legitimacy of the receiver's emotions by assuring the receiver that he need not feel bad, or that he is overly anxious, though often intended as support-giving, may not be accepted. The combination of understanding and empathizing, with no accompanying effort to change the other person, is apparently very supportive.

7. When a patient communicates to another that he feels superior in position, power, wealth, intellect, self-awareness, or physical characteristics he arouses defensiveness. The feelings of inadequacy that are engendered in the listener cause him to focus on the affective loadings of the statement rather than upon the cognitive elements. The listener then reacts by not hearing the message content, by forgetting it, by competing with the sender, or by becoming jealous. The person who is perceived as feeling superior communicates that he is not willing to participate in a shared problem-solving relationship, that he probably does not desire feedback, and that he does not require help.

Further Relationships Between Feedback and Self-Disclosure

Sensitivity training originated with the introduction and development of the T (training) Group. Meeting in a small group environment, the T Group operates on the assumption that understanding of oneself and others can best be accomplished through the sharing of perceptions, feelings, and reactions to self and others in the here and now. Out of this "learning how to learn" experience comes the knowledge of the self and the dynamics of group interaction, which, hopefully, each individual will be able to incorporate into his ordinary life setting to improve his level of communication skills and increase his ability to help others.

Feedback is a way of helping another person to consider changing his behavior. It is communication with a person which gives that person information about how he affects others. The technical term comes originally from the field of automation. For example, the thermostat gives feedback to a furnace on how well the furnace is heating the thermostat. It is a term which applies equally well to what goes on in group. Helpful feedback should be:

Descriptive. It has already been mentioned that descriptive feedback is an improvement over inductive feedback. Describing one's own reaction leaves the individual free to use it or not as he sees fit. Avoiding evaluating language reduces the need for the individual to react defensively: for instance, "Susan, I can't hear what you are saying. Could you talk a little louder please?" This gives a different feel from the statement, "Susan, you talk too low." The latter sounds condemning and puts all the responsibility on Susan. The former shares the situation between Susan and the speaker and contains the complimentary rather than accusing note. Some other examples of feedback comments are:

"I felt hurt when you didn't listen to me," *rather than* "You are rude!"

"I feel hurt and humiliated," *rather than* "Why do you always put me down?"

"I am disappointed that you didn't remember our appointment," *rather than* "You don't care about me!"

"I am too angry to hear what you are saying now," *rather than* "Go fuck yourself."

The best way to describe feelings is by name, simile, and action urge, conveying it as information about one's inner state and not as an attack or coersive demand on the other.

Specific. It is specific rather than general. To be told that one is "dominating" will probably not be as useful as to be told that "Just before, when we were talking about the party, I felt I had to do what you wanted or you would jump on me."

Appropriate. It takes into account the needs of both the receiver and giver of feedback. Feedback can be destructive when it serves only our own needs and fails to consider the needs of the person on the receiving end.

> A husband and wife had been working on a serious sexual problem for about six months in a couples group. Their difficulties were very complex and subtle and this particular evening, the group was successfully clarifying one aspect of their conflict. In the midst of this, one woman impatiently blurted out, "Oh, why don't the two of you have a couple of drinks and go to bed already!" When feedback is drastically out of tune with the tone of what precedes it, the person who is addressed usually turns off and begins to feel that he has overstayed his leave.

Useable. It is directed toward behavior which the receiver can do something about. Frustration is only increased when a person is reminded of some shortcomings over which he has no control (e.g. "Your voice sounds feminine").

Requested. It is solicited rather than imposed. Feedback is most acceptable when the receiver himself has formulated the question which those observing him can answer.

> Jerry by his physical presence showed that he wanted something from the group but never made it clear what he needed. When members offered reactions to his behavior, he would either nod his head yes, say a few words, or appear only mildly interested while speculation concerning himself swirled around him. After a few months, group resentment and antagonism grew as members started sensing that behind the passivity was a great deal of control and subtle hostility.

Timely. It is well-timed. In general, feedback is most useful when offered at the earliest opportunity after the given behavior (depending, of course, on the person's readiness to hear it, the support available from others, etc.). However, a commonly encountered group resistance takes the form of denying the legitimacy of potentially threatening feedback by criticizing the speaker for not talking when the event in question happened.

Clear. It is checked to insure clear communication. One way of doing this is to have the receiver try to rephrase the feedback he has received to see if it corresponds to what the sender had in mind. "Do you mean . . . (statement). . .?" "Is this . . . (statement) . . . an accurate understanding of your idea?" "Would this be an example of what you mean? (giving a specific example)."

Another way of sharpening reception skills is to engage in a perception check: that is, describe what you perceive the other person feels—tentatively and without evaluating him. "I get the impression you would rather not talk about that. Is that so?"; "You were disappointed that they didn't ask you to go along?"; "You look like you felt hurt by my comment. Were you?"

Accurate. When feedback is given in a therapy group, both giver and receiver have an opportunity, with others in the group, to check the accuracy of the feedback. Is this the impression of one man or is it shared by others? It is highly important to remember that not all members in the group see and read the data in the same way. We all see what we are prepared to see. We are affected by the speaker's output in conjunction with what each of us brings to the encounter. A statement which makes one person bristle might amuse another. Therefore, it is more accurate to say, "Jack, what you said just now ticks me off," rather than "Jack, you always talk provocatively." Categorical comments of that sort are more apt to be a false than a accurate summary of the group's reaction. At least, they need to be checked out for their applicability.

Trusted. A trusted, nonthreatening source helps to make feedback more palatable. It is very different for someone who is concerned about our welfare to advise us to go on a diet or to cut down on our smoking than for somebody to nag us or use our bad habits as a "sweet, reasonable" excuse for hostility.

Feedback, then, is a way of giving help; it is a corrective mechanism for the individual who wants to learn how well his behavior matches his intentions; and it is a means for establishing ones identity, for answering who am I.

To summarize, some appropriate standards for giving feedback are:

—Speak to data
—Speak to one specific datum at a time
—Check with the target patient
—Give feedback at a useful level
—Offer rather than impose feedback
—Talk about behavior you can see
—Give feedback as soon as possible
—Give it directly; don't hint or allude to it or filter through a third party
—Give the other person a chance to explain
—Set the climate for feedback
—Give it caringly
—Don't nag or hound a person about his behavior unless he has told you that he wants your help
—Don't probe the why of behavior, just deal with what you see
—The way we *feel* as a result of another's behavior is genuine and authentic

Tell *how* it makes you feel

—Don't beat around the bush
—Don't use sarcasm or a condescending manner when giving feedback
—Show the positive too
—Don't judge

Examples of feedback comments are

Not "You were insecure" (personal imputation) *but* "It seemed to me you often did not speak when the group was tense or upset" (report of perceived behavior)
Not "You were trying to take over the group" (attack, imputed motives) *but* "I don't know how you saw it, but the impression that came across to me was that you were trying to control me.

How did you feel about it?" (here is my reaction to your behavior; what is your view of it?)

Not "You are a pleasant, well-adjusted person" (personality generalization, stereotyping) *but* "Whenever you spoke, I felt warm and accepted. You never did anything that threatened me " (report of the way you affected *me.*)

Not "The group thinks you are very smart" (imputation of opinion to the group) *but* "You struck me as making a real contribution to our thinking, for example while we were trying to decide when to meet for the alternative session. Do other group members share this feeling?" (here is my view, what is that of others?)

Self-disclosure has to do with how and to what extent the individual makes more of himself known to others. Feedback is often directed at those patients who are willing to share information about themselves. Relatedly, appropriate feedback often will elicit self-disclosure. You have to give in order to get. The great significance of feedback and self-disclosure in a therapy group is easy to see, but hard to capitalize on. One step in the right direction is to sensitize patients from the very beginning to the most important dynamics operating in the group. This seems to further greater involvement and participation in the common good.

Some of the points I either make directly with patients or apply in the course of my interventions:

1. If you want to get worthwhile feedback, try to disclose self-information that has revelance and meaning for the events in which you are currently participating. If you change the topic, make lots of small talk, or break a mood, be prepared for a neutral or negative reaction. Appropriateness of self-disclosure increases the liklihood of positive reactions. This does not imply that you should not take risks by going beyond group norms. On the contrary, many valuable experiences emerge as a result of persons taking risks. But essential to the meaning of "risks" is that its effects may be far less than optimal, and the discloser must take the responsibility for risk taking.

2. To the extent that the communicator is congruent, the receiver is likely to accept his participation at face value and be open to viewing his communication favorably. A fairly common type of patient seen in therapy groups is the help-rejecting complainer. At

first, group members are sympathetic and giving when the patient presents his problems. Disillusionment sets in when, time after time, the patient manipulates the group by continually rejecting what is offered, never seeming to be satisfied, but always asking for more.

3. All concerns are the property of the group as a whole. A good group therapist should never sit passively by and allow the group to become just a bunch of onlookers, while only two members interact. If two people are fighting with one another in front of the group, the therapist should encourage other group members to comment on the relationship and how it affects them and the entire group. This is often difficult. People don't like to butt in. They feel that it is none of their business. Often the other members are afraid of the feelings involved in the interchange. Many participants are too polite or too inhibited to interrupt noninvolving group action (or dyadic action, as the case may be.) The therapist should constantly remind the group that there are no "brownie points" for excessive good manners. Everyone should feel free to speak on every issue and should actually take advantage of their freedom.

One of the violations of the everything-through-the-group standard is siphoning. Two or more members get together outside the group in order to work out their relationship. They return to the group changed, and this interrupts the rhythm of the group. Or worse, one member will pair with another member outside the group in order to discuss and work out feelings toward a third member. This dilutes group process and manifests negative feelings toward, and mistrust of, the group. It is only natural that a certain amount of pairing take place outside the group, but whatever significant interactions this involves should be made public to the whole group. Pairing may be encouraged or planned, however, if it helps make the group sessions more meaningful. For instance, one of the group members might find it quite difficult to engage in self-disclosure. So outside the group, he tells what he thinks is important to another group member. This breaks the ice for him and enables him to be open in the group. Many therapists see patients in combined treatment (individual and group), using the less threatening atmosphere of the private session to further explore insights that have been gained in group. If proper caution is taken not to prevent sharing with the group, the coordinated effect can be very advantageous.

4. Try to talk directly to what is going on in the group. Make the

basic focus what is happening at the moment. A person's capacity to be well-integrated is enhanced to the extent that he can deal realistically with his present (Clark 1967). One of the therapist's prime functions is to help patients to talk as much as possible about data that is directly verifiable. The problem with the past is that it causes boredom. It makes group members lose contact with one another. The group cannot survive, much less operate effectively, unless certain of its needs are fulfilled. Prolonged dealings with concerns that are too distant is like cutting off the oxygen supply of the group. A kind of suffocation takes place. Therefore, group members have to search out meaningful ways of rendering their "then-and-there" concerns to the members in the now. If these expressed concerns and genuine and not used for manipulative purposes, then they define the speaker. They color him and his activity. In other words, in the course of relating an outside event, the speaker is interacting with the audience and giving it a chance to validate his outside story in the here and now.

> A patient was describing his wife's selfishness and control. "Everything has to be done her way, she never lets you put a word in edgewise." In the meantime, this man had monopolized the group for thirty minutes, was unaware of the group's irritability and restlessness, and had passed over four or five comments by fellow group members, pausing for a moment each time and then continuing as though nothing at all had been said.

The therapist can be very helpful here, by modeling ways of transporting then-and-there concerns so that they become relevant to the group. The inept group therapist falls back on the expedient of using the group as a locus for multiple individual therapy. In this regard, Carl Rogers (1951) has commented:

> It should also be mentioned that in this concept of motivation all the effective elements exist in the present. Behavior is not "caused" by something which occurred in the past. Present tensions and present needs are the only ones which the organism endeavors to reduce or satisfy. While it is true that the past experience has certainly served to modify the meaning which will be perceived in present experiences, yet there is no behavior except to meet a present need. (p. 492)

Too often in group therapy, patients become preoccupied with there-and-then concerns not because they are more meaningful, but because they are safer. If they are really meaningful, they should be translated into the here-and-now concerns and becomes vehicles of involvement rather than modes of flight.

5. It is terribly dull to listen to a conversation filled with vagueness and generalities. Truax and Carkhuff (1964) have indicated that concreteness and specificity in the therapeutic dialogue may well be variables worth exploring. They define concreteness as follows:

> A *low* level of concreteness or specificity is when there is a discussion of anonymous generalities; when the discussion is on an abstract intellectual level. This includes discussions of "real" feelings that are expressed on an abstract level. A *high* level of concreteness or specificity is when specific feelings and experiences are expressed—"I hated my mother!" or "Then he would blow up and start throwing things"; when expressions deal with specific situations, events, or feelings, regardless of emotional content (p. 266).

Such concreteness definitely makes interactions more immediate and personal. Some of the rules for immediacy that I try to convey to my patients are:

The use of "I." When the participant is speaking of himself he must use "I" and not some substitute such as "we," "one," "you," "people," or some impersonal expression such as "it happens." Any substitute for "I" entails a loss of immediacy, and puts distance between any speaker and the state or action he is discussion.

Concreteness. The speaker should avoid vagueness, abstractions, and generalities. If he does talk about something abstract, such as a principle, he should illustrate what he means by a concrete example, preferably from his own experience. In general, he should talk about his own experience. If he talks about the experience of others, he should talk about the impact that the other experiences has on him.

Speak to a particular person. The participant should, in general, address specific people in the group rather than the entire group. The participant who always speaks to everyone often speaks to no one. It is more immediate to address the whole group through a specific member. For instance, someone might say: "I think that there is a lot of running away going on in the group. John, you tend to talk about stuff from the outside all the time. Bill, when called, you're always uptight and very defensive. You don't open up and examine the issues at all." The person who addresses the whole group tends to talk about generalities and to give speeches. Both are deadly to group interaction.

Questions. The participants should not ask too many questions, especially the question "Why?" Pointed questions that demand concrete answers help keep the interaction concrete. The question "Why?" usually demands an interpretation on the part of the respondent. Interpretations tend to become vague, highly intellectualized and hypothetical and are therefore antithetical to the immediacy desired in the interaction. "Did you hit him?" gets at the facts of the respondent's behavior. "Why did you hit him?" can lead anywhere and thus nowhere.

Cut down on filibustering. Don't let the patients grab the initiative in establishing their typical character defenses by permitting them to talk in lengthy paragraph form. Feel free to interrupt.

I see a parallel between the cadence of a person's speech and his style of defending. If a person talks typically in terse, abbreviated statement form, this may be an anxious avoidance of revealing too much. In this instance, encouraging elaboration and not letting him off the hook with summary statements, is advisable. If, on the other hand, a person thinks and speaks in lengthy paragraph form, the best way to break this character resistance is for the therapist to intervene after the first couple of sentences. What I am stressing here is that the unexpected is the best way to deal with character defenses. The therapist must seize the initiative. The breaking into ingrained sentence structure patterns is the surest way to shake up an overlearned, prefabricated resistance. For example: *Patient,* "Well anyhow, I . . ." *Therapist,* "It made me think you wanted me to forget something."

Don't accept pat answers. Try to find out how the other person actually feels about what he is saying.

Let me summarize the principal communication-reception skills that I try to transmit to my patients, and in the process, emphasize and flesh out some of the points that have already been made:

Ask for feedback. The special combination of someone requesting help and doing this when they feel most open-minded to the feedback forthcoming is most conducive to worthwhile communication.

Try to receive it openly. Hear people out. If you frown early in their communication attempt, interrupt their statement, find excuses, or argue back, nothing will be accomplished. Try to entertain the other person's opinion and give it a fair chance to see if it's worth anything.

Don't make excuses. Finding excuses or rationalizing turns people off. They feel as though they have to get over a difficult hurdle to reach you. Accept what is said, even if momentarily. What's so terrible about that?

Acknowledge the value of feedback. If you want continued feedback, the supplier must feel that it's worth it. People lose courage and interest in giving feedback if they don't feel their statement is making any kind of impact.

Don't just sit there with a blank stare. If you disagree, that's all right. But complete indifference is destructive in that it discourages sustained involvement, and also it is false.

Occasionally at least express appreciation that people cared enough to give you the feedback. Group members deserve acknowledgement for their efforts. It is a message to "try me again even if this time I can't connect up with you."

Discuss the feedback. Don't just say, "Thank you" and let it drop. Make the feedback part of a shared quest for mutual understanding. Don't let communication be a one-way street.

Try to be objective. That is, don't personalize if you can at all help it. A wife told her husband one night that she was depressed. The husband construed this to mean, "What did I do wrong lately?" He spent the rest of the evening ticking off all the nice things he had done for her (but he still didn't know what was bothering her).

View feedback as part of a continuing exploration. If someone makes a comment during a particular session and you are only able to work it through up to a particular point, do some thinking during the week. Don't let the slender thread break. Bring your new observations back to the group. When someone knows you've been thinking of them, they begin to think of you and to take you more seriously.

Indicate what you intend to do with feedback. People like to know what happened to their offerings. The significance with which you treat feedback, how you are going to allow it to affect your life, are of consequence in determining future patterns of giving in the group.

Get the reactive feelings out quickly. Don't carry a grudge, if possible. The longer you hold feelings in, the more likely they are to get twisted, distorted, transformed, and justified. The sooner that you speak up after the critical episode, the more likely it is that you can get satisfactory closure.

Don't automatically look for motives and hidden meanings. Don't discount the literal meaning of what people say by seeking out their deeper meanings.

> A patient was once accused of being cheap because he always mooched cigarettes but never bought his own pack. He tried to interpret this to mean that he was overprotected as a child and spoiled, so that as an adult he wasn't capable of giving. "Oh no", said the woman sitting next to him, "You're a cheapskate. Specifically now, why don't you smoke your own cigarettes?"

Seek clarification. If you don't understand something, ask the person who said it what they meant. Therapists would benefit too if they took the role of the intelligent but naive observer who asks questions until he is satisfied as to the other person's intentions. Many therapists masochistically assume an omnipotent position and feel impelled to interpret on the basis of minimal information. They foolishly view help-me-to-understand questions as reflections of their inadequacies unless they come up with a "quicky" profound answer.

Think about the feedback and try to build upon it. This is a continuation of point nine. Test out the feedback. See if it applies to outside relationships. Seek validation from other group members as to whether they see you in the same way. Try to crystalize in your mind under what conditions the feedback statement might possibly be accurate.

> A woman was describing how her boyfriend said, "Don't take this relationship seriously," and she went on to deny any hurt or angry feeling stemming from the remark. Another member, Sally, confronted

her with her avoidance of strong emotions. She kept warding off this
feedback by saying that she was "not really that way", and asked the rest
of the group for confirmation. People in the group noted that in the face
of Sally's challenging attitude, her body language and defensive
verbalization betrayed feelings of resentment and a sense of being misunderstood. In contrast to this the content of her words were weak,
apolegetic and self-justifying. This massive dose of consensual feedback
helped to highlight her dissonance, and successfully broke through the
denial mechanisms to the extent that real feelings began to emerge.*

Confrontation is usually directed toward the defenses of the
target patient. This questioning of defenses, although ultimately
growthful, can entail temporary disorganization. Every individual
has a characterologically established self-image protected by a
unique system of defenses. Such mechanisms are resistant to change
because they are always associated with anxiety reduction; that is,
they insulate the self-image against threat.

A patient who was hurt by her husband's spending much time away
on business trips, tended to rationalize her feelings by saying it didn't
matter because she didn't love him and no longer felt close to him.
Several sessions later the patient realized that if she were to acknowledge
the extent of her hurt feelings this would open the floodgates of terrible
feelings of desertion and abandonment. This anticipated dread was
closely related to actual traumatic events of her childhood that she was
trying to avoid recapitulating.

In the therapy group, when an individual's typical style of
interacting is interrupted and his defenses focused on, considerable
anxiety results. Such anxiety constitutes a force for new learning
because, if the group experience is a successful one, new methods of
anxiety reduction are learned. If the group climate is supportive and
growth-promoting, these new adaptations will have more utility for
the individual in coping with his environment than did his old
dysfunctional behavior. Thus, anxiety serves a purpose of shaking
the participant loose from preconceived notions and habitual forms
of interacting so that feedback may intensify its effect. Without such
"unfreezing," feedback is ineffectual (Campbell and Dunnette
1968). Harry Stack Sullivan (1953) was pointing to these
possibilities when he suggested that each person has a composite of

behavior patterns called *dynamisms*. These are largely hidden from the individual but are immediately apparent to others. In group, the feedback from others about my behavior would be mostly a reflection of these unseen behavior patterns of mine; the process of conscious awareness is greatly enhanced so long as free interaction is built into the communication network. I then have choices where before I was a victim of forces beyond my control.

The strength of the confrontation must be commensurate with the ego resiliency of the target patient. Confrontation represents a direct challenge to the patient's illusions. Even though the patient's perspective is distorted, it feels "solid" to him. I would suspect that except for wild, untrained leaders who do their thing by hammering away at defenses with no awareness of relevant dynamics, proper timing, or developmental readiness, many therapists avoid active confrontation because the anticipated reaction scares them. Saying things in carefully phrased, cautious ways dilutes the strength of the message to be delivered. In the process, their patients lose the chance for "beneficial uncertainty," which is a step toward growth rather than toward dissolution.

One way of illustrating and concretizing the norm or climate of trust and caring leading to greater sharing is by means of the Johari Window (Luft 1955). The leader begins by drawing the Johari Window on an easel sheet and explains that "there are some things about me that are obviously known to you. The color of my shoes, the style of my hair, whether or not I have a beard. These things are public information. You know them; I know them. They are my public self (box 1). There are things about me that are unknown to you. You aren't aware of them unless I tell you about them: What my concerns in life are, how I feel about my job, my ambitions, my goals, my dreams. These things are hidden from you. They are my private self (box 3). Then there are some things about me that are unknown to me, but that you know about me: what kind of impact I have on you, for instance. I don't know how I come across to you

---

*Obviously these skills present standards impossible for anyone to continuously live up to. By identifying them as desirable, however, the therapist can later refer back to them and slowly educate patients to take a greater measure of personal responsibility for the impact they make on others. Moreover, transference reactions can be seen in a clearer light. If patient A is rigidly rejecting practically everything that patient B says, even though patient B is living up to his end of the "good communication" contract, then patient A is confronted with the challenge of teasing out his explanation of why he has this irrational negative response.

unless you tell me. That's a blind area for me (box 2). Then there are things about me that you don't know and I don't either. These things represent the unconscious an untapped potential (box 4). The whole goal of therapy is to increase the area of box 1 in relation to the other three areas. The more I know about myself, the more consciously I can govern my life. The less energy I have to use hiding from you, the more I can concentrate on being what I am. The more we can be open with each other, the better chance we have to understand each other and work together effectively. For this to happen there has to be a norm of caring and trust. Sharing is often uncomfortable and difficult. No one will do it if the climate isn't right. Under the proper circumstances, two people can be so trusting with one another that even box 4 data can be unearthed."

JOHARI'S WINDOW

FEEDBACK

		Known to Self	Unknown to Self
D I S C L O S U R E	Known to others	1. Public Area	2. Blind Area
	Unknown to others	3. Hidden Area	4. Unknown Area

But even under the best of circumstances, people don't accept the "truth" about themselves. In a broad sense, the reason for this resistance is that no one likes to believe that he is acting neurotically out of choice. Patients constantly struggle against awareness that their life has no predetermined meaning and therefore demands self-definition. The key to understanding the successful self-disclosure-feedback-insight process is that if you make a person enough aware of parts of himself that he has denied, he will gradually repossess himself, begin to see alternative ways of behaving, exercise greater control over his fate, and take ultimate responsibility for himself. The Johari Window concept, though somewhat simplistic, graphically suggests that the more we make ourselves congruent and the more we increase the area in box 1, the more self-directed and related we can become. In this context, I view resistance as a function of the guilt and fear of assuming personal responsibility. Parental introjects forbid the patient from experiencing satisfaction and so he appeases his conscience by surrendering a part of himself. Johari Window provides the basis for setting the record straight. It places what has happened to the patient and why he believes he must act the way he does, in an intellectually understandable framework. Once the basic pattern is clearly delineated so that the patient's observing ego is recruited as a conscious ally, the working-through process can be made somewhat easier. The appropriate application of some of the exercises described in chapter 6 can now be used to focus on the dissolution of guilt and the reestablishment of "I," with a much better chance of success.

The way I tie the Johari Window concept into feedback and self-disclosure is by asking the group members to perform the following tasks:

I ask each participant to list all the good things and bad things they have revealed about themselves since they began in group. Then I ask them to make a separate list of traits they haven't yet revealed.

I ask each member to repeat the first task with regard to every other participant.

I then collect the feedback forms and read them aloud anonymously.

Members have an opportunity to see whether they are primarily seen in terms of what they think they have revealed rather than in terms of their blind spots. An exploration of the negative points in area 2, sometimes leads to anxiety but this is usually counterbalanced by unexpected positives that people don't anticipate (everybody tries their best but expects the worst). This discussion frequently is enriched by members being stimulated to share their area 3 secrets.

Patients are frequently surprised by how much of themselves has been noticed, or they are confronted with how little they have chosen to reveal. They become curious why others don't realize certain things about them. They often openly discuss their reasons for remaining guarded or they inquire why others resist seeing the obvious.

> I once saw a man in treatment who was a child molester. After about a year of individual work, I suggested group. The patient was frightened on grounds that his perversion would shock others and they would see him as disgusting. When he finally joined the group, he took about three months to reveal his secret. The members made a few perfunctory remarks and then continued on to another theme. During the next two sessions the group totally denied the revelation. The patient confronted the group and made them see that their avoidance made him feel as though he didn't exist (which he felt was worse than being seen as a pervert).

SUMMARY

In many ways those of us who are practicing group psychotherapists have tended to overlook the obvious, assuming that it is too superficial or irrelevant. We've been trained to focus on problem solving while working primarily with rather severe conflicts. Traditional group approaches have relied heavily on resistance and transference analysis and by restricting their interest to interpretation and the encouragement of different forms of free association within the group setting have not shown much interest in examining communication patterns themselves ("the how of things"). And yet to my way of thinking, the deep understanding and appreciation of intrapsychic and group-content dynamics must share in importance with other, often neglected parameters that a good leader can offer to a group. Thus, this chapter is devoted to illuminating how the leader must take responsibility for helping members examine group and dyadic processes by clarifying, interpreting, and offering suggestions, while encouraging the data flow.

To summarize, honest self-presentation in the here and now is the genesis of intimacy and an experience in interdependency. The key ingredient in reaching this goal of intimacy is time—not chronos (linear time) but karios (quality of time). We can make the passage of time into a supersaturated, fertile soil for growth by strengthening the communication skills described above. In reaction to open disclosure, other members are encouraged to respond wholly to the person, and not to the verbal message. This in turn prompts a counterreaction of how I respond to your responding to me. The process continues until someone else rewrites the agenda and gains the group's attention. In the course of this process, the participating members have an opportunity for feedback, to appraise their self-perceptions as well as to reevaluate their prediction of the other's perception of him.

Specifically, I strive to accomplish the following learning tasks during the crucial first three months of a patient's entrance into a group:

1. To get the target patient to relate his behavior to the subsequent responses he evokes
2. To get the patients to evaluate their goals in terms of their current behavior
3. By means of a leveling process, to gain experience in responding as a coequal with other group members
4. By establishing the norm of honest self-presentation and straight feedback, to make the group safe for continuing interaction (trust)
5. To help members realize George Bach's motto: that constructive aggression leads to intimacy, not alienation
6. By making patients take responsibility for their behavior, to get them to see that they can create opportunities rather than passively accept the "natural flow of life events" as givens
7. By causing patients to see that a loosening of their defensive postures allows for greater room for experimentation and contructive energy to cope more creatively with crisis events in their present situation.

Again I have to state that these communication guidelines are not enough by themselves to effect deep psychotherapeutic change. Coupled with traditional clinical skills, conceptual understanding of

group and individual dynamics, and a resistance analysis orientation, they provide the leader with something extra to offer to his
patients. Not only do transmission and reception skills promote a
growthful group climate, but they provide each participant with a
useful framework for applying these skills beyond the confines of
the group subculture. A sizable proportion of patients who report
minimal short-term positive change as a result of group exposure
terminate early. In working with these dropouts from other groups,
I have instituted some of the procedures described in chapters 2 and
3, with very positive results. Many poor-prognosis clients improve
their motivation to work once they can see something tangible about
how they talk and how they listen. Of course, these communication
interventions are woven in and out of the problem orientation, so
the patients themselves don't feel basically frustrated because
"they're not talking about what they came in for." For those sceptics
who question the validity of this approach as being limited in value
to highly intellectual, sophisticated patients, let me just say that this
format (with appropriate revisions) has proven equally successful in
a black agency with a low-income catchment area, in a Catholic
agency servicing many welfare clients and also with a group of well-
educated, middle-class patients in private treatment.

4

Attitudes
Toward Structured Exercises

In this chapter three prominent group psychotherapists will be interviewed concerning their experiences in using structured exercises and encounter techniques in their ongoing therapy groups. The following areas will be explored:

1. How did you go about introducing new techniques (nonverbal, games, Gestalt) into your ongoing groups?
2. What do you think the effect on resistance is when a patient is encouraged to "act in" his problem through the vehicle of a game or structured exercise?
3. Is the nature of the transference affected by the leader's being more structuring and directive (e.g., suggesting tasks)?
4. How do you handle patient resistance to assigned individual or group tasks?
5. How do you determine when it is appropriate to introduce a game or exercise and when such an intervention would represent a counterresistance?
6. Have any games or exercises backfired? How do you handle this?
7. Have any new games or techniques spontaneously emerged in your group? If so, can you describe them?

George D. Goldman got his Ph.D. from New York University in 1950 and his certificate on completing Psychoanalytic Training in 1958 from the William Alanson White Psychoanalytic Institute of Psychiatry, Psychoanalysis, and Psychology. He was trained in group psychotherapy in the early 1950s with the Veterans Administration and later in workshops with Alexander Wolf and Florence Powdermaker. He has been doing group psychotherapy for about twenty-five years and is a fellow of the American Group Psychology Association. He has published four papers and edited two books on the future of group pscyhology and group process.

TS : What's your conception of group therapy?

GG: I don't use the group situation to focus on real life problems, for the most part. I try to have patients visualize the group as a microcosm of society and use it to bring data into the individual session that is more vivid and intense than the data that they might bring from the outside.

TS : When patients try to bring things in from the outside, how do you handle it?

GG: For the most part the group handles it and discourages it and says, "What does that have to do with us? What does that have to do with your relationship with us?" Especially with a group that's been going on for any length of time, there's no problem bringing things back to where they should be.

TS : Patients pick up their cues from you in that aspect.

GG: Yes, I do a lot of educating in the beginning. Once I have oriented them to it, they pick it up.

TS : What's been your feeling about these new techniques, the encounter techniques, the Gestalt approach?

GG: For the most part, I think they're too gimmicky. I have on occasion used them and I have, for example, used them in marathons. I have used them as a carry-over from my own experiences in encounter groups, but for the most part I avoid them as antithetical to my view of group therapy. I want to work with group dynamics; I want to deal with transference; I want to work with ego-psychology and the person's use of himself and the evolving of personality. If I introduce too many outside agents, the personality of the group isn't changing at its own rate, not growing by its own efforts. It's as though some artificial method has been induced that's not a reflection of the egos and I want egos to have participated in their own growth. So, even though I have used these things, at the moment I do not. I run a straight analytic group.

TS : You make it sound as if you've gone through different phases of your own thinking because of the experiences you have had in your enthusiasm for or your questioning of these approaches.

GG: This is true. I have found that often a group had gotten to be too intellectual, that I felt it was going too slowly, that progress might be intensified for one particular person by some more dramatic technique, and I had seen remarkable results at times using these games. But, in the long run it's not my cup of tea and I gave up using it.

TS : You indicated before that one reason for that was that you felt as if there was something the leader imposed on the patients so that patients weren't "coming from within themselves" because of it.

GG: Right. In other words, I try to do a very patient-centered, ego-psychologically modeled psychoanalytic psychotherapy, and if I interpose all these techniques, the timing of the unfolding of conflicts in the person involved is going to be interfered with, and he might not be really ready to integrate them. He might not be ready to share this with a group of people and since this is what I believe in most, I don't do that. The other thing is that one of the major techniques I use is the unfolding and gradual development of the group process (how a patient affects the group, how the group affects him, what is literally happening in terms of the feelings at the moment in the group). My whole sensitivity to this and my whole use of techniques gets fucked up if I start bringing in intervening variables that I have no control over and I don't know what effect they're going to have on the patient or other people.

TS : Speculate for a moment about what effect you think it does have when these things are introduced.

GG: Well, let's take one of the things that I did introduce. I brought a big pillow from the couch onto the floor and suggested that lying on it and kicking arms and legs and having a childish temper tantrum might help members to work through certain problems. I used it with a particular patient and it seemed to have released a great deal of terror, because what came out was eventually a cry for mama. It was really connected with all her dynamics and I chose that technique because I really thought that was her problem and she needed a release and she needed to feel it. Now, the other group members thought it was gimmicky. They were angry at me for introducing it. They felt it had destroyed the group feeling and that I was doing individual therapy in a group setting. There was no awareness of what might have happened or the reason that I had chosen her to work on. They were really angry at me.

TS : Could that be more a function of your not preparing them well enough, than the introduction of the technique itself?

GG: I don't know if it's a matter of not preparing them well enough; it's a combination of having spent, with some of them, years orienting them the other way, so that it's like with my kids. They were raised in a sort of kosher house atmosphere; if I suddenly said "Here's a slice of ham, it's good, taste it," all the preparation in the world is not going to get them to accept that if it goes against every value they have. So, I identify as a psychoanalyst and my patients identify, for the most part, as psychoanalysands. They accept that group dynamics and intragroup interaction is the model we're going to use. Now, with that as something they've incorporated and accepted, these things are not intragroup dynamics, they're from an external source, brought in.

TS : Now aside from the group opposition, did you find too that the resistance emerging during that particular session was because the technique was premature or precipitous for that particular patient?

GG: Well, it didn't seem to have lasting effects. I've used other things. I've used the active trust experience, passing the body around and picking it up and rocking it and all of that; and again, with a patient who was a particularly paranoid, distrustful person, it had a good effect. Then with another distrusting lady, while someone was lifting her, they had their hands on her ass and, I don't know if they moved them or what, but instead of becoming a trust experience it became a distrust experience and it sort of acted as a precipitating thing for, well, a lot of grist for the analytic mill, but it certainly didn't do what we were intending to do. Just bare hands on her body threw her into a panic so that I eventually got to feel it wasn't doing what I wanted and that frankly I had brought these things in out of desperation when I felt that my analytic techniques were not working. So, they were in some sense manifestations of countertransference feelings of helplessness. When I felt a lack of faith in myself and a lack of faith in my analytic techniques I would ask, in a sense, for magic. "God help me with this magic gimmick," and it was an external magic gimmick that was antithetical to everything I believed in and I had been trying to get the patients to believe in.

TS : Do you feel that this would be one of the primary aspects of countertransference that would be responsible for the introduction of games?

GG: For me, yes. In my own analysis, I had sort of gone back into analysis and it wasn't going as fast as I wanted it to go and I was acting out a faster method, as though I was asking "Why doesn't my analyst do something faster with me?" It was a sense of helplessness. It was trying to be current. In other words I am very aware that it's a fashionable thing to do and that I wanted to be up on what the new generation of therapists were doing. I didn't want to fall behind the times so that as each new thing came up I would take a course or a workshop in it and try to see if I could integrate it so that I would be up on things. I had to prove to myself that I wasn't stagnating so I would try to use these things, but they were so alien to my frame of reference that I couldn't integrate them.

TS : Could you speculate for a moment about what you expect to happen to resistance as these techniques are introduced to patients?

GG: Well, there are two different ways of approaching resistance. One is manipulating the resistance of the patient and in a sense beating the resistance out of them; overpowering the resistance, not respecting the resistance, or not respecting the defense. The other way is that by bringing it in at a time when the patient's natural senses are not ready, some foreign thing only builds up resistance and resentment toward you and resentment toward the treatment, and all the person's defenses are not geared to face whatever insight you are giving him. The whole concept of timing is important here: that timing is a very sensitive thing; timing is an interpretation, timing is an awareness based upon your knowledge of the person, his dynamics and your knowledge of his readiness to face it by his giving you enough cues and clues—that this is what he's ready for. In fact, all of group therapy does in some sense mess up timing because the patients aren't cued to the way things might best unfold.

TS : How do you think that affects the natural unfolding process, the fact that patients react spontaneously, and randomly, and not according to prescription?

GG: Well, there are some analysts who say that you should never use group treatment because you can't really do psychoanalysis any more once you've introduced a patient to a group. I don't go along with this. But I do know that there are times that it can bring awarenesses that the person is in no sense of the word ready to accept. I have a patient now who was probably put back a year or so in his treatment because of a precipitous interpretation that he wasn't ready for.

TS : By another group member?

GG: Yes, there was a fellow who had a homosexual conflict and another person who also had a homosexual conflict but was not really able to talk about his own, except that he was fantastically sensitive to problems of the kind in someone else and he'd start mimicking this other guy's effeminate traits. The other guy was a big, burly, fairly masculine-looking type and the first guy went into practically a homosexual panic and then built up monumental defenses against this afterwards. This didn't happen with an encounter technique. It happened with a group technique.

TS : How do you feel transference is affected by the introduction of these different games?

GG: Well, first there is the natural role that you would sort of project onto the analyst. The analyst can have a transference to his own role. He is in a sense playing god, he is the powerful one, the doer, the healer, and as long as this distortion of transference occurs it's not going to allow the patient to get to any kind of independence. Instead, it's going to distort the picture of the therapist and who he is. It's going to change the levels of expectation; it might reach more infantile levels. It could be good or it could be bad; but it's not going to be the same transference that existed, and that may not be a bad thing.

TS : You're saying that the patient, as a result of the therapist's introducing such games would built up a certain expectation that the therapist would have them at his disposal whenever a problem arises?

GG: The therapist is by implication saying, "I have the answers." It's changing analysis from a patient-centered way of removing blocks from the growth process. In colloquial jargon it's the difference between helping patients grow and raising them. When you do things, you're raising your children; you're doing it in a way that is going to make them grow, you're going to make them better. All of this is antithetical to my view of what an analysis is and of what has to be done in terms of growth and development.

TS : Some people who use these techniques might add to that by saying, "But doesn't the traditional psychoanalyst by way of his interpretations and his theoretical understandings presume that he knows the difference between an Easter egg and a rock?" Why doesn't it create the same aura of expectation for the patient when their therapist sits there and says, "Yes that's good" and "No that's bad?"

GG: I haven't tried to be that kind of a therapist, in the sense that I try to use in my model of the good hour, the unfolding of an unconscious process, and I take my direction from where the patient is. In group I can't do this. But, at least I can take direction from where the group is. I don't interpose my interpretations unless I see that's what seems to be going on in the group.

TS : Yes, but you know all of us as group therapists have general notions about what we'd like to see happen in the group and what we don't like to see happen and we can't help but bring that interplay about in some way.

GG: In other words, you are saying that one's image of man in terms of what we think is human or what we think is a decent human being affects our interventions?

TS : I am saying something more specific: that with each patient we have a general idea of what we would like to work through to for them at this particular stage in their treatment, and that certainly enters into what we encourage or what we discourage during a particular session.

GG: I don't.

TS : You don't feel that?

GG: I try to follow where they're at or where the group dynamics are at. I try to work on that. In other words I don't have a predetermined agenda. I walk into a session trying to know what the patients have talked about and are working on, and I then let them see what they're working on and try to work with that.

TS : Going back to something you said before: Bob Holt gave a speech at the New York Society of Clinical Psychologists and one of the statements he made was that . . . he was not talking in terms of these new techniques but he was talking about defenses, and he said what some people fail to remember is that defense is a process. It's not a "thing" and so when we talk of magic when we remove a defense, it's a bogus hypothesis because a defense is something that takes place over time and the removal of a defense or the working through of a resistance is time-bound. That seems to relate to what you were saying earlier about the fact that you just can't interrupt the natural flow of the patient's defenses. But what I was wondering was this: we seem to have a sense from the way we work, or the way our own personal analysis worked, of a "correct" pace at which therapy progress is supposed to happen. But that is a very fixed model, a fixed set in our own mind. Now in a way, that fixed notion prevents us from allowing for the possibility that a certain intensification or facilitation might be possible.

GG: I don't know that I have a fixed set concerning rate of progress or things like that. The only thing I can say is that in my very limited experience with these gimmicky techniques the results were not long-term, there didn't seem to be "real" change, it didn't seem as though the person was actually ready for the abrupt shift; and besides it was superficial, it was external, and it didn't last.

TS : Could you think about any particular patient where you did introduce a technique like this and it did seem to work at the moment? I would be curious about what you did in terms of the working-through process. After you dealt with the resistance and some strong feelings did come out, what did you experience in the working through when, for some reason or other, it didn't carry over? Why do you think it didn't carry over? For example with the woman who was kicking and screaming, despite the group's objections, did she at the moment feel as if something important was happening?

GG: She felt it was very good and very helpful.

TS : At that point in her life was it desirable for her to get some anger out?

GG: No two ways about it.

TS : What were you trying to work out in terms of her anger at that point?

GG: I wanted her to experience on a deeper level the feeling of anger, get in touch with its origins, and see for whom it was intended. She was demanding attention all over the place and aware of the annoyance that other people had toward her. Perhaps I wasn't tolerant enough of her slow progress and the persistence of her demands. I suppose her demanding attention all the time brought out a countertransference problem on my part and maybe I wanted to get through this phase faster. It did make the group and myself very aware of the infantile aspect of her deprivation, the deep-seated anger toward mama, and the call was "give me more mama."

TS : After that emerged, I am not sure what you did with her subsequently in group or in individual. Looking back on it, what do you think the right approach would have been? What would you have wanted to work out after that emerged? What would be the next thing you'd want her to see?

GG: That she has generalized her mama to everybody. That she feels that everyone is going to defy her. And that what she does is try to beat them to the rejection by asking too much of them and that the end result is that she makes them reject her because she is so insistent and so demanding.

TS : What do you think happened when you tried to bring this to her attention soon after these feelings started coming out? Why would the working through fail at that point? In other words, the emergence of the infantile feelings was the desirable subgoal within the group. Why would working through fail at the point subsequent to that?

GG: I would imagine it's something to do with the length of time one has to work something like this through. She achieved an immediate catharsis and perhaps an intellectual identification of the process, but this isn't really working through or really experiencing the infantile deprivation and the infantile rage reaction against mama. It was easily identified as that, but maybe the insight was more on an intellectual level and she certainly didn't really experience this herself, in her way, at her time. In any case, it didn't work out.

TS : So what do you think of something like a Janov technique where patients claim they do truly experience primitive feelings in such a way as to explosively remove neurotic barriers to growth?

GG: I think it's full of shit. I think it's the biggest hoax to hit psychology in years.

TS : Only in terms of its claims of cure and rapidity?

GG: I think that this idea of a two-week period of Janov devoting himself totally to them is bizarre and doesn't really do anything but make for some sort of transference, some sort of regression, some sort of infantile "making them special." It might work with people who need this kind of feeling, being special.

TS : The reason I brought it up is that one of the statements you made before was that she didn't experience the deprivation of her mother in a true way; it was on a more cerebral level. Now, if the experience were more primal, if the experience were more aggressive, if the group was a supportive group which would have permitted her to regress fully into that experience, do you think that the working through might have been an easier task?

GG: Conceivably, but I don't know if she would still have spent the amount of time necessary for working through.

TS : As I was listening to you I realized something. I remember hearing Zane Liff mention that he sees the therapy process as taking place in two phases. The first stage can be seen as breaking down defenses; the second phase as working through. Now, what would you think of the conception of using these games primarily as ways of getting defenses to reveal themselves more clearly, tapping into the stuff behind the defenses, and then the working through process begins where the clinical skills of the therapist can be used and his training and experience?

GG: I don't break down therapy in the same way you do or Zane Liff did. I said 1) that in an interpersonal sense, I'm trying to get patients to see what they are doing that is characteristically maladaptive, 2) going into the why (this being an historical exploration) and 3) working this out by reexperiencing in the individual session. So, in some sense something that I had relegated to an individual part of the treatment I tried to interpose in the group session and I was in a sense not giving her or the group something they had any experience in handling. They have just become expert in and used to identifying processes and all my people do is react. All I train them to do is to just give their feelings, their reactions, be whatever they are; what do they feel, what do they think is more or less important?

TS : You raised the issue before about your group being very much like a highly trained, well-honed, finely tuned group in their reacting. Wouldn't this act as a counterforce against the introduction of any new approach when you thought one appropriate? This might be a very common problem for therapists who have created a certain climate and style for their groups and then when they want to introduce some of the new learnings that they've acquired, it always is very difficult to get your patients to see the new "you."

GG: Especially since the new me is something I was ambivalent about. They probably picked up the ambivalence as well as everything else that annoyed them. I was in no sense really committed to this new technique and who is to say what would have happened if I had been. I have used them in marathons. I have had a cotherapist who trained with them and used them and it seems to have worked. I had brought her in particularly because she was expert in all these methodologies. It kept the marathon alive but in retrospect maybe turning to these techniques too easily is a function of my own insecurity.

TS : Yes, Max Rosenbaum once said in this regard, "Excitement isn't change," but it sure helps to give patients the impression of movement.

Dr. Elizabeth Mintz, who holds the Ph. D. in clinical psychology from New York University, was trained originally in classical psychoanalysis under Theodor Reik. She still considers psychoanalytic theory as the best approach to understanding psychodynamics but has departed radically from the Freudian technique. She now specializes in intensive, time-extended workshops, using the Gestalt approach (learned in studying with Fritz Perls); psychodrama; bioenergetics; and encounter games. She has been invited to universities and growth centers all over the United States, in Switzerland, and in Holland. She is the author of the book *Marathon Groups: Reality and Symbol,* published in hardcover by Appleton-Century-Crofts and reissued by Avon Press.

Dr. Mintz is a Diplomate in clinical psychology from the American Board of Professional Examiners. She has held the post of adjunct professor at Adelphi University and associate professor at Cornell University Medical School.

TS : How did you get interested in the introduction of games or structured exercises?

EM: It was a very gradual process. I had a very conservative classical psychoanalytic training and although I have departed from the techniques of psychoanalysis somewhat, I still believe in the theory. I find that my early, very firm, very rigorous analytic training was invaluable and this I obtained at the National Psychological Association for Psychoanalysis under the auspices of Dr. Theodore Reik. Fairly early I began to feel that the personality that was sitting behind the couch and the sparsity of the analyst's comments did not really create a therapeutic climate. At first, I would say to myself, "Well, this patient obviously has borderline components and I have to more realistic and more related and keep communication going." Then I began to feel that you didn't have to have borderline components to be the kind of patient who needed more contact, and at this point I began to feel that the only kind of patient with whom one should begin with a classical approach is the one who is so terribly anxious, borderline or not, that he really cannot tolerate much human contact or communication with his therapist. People like that usually need a preliminary period of ultraclassical analysis and then one can get into other work. Now this is on a one-to-one basis. My first violation of the classical analytic procedure, which I still remember vividly, was with a young woman who had formerly been a prostitute and was bitterly ashamed of this. Here she was talking to this nice middle-class, middle-aged lady and she was terribly embarrassed. The first time she told me about it, I put my hand on her shoulder as she left the room and said, "See you next Wednesday," or something like that. I found myself doing this whenever she spoke of her periods of life as a prostitute. She was not a psychopath but she was a masochist. Then I began to think through when one should use physical contact with a patient and when one shouldn't. I thought it through very, very carefully. I'm still unalterably opposed to any kind of sexual contact with a patient. I thought that through and the real reason for it, of course, is that healthy sex is mutual, whereas the therapeutic relationship is dedicated to the interests of the patient. There are all sorts of other reasons. Anyhow, I began to do group therapy in about my third year of practice, and this was fairly traditional except that I did not impose taboos. I did not prohibit physical contact. I think it's absurd, after somebody has been crying their hearts out over a terrible memory of chilhood or something very unhappy, that nobody in the group should be allowed to reach out and hold his or her hand. It still seems ridiculous to me. It's such a contradiction of the values we try to develop in therapy.

TS : And the ones we allow in the group.

EM: Yes. So this was my first unconventional or innovative step. And then I had a fantastic year; I think it was 1965. It began with the National Training Laboratories in Bethel, Maine, where I went for a nice vacation and probably for want of some new group techniques. And there it happened that my trainer was none other than William Schutz, which was just a coincidence. Bill, at that time, was also experimenting with innovative techniques and he was actually just beginning at that time to think of using wrestling and physical contacts. Anyhow, I was Bill Schutz's first lady wrestler. He got me into a scuffle with a guy who was about six foot five. This was a very interesting thing; it appears in *Joy*. The story is told where I am disguised as Ginny and the thing was that the group, and Bill too, were shocked. He didn't think we could really wrestle, and I knew I was safe because I knew that a man that big and strong could get me down without hurting me no matter how hard I fought. I felt perfectly safe which I might not have felt if I had been up against somebody who is more nearly my size and weight; in that case it might have been risky but this wasn't risky at all. Two members in the group said that they had seen a man beating up a woman; not a hair on my head was ruffled and it was fun. They were ready to jump in and, oh my, this is so different from the climate of today. You wouldn't believe that it was only in '65. So from Bill I got more freedom in using contact not just for comfort and warmth but also I learned the arm-wrestling technique which is absolutely terrific for expressing and dissipating hostility and competitiveness. I don't think I've ever had two people arm-wrestle in a group without their feeling more friendly afterwards than before, regardless of who won; and all sorts of valuable material also often comes out. I do want to say, which I'll be saying during the course of the interview, that with any of these games, the meaning of them to both the participants and the onlookers has to be discussed afterwards so that we have insight in addition to the emotional experience and, hopefully, a kind of cognitive integration. This means that instead of its just being an interesting experience, like seeing a movie or something, it has a genuinely enduring therapeutic effect.

TS : You're very oriented toward introducing these games in an integrated way and it seems very natural to you. However, a lot of therapists who might be interested in using these things have ongoing groups where they have not yet introduced anything but would like to. How do you suggest such a person bring this into the group's experience?

EM: Well, let's say arm-wrestling, because that's one of the basic techniques. I think I would almost have to give examples. I don't find today that group participants are as reluctant or, as surprised at the games as they used to be. They more or less expect it. Now this may be a function of the kind of practice I have and the environment in which I practice. But I think I would wait with arm wrestling. For example, let's say I have a group that has heretofore been conducted along classical lines with just talking, and I do want to make it clear that both in my ongoing group and my marathon group there is a great deal of time spent with the same kind of verbal give-and-take which would occur in any kind of more classical group; that at least half the time, maybe more, is spent in verbal exchanges and the only difference between my group and the classical one would be that I am more active, I participate more. Let us say that we have a group in which two men have a lot of antagonism toward each other and a lot of hostility, and that it is my feeling as their therapist that this is primarily on a transference level; that is, that they don't really see each other as human beings and as people. So, I might invite them to wrestle. Arm wrestling must be conducted on the floor; it is not safe to conduct it on the table. It seems less threatening if it's conducted on the table but actually it is more dangerous because there's the chance of a dislocated shoulder, and in any and all of these games I do my very best to avoid any kind of damage. There are all sorts of safeguards that are important. Actually I like to work with gymnasium mats on the floor. To get back to our two men; I might suggest that they express themselves physically. I explain how it's done. More often than not some other man in the group knows better than I how to set up the arms and he will take charge and say "one, two, three, go," and that gives him a bonus because he is doing something active in which he takes responsibility; but if nobody volunteers, I'll do it myself and tell them to look into each other's eyes while they wrestle. A number of different things can happen. Minimally, they get a chance to express themselves physically. This is a situation in which you can put forth your maximum physical strength without injury to yourself or the other person and there aren't many situations like that in the world. So at the very least, some of the tension and hostility is dissipated and they are better able to explore why they feel the way they do about each other because they will finish in a more physically and emotionally relaxed condition. Sometimes, and I don't know why this is, the hostility will simply dissipate completely and they'll be patting each other on the shoulder and hugging each other and saying, "I don't know why the hell I dislike you so much; you're a nice guy after all." Sometimes, very important feelings about competition will emerge; for instance, a man may realize that he gave up when he was really at the point of winning, because he was either terribly afraid of winning or terribly afraid of losing. That's how I would introduce arm wrestling. Does that answer your question?

TS : Yes it does.

EM: I'll take another of the basic techniques and that's the fall-catch response which I don't have to explain. Let us say we have a woman who has a great deal of difficulty in trusting men. I ask her if she would like to translate that into physical terms. People usually are pretty open to this, although with a group therapist who has never used these techniques and is unfamiliar with them, I would recommend that he or she choose as a beginning the people in the group who are most at home with their bodies, who have some experience in sports, dancing, swimming, for instance. I think it was no accident that Bill Schutz picked me as the first woman to do a wrestling experiment with and I don't think this is because I'm assertive but more because I'm a tennis player, a swimmer, and a dancer and like to do things with my body; at least I hope that's why. So I think one has to begin with the right people. In other words, you don't begin with the shyest, most schizoid, most detached member of the group to introduce games. You begin with outgoing people who are at ease with their bodies. I don't mean athletic; I mean have a sense of enjoyment with the body. So with the trust-fall, I might say to this woman, "See if you can translate this into physical terms." By the way, I never press, even when I have a group that is very familiar with the physical techniques. I never insist upon a game if there is resistance, particularly physical-contact games. I feel that it is outrageous to force people into physical contact if they really don't want it and if they aren't ready for it. It's an insult to the integrity of the person. But let's say she says, "Well, okay." I would then ask her to pick the man in the room whom she would most trust to catch her and of course, she usually picks the biggest, strongest guy there. If she's mistrustful and if she's unfamiliar with this game it will take her quite awhile to fall and I will stay with her and I will be very patient and I will instruct the catcher to stand very close to her so when she finally does it, she finds that it's nothing. Then the guy can stand further and further away from her. Now, this can take a long time but groups are usually quite fascinated by it. I have had a woman who took half an hour to fall and finally had a remarkable sense of exuberance and delight. It's like overcoming a phobia; she finally insisted on being caught by every man in the room. I think it's interesting that if one wants to adopt the behavior therapy structure of therapy, you can see this as a desensitization procedure. Of course, it is on a symbolic level but the body and the feelings are so close anyhow that it goes somewhat beyond symbolism.

TS : Have you ever conceptualized what the experience is like for the patient and his resistance as looked at from a classical point of view?

EM: From a classical point of view, no. I was so pleased when I recognized how easily it could be interpreted as behavior therapy that I would say it is a corrective emotional experience on the oral level of psychosexual development. Even though the eating is not directly involved, it is an experience which resembles the very early times when the human baby is picked up and carried. It is a corrective emotional experience, which many of the games are. Incidentally, again, as to introducing this particular technique which you call trust-fall, if someone really can't fall I ask them to catch. I pick out the lightest person in the group and I say will you catch so-and-so. Having once caught and found that she can trust herself, she feels an extension and thinks perhaps she can trust others. Mind you, I'm not saying that such a woman goes into the world and fully trusts men; I'm just saying that a little bit of the mistrust may be chipped away or she may get an insight. For instance, a couple of people have had the paranoid fantasy that I was going to wink at the person and get him to drop them; that I'd get the catcher to drop the person who was falling. From there we get right into fantasies such as "I couldn't trust mother," and then we have analytic material with which we can deal analytically.

TS : I have taken a similar position with people who are more analytically oriented. They seem to feel that treatment has to take place over a period of time and that somehow or other the intervention of the therapist in accelerating trust, before the resistance has been worked through in a more classical way, can rigidify resistances. They can't understand how this isn't precipitous and doesn't put the person in a vulnerable position, you know, before he's had a chance to discover his own pace.

EM: I haven't thought that through enough but I would like to say that the fact that someone cannot understand something does not prevent it from existing. I do think that any of the games work best in the context of ongoing therapy. I found, for instance, that in the marathon groups, the intensive weekend groups which are my specialty, the people who get the most out of them are people who have had a period of one-to-one therapy so that they have enough self-knowledge to give them a framework for the intense experience of the games. I doubt very much if genuine therapeutic growth can be achieved in, let us say, a three-hour session devoted entirely to physical games. I don't think it would have much more meaning than a good game of tennis or a really nice party where you meet some people you like. In terms of lasting personality change I can't see it as meaningful.

TS : You're saying the working through process requires time.

EM: Absolutely. The time can come either before or after the game experience. Sometimes people will come into a marathon who have had a period of intensive one-to-one therapy in the past and they know a good deal about themselves and where their problems lie and they can get a great deal out of it.

TS : One common problem that I find in therapists is that they can't determine whether their impulse to introduce a game is a function of appropriate intervention or a countertransference reaction reflecting their own problems.

EM: This is an absolutely valid point. However, the same point applies with equal validity to any purely verbal intervention and one of the basic tasks of the therapist is to learn to know himself well enough so he can tell when he wants to do something in his own emotional interests and when he is really working for the patient. I don't see any difference between introducing a game and introducing an interpretation on a purely verbal level about the oedipus conflict, or repressed hostility, or whatever.

TS : That's true. However, are there any rules of thumb that you can give the therapist as to how he might make this discrimination in his mind? Is it difficult to do that on a general basis? For example, when you either supervised or observed other therapists in action, did you come across cases where the person was indeed introducing a game in a way that was a function of counterresistance?

EM: I am sure that I have but I have not had any experience in supervising someone primarily to help them use games. I supervise people to help them use interpretations, the ongoing therapeutic relationship, transference in analysis, possibly games, possibly Gestalt. It's a package deal and when I pick up a countertransference to a specific patient, I do it in a general way and it's more likely to be something like being overactive with that particular patient, picking him all the time in the group to play games, etc.

TS : Are there any special types of countertransference reactions you might expect from the use of the games?

EM: I would not expect anything different in association with the games than in an ultraclassical one-to-one relationship. I would expect exactly the same kind of countertransference problems that you would get anywhere and for the same dynamic reasons, and I don't know that there is too much point in going into them. There is one thing: the anxiety is often expressed that a sexual attraction between patient and therapist might take the form of introducing physical games which would bring the therapist himself into physical contact with the patient. How this has not to my recollection happened to me but if I were to find myself having strong sexual feelings toward a man in the group I think I would avoid the introduction of any game which would bring me into contact with him and would instead ask another woman to take part as the mother, the sister, the wife, or whatever. This hasn't happened but I can imagine it could happen and I guess I'll retract what I said before, that sometimes perhaps games do have pitfalls. The sexual attraction, if it were there, would be there anyhow though and would make it necessary to watch out for even in a purely verbal therapy because you can be seductive without contact.

TS : Let me share some of the problems that I've experienced myself. I went to NTL also and was introduced to the trust-walk exercise. So I came back in September and I had an ongoing group that was in a high state of distrust and suspiciousness.

EM: Because you'd been away.

TS : Perhaps, but for other reasons also. Anyhow, I introduced this game and it didn't succeed. I mean the game happened and the people processed it and discussed their feelings but I was aware that somehow it was not being worked through and discussed in the right way. When I finally got in touch with was that to impose a game that's supposed to create trust in a group that is in a state of high suspiciousness, without first working this suspiciousness through, suggests that the group was actually being healthy when it rejected the exercise.

EM: You are absolutely right. This is actually one reason why I am very careful in introducing games to the group as a whole. The games that I do introduce to the entire group are always games which are nonthreatening. Sometimes they are games where nonverbal expressions can be shared, and I can give an example of that. What I do is simply work along with the group and when it seems time to introduce a game in terms of the dynamics of one or two or perhaps three of the members, then I will do it. But I don't like—I would not suggest to a group as a whole that they do a trust-walk with everybody pairing off.

TS : Because the dosage isn't appropriate for each person.

EM: It's not appropriate for each person, just as I would never say to a group, "Now we are going to work on anger; everybody get a pillow and start beating," because there may be people in the group for whom anger is not at that particular moment an important issue. I do agree that, essentially, it is an important issue to everyone but you have to deal with what is on top for each individual at the time. From a purely verbal standpoint, let me make a rather ludicrous analogy. We all have oedipal problems or electra problems and I would not say to a classical analytic group, "Well now, tonight we are going to work on our oedipal and electra problems; I want you all to think about the parent of the opposite gender." You simply wouldn't do it. It would be grotesque. Well, to my mind it's equally absurd to say now we're going to work on anger and we are all going to pound pillows. People are at different places. Usually when you get somebody pounding a pillow the exercise is initiated by someone in the group saying something like, "I feel so angry and I have trouble expressing it." That's tailor-made for introducing a pillow pounding and I'm willing to introduce it. First I will say, "Is there anybody else here who feels the same way?" My favorite expression is, "Would you like to be Joe's brother and pound with him?" And usually there are a couple of brothers and maybe a sister too, and the rest of the group watches and then, of course, is asked to share their feelings. I may be getting away from the question. But physical-contact games in particular are never imposed on the group as a whole even if the group has been together for years.

TS : One comeback that I've heard therapists make is that if the therapist is too much the gimmicker, the magician, then it puts the group in a more dependent position with him. They expect magical tricks all the time.

EM: I have heard this also. I think it simply does not occur unless the therapist is an authoritarian personality anyhow. If the therapist is authoritative or if he likes to have people think he's got magic, that's going to come through even if he sits back in his chair and never does anything except say, "Doesn't she remind you of your mother?" It's going to come through. I don't like the expression "games" but I . . .

TS : Do you prefer structured exercises?

EM: Structured maybe, but I don't like the word "exercises."

TS : Experiments.

EM: Yes. The use of the word "experiments" is very acceptable. This gets back to the point you made about how does one introduce the games. I find that if I say to people, "Will you try an experiment?" I am almost guaranteed a yes. There is something about it they like. Whereas if you say, "Will you try an exercise or a game?" they're more apt to resist until they know more about it. Anyhow, what I was going to say is that in a group where games are used, the therapist typically sits on the floor if the patients sit on the floor. I certainly feel very silly in the chair with everybody else on the floor. Also, I engage in some of the games myself. For example, if someone is picked up and rocked, I join the group in picking up and rocking. If someone wants to arm-wrestle with me, I don't accept if I am too tired, but if I feel it's appropriate and if I want to, I will do it and this counteracts any of the magician effect. See, I don't really think that the pitfalls of the games are any different from the pitfalls of any other form of therapy but just because the games are still controversial, we worry more about them. I think that the therapist is equally apt to appear as an authoritative magician if he maintains the cool detachment role of the classical analytic condition. Then people say, "Oh this guy really knows; if he would only talk more and tell me. He's got the secret wisdom."

TS : Some therapists I have talked to feel that the patients become very hip and knowledgeable about what other therapists are doing in the introduction of these experiments and there is a sort of coercion on the therapists and the other group members to participate prematurely in these things, like, "How come we don't do what other groups do?"

EM: That's the therapist's responsibility. I think you're describing the "assistant therapist" in the group, which, of course, is one of the roles we are all familiar with. Now, you get an assistant therapist in any kind of a group. You can get people who are specialists on oedipal material or oral material or anything; but if somebody says why don't we do this, the therapist himself has to take responsibility for doing what he considers appropriate and not what somebody down the block is doing.

TS : And for finding out what it means to the patient who raises that as an issue.

EM: Yes, of course. What's your fantasy? What do you think would happen if? What would happen to you, not what would happen to them?

TS : Then from your viewpoint, transference isn't differently affected in this kind of experience than in the more classical group analytic experience?

EM: I have been really astounded by the kind of transference reactions that come through to me; the classical transference reactions in a situation not only where I am using games or where I have been participating in games—sometimes in a residential group where I have been walking and swimming and dancing. I had a marathon group just this last weekend which was a therapists' group and I participated very vigorously. It was a good group, and my natural temperament is very informal and where I have to watch my step is in being an oversolicitous mother. So, after the group is over, several of us were sitting around drinking coffee and one of the participants said to me, "You know, Elizabeth, I would like to tell you how I feel about you. I think you're a very competent therapist but I am put off by your coldness and formality." A kind of a yell of astonishment went up from the others; but here is pure, pure transference. I wasn't even working; the group worked. I was having coffee because I was tired. But it took about ten minutes for him to see that he was speaking of his mother. This was such a striking distortion. The only difference is, and here there may be some disadvantages, the transference reaction is apt to occur in a more forward form, occur more quickly, and be dissipated more quickly so that something which is lost is the value of the patient's seeing week after week, month after month, how his transference to his therapist colors the material he brings his therapist. I think here, it's six of one and half a dozen of the other. I'm not sitting here and saying games are perfect and have no disadvantages. Where you have the transference reaction emerging suddenly and dramatically and then being worked through quite quickly, you have to say to the patient, "Since you felt this way about me and since you now see it was your mother, it's your job to look around you and see where you have this similar reaction in other aspects of your life." Which again, is what one would do in classical analysis.

TS : Do you find that because you have been identified with a particular orientation that you are the marathon lady in New

York? People know about your book, a special expectation is set up, and perhaps patients come to you because of your reputation?

EM: No, I find that, well, a lot of people do come to me specifically for marathons, a lot of them come from other therapists who have patients wanting to be in a marathon but who don't want to give marathons themselves. I also find that people are sent to me for one-to-one work but because of my marathon reputation, they sometimes do expect magic. Occasionally, someone comes in and feels they've been oversold, because all they find is a good, capable group leader with a knowledge of a number of unusual techniques and then they go away disappointed. This has happened with two or three people, maybe more, as many as half a dozen or more. People who are very glowingly recommended and expect magic, and maybe I wasn't really tuned in to them either. This does happen.

TS : Do you have ongoing groups?

EM: I have one.

TS : Do patients from your ongoing groups occasionally participate in your marathons?

EM: Yes.

TS : Have you thought about the relationship between the marathon experience and the return to the ongoing group? Have you ever had any backfiring effects or has it always been a helpful thing?

EM: It's usually been helpful to the patient. Sometimes people who have been in a marathon are disappointed upon returning to the ongoing group because it lacks the typical intensity of the marathon group. But this isn't a pattern. It doesn't happen that frequently. Mostly the patients kind of divide themselves into those who prefer the experience of an ongoing group and those who prefer the experience of an occasional marathon. People I work with one to one also go into my marathons; I almost stipulate it for taking someone on because I find it accelerates therapy so much.

TS : Since you wrote your book, have there been other techniques, other experiences that you have introduced into groups?

EM: Oh yes. I would hate to think that I would stop growing once my book was written. There have been loads of techniques.

Actually you know, one almost invents the techniques as one goes along, once you get into the right frame of mind. It goes like this: translate this situation into the here and now and if possible translate it into the physical terms. Once you get into that way of thinking, you find yourself inventing new techniques all the time. I think I am much more a Gestalt therapist than an encounter therapist. We know that Gestalt therapy is a way of looking at a situation. It's not a group of rules. There are certain principles that Fritz Perls, the founder of Gestalt therapy, enunciated, like, "Turn that question into a statement," and so on; but the point is that every Gestalt experience is totally different and should be different because you base your intervention on where this particular patient is at in this particular moment. That is an absolutely unique event; the individual patient has never before been exactly where he is now so that new approaches are constantly emerging. I feel that if I reached the point at which I couldn't invent a new approach, I'd be through.

TS : What are some new things that you have done recently that you've gotten a kick out of?

EM: I got rather a kick out of group fantasy which I sort of resisted at first. In my ongoing group, just last night, I got the feeling that they had fallen into the habit (which was quite good in a way; they've been together a long time, they have a lot of confidence in each other, and they share very freely the most intimate details of their personal lives. They share their reactions to each other very freely and this is good) of being too outer-directed. They'd come in and they're very eager: "What happened with your boyfriend?" "What happened with your job?" "I had a dream about you the other night," and so on. I decided it would be fun to have them get into themselves so I asked them if they would care to spend part of the group time in a group fantasy and I told them why. I told them pretty much of what I just said here.

TS : What is a group fantasy?

EM: Something like this. The words would be different every time I say it; I never have prepackaged directions. I give the directions every time but it goes something like this: "Close your eyes, be in a comfortable position. Lie on the floor. Now you have a box; this box may be of any shape, it may be square, it may be rectangular, it may be any shape you like. It may be any size. It may be small, it may be very large. It may be made of any material, it may be made of paper or metal or anything else you like. You have the box." Now looking around, I got the impression that everybody had a box. Then I say, "Now open the box and see what's inside the box." Pause, quite a long pause. Then finally I say, "When you're ready, open your eyes," and everybody opens his eyes at a different pace and then I say, "Do you feel like sharing with the group what your box is like and what was in the box?" The question, "Do you feel like sharing?" is very important to me. I would never go around and insist that everybody, reading from left to right, tell the group what was in their box. But, everybody wanted to and I think this is likely to be true in any group that has been going on for awhile. It was quite fascinating; for example, one man had a glass box and he was inside it, and this of course expressed his relationship to the world, but the glass on one side was more like plastic and you could break it and this also expressed his relationship with his world in that he was moving out more. My colleague, the man I work with in this group, had a rather small box and when he opened it there was a beautiful diamond in it and then he realized this diamond was his first grandchild who had just been born and he shared this and the group was very pleased because he is a rather reserved person and he doesn't share very much. I think I've told you enough to indicate what a group fantasy is.

TS : So a group fantasy sort of helps people to get back in touch with themselves and also, since you're presenting the same task to the entire group, it helps everybody to share together.

EM: That's right.

TS : What other directions have you moved in recently? Is there any extensions of what you've done before?

EM: I hope very much that there are extensions but I don't know for sure—I think I have further developed along the lines of the Gestalt approach, which I began with Fritz. I hope I've developed more skill; I think I've developed a little more imagination in the use of games, but it's very hard to take my book as the watershed for what I've done before and what I've done since. But I do think that anybody who learns ten games and stops there is in exactly the same position as the analyst who has three things to say, like "Why do you say that now?"

TS : One of the criticisms of the Gestalt approach as applied to group is that it tends to focus on individual patients for extended periods of time and it breaks up a certain kind of group climate.

EM: Well, I don't do pure Gestalt. I think if I had to describe my approach now I would call it Gestalt-Interaction. I find that if you take a group participant through a Gestalt experience, there is a lot of identification and empathy in the group and then a period of time afterwards is devoted to people talking about how they felt while this was going on and what this meant to them. This will almost always get into interaction, real group interaction, and an exchange of feelings and ideas, sometimes on a level of "I'm remembering something similar happening to me as a child." Usually, the group will communicate on a more intense level after a good Gestalt experience. Also, many times when one is working in a Gestalt way, it is possible to use the group itself as a therapeutic medium, as one sees most brilliantly in the work of Fritz Perls. For example, here is somebody who says she is afraid of people and she doesn't know why. This isn't a terribly subtle example. She goes around the group and says to each person, "I am afraid of you because. . ." letting the sentence finish itself; "I am afraid of you because. . . ." And since you've instructed her to let the words change, she may say, "I'm not afraid of you because. . ." as she approaches the end of the circle. The movement around the circle is almost always from pathology toward health. So I don't think it's necessarily true that a Gestalt group involves a one-to-one; it depends on how you operate it.

TS : It can be integrated.

EM: They definitely can be integrated with group interaction. In fact I think the great thing about Gestalt is that it will integrate almost anything. I can't think of any technique that Gestalt can't be used alongside of.

TS : How much do you participate?

EM: Some people who specialize in encounter and experiential therapy see themselves as role models and they will begin the group by as intimate a self-disclosure as they can possibly bring themselves to make, with the thought in mind that they will serve as the model of self-revelation and trust to the other group members. Other people, of course, are somewhat aloof and even when they use games, they direct the games. The classical analytical therapist, remains completely aloof and shares no information. Now this is something I've thought about a lot and I really think I know where I'm at. I participate to the extent that I think will be useful to the group. I do not ordinarily bring in my own problems and hangups because I feel after all the group is paying me a fee. I have the position of responsibility; the group is not assembled there to help me solve my problems. They didn't come to my office with a check in hand because they wanted to help me. I do participate physically. That is, if there is holding someone down, or lifting and rocking, I take part as a member of the group. Some of my procedures do involve physical contact, specifically with me. For example, the hand pressing, in which I invite a participant to press hard on my hands, shut his eyes and say to his mother what he always wanted to say to her and never said. Here, I obviously am participating in the sense that I'm in physical contact. I'm role-playing the mother as accurately as I am capable of doing and if this is worked through successfully and if the protagonist succeeds in discharging either repressed feelings of hatred and anger or repressed feelings of love toward his mother, he will almost always open his eyes and gleam at me and give me a hug and I hug him back. This is not a technique, it's just something I feel like doing when I can't help it. If I felt lonely in a group, I would not state it; I don't think I ever did feel it but if I did, I wouldn't say to anyone, "I feel lonely, will you hold my hand?" I probably would not say I feel lonely, unless I thought there was something specifically happening in the group, not just to me; only if it would be a good thing and would get the group moving. Then I would say, "Yes, I feel lonely." I try to express my feelings only to the extent that will be useful to the group. It goes a little further though. There are times (usually it doesn't happen because I get so involved in a group that I generally forget most of what is going on in my life outside) when I'm coming in for a marathon weekend and it might happen that on the highway I had a slight accident or something and I'm all shook up, I'm shaky and I'm upset. Unless I could get on top of myself right away, I would probably say to the group, "You may notice I'm kind of off base. I'll tell you why. This is what happened." That will help me get past it in about a half hour.

TS : Once you say that, it sort of serves as relaxation.

EM: It goes away, it really goes away and I don't have to go into it and talk about what an accident means to me or my fantasies about this or about that. Just sharing it somehow makes it go away. I don't work on my own problems, but I may share them if they impede the group.

Dr. Zanvel Liff is a psychoanalyst who has been engaged in private practice of individual and group psychotherapy and psychoanalysis since 1952. He is Director of Psychology, faculty member, senior supervisor and training analyst at the Postgraduate Center for Mental Health in New York City. Dr. Liff has been a member of the Institute on the United Nations of City University of New York since September 1968, and on the national board of governors, Council for the Advancement of Psychology as a Profession and Science since 1971. From 1972-1975, he was a member of the executive committee, Clinical Division, New York State Psychological Association and from 1972-1976 on the board of directors as program committee cochairman of the American Group Psychotherapy Association.

Zane Liff was the president of the Eastern Group Psychotherapy Association from 1969-1971 and, in 1967, was president of the Professional Association of the Postgraduate Center for Mental Health.

TS: Zane, what would you consider to be your basic strategy in group therapy?

ZL: My strategy is first to break through the patient's resistances. I find that group is the best approach to get through the character defenses, which represent the first level of resistance. The group is more influential than individual treatment and has greater impact on the individual.

TS: Why?

ZL: Because you have peer impact, the collective pressure, collective challenge, collective confrontation and you have a basic therapeutic support structure. I believe that the group is the treatment of choice for character disorders. But I find that a lot of these newer techniques, the primal technique and the encounter techniques, if they don't have real psychoanalytic orientation, stop at this first phase. I see working through in two stages.

TS: What are the two stages?

ZL: Working through the character defenses and working through the resistances to growing up. If you break through defenses, you get down to the infantile transferential level and get the early fears, the early wishes, the early pain and rage. This is the basic underlying structure from which the transference emerges. Often there is a transference denial in character disorders. These individuals resist really getting into therapy. They feel vulnerable to the point where if they let themselves go, they'd be swallowed up, rejected and abandoned. Right underneath the character defenses are the very polarized transferential wishes and fears and rage. The wish for the parent as well as the fear of the bad parent depriving you or destroying you. These patients guard against this happening. They try to function on a defensive level of self-maintenance. They use power and try to build more power and attempt to preserve what power they have. They fear anything emotionally substantial developing. They don't want to get caught up in a close, intimate, intense relationship. Anyhow, this transferential material is brought out during the first stage. The second stage then involves working this material through. There's also a resistance to getting out of therapy, a resistance to separating and growing up. In order to go through a successful therapy, you have to defensively deindividuate and then reindividuate on a more separatistic level.

TS: You mentioned earlier that the newer techniques stop short in some ways.

ZL: They stop short and leave people hanging. Then what happens is people go out into the world, and if there is not a follow through of the working through of the second stage, a numbing takes place, because society with its reinforcement will reactivate the defenses again. The analytic approach considers opening up character defenses as just one step or stage, and the second stage is more difficult but most urgent because that's really working through the deep transferential material which is beneath and behind the defenses.

TS: Do you believe that the very introduction of these techniques has an effect on the transference itself?

ZL: The transference is highly affected by it.

TS: In what way?

ZL: If the patient is deeply rooted in a very primitive level of experiencing, the introduction of these games can carry an antidepressant charge which patients can easily become addicted to. It's gratificational, but does it make for permanent change? Patients can surrender to the positive thrust of the group plus the leader and give in. It might seem at times like they are incorporating a new introject but the cure might be more charismatic than real. What's the sustaining power, what's the duration of change? There might be more carrying power (personality reconstruction and reintegration), if these techniques were used adjunctively with the regular methods.

TS: You mentioned gratifying patients, which of course could set up one type of transference, an exaggerated expectation that the therapist in some way or other, will be omnipotent enough to always be able to provide gimmicks.

ZL: Yes, this feeds into the omnipotent magical thinking of the patient.

TS: Also, the analyst could use the games in a countertransferential way to control the group by throwing them off if some resistance is bothering him.

ZL: You're touching on the two main countertransferential polarities. The therapist can set up the group as a source of nurturance, as a feedback mother figure to overcome his own depression. In order to get adoration from the group, the therapist has to very good to them: giving, resourceful, lots of new games, new exercises, new gimmicks, the latest in Gestalt, transactional therapy, all the instant cure stuff. It boiled down to the formulation described by Kohut—the grandiose self searching for the idealized object. The therapist's narcissism makes him perceive the group collectively to be the idealized object. If they can feed his grandiosity by appreciating his contributions, everybody's happy. On the other side of the coin, there are therapists who are trying to overcome their own counterphobic needs because of bad, threatening, destructive introjects. Under these conditions, it's like walking into a lion's den. The group becomes a dangerous, projectively destructive, annihilative preoedipal mother or castrating oedipal father. In order to overcome this aggressive, threatening climate, the therapist becomes very authoritarian, coercive, controlling and managerial. He dominates inappropriately and tries to run the whole group. In this form of countertransference, the therapist is acting out of a counterphobic tendency. In both types of countertransference the therapist's needs take priority over the patient's; where the specific patient is, becomes secondary.

TS: What rules of thumb should the therapist use in order to guard against using countertransference?

ZL: He has to have worked through this in his own analysis. He should have gone through a substantial analytic experience and have worked through his early derivative unfinished business that comes into play, especially in attraction to groups. Secondly, he has to really work with each patient where the patient is at, since every patient is somewhere different. Yet, at the same time there are group dynamics and you can think about the group as a whole, but you have to be careful with not obscuring where a particular patient is at. You are trying to help the individual.

TS: In your own experience have you used some of these different techniques in on-going group therapy?

ZL: Occasionally, I do use them.

TS: Do your patients, having been accustomed to previous methods, require any special kind of orientation and how do they react to it?

ZL: If they understand the legitimacy and validity of it they'll respond very quickly. I think patients want to understand the process. If they can understand the process and are motivated, they will go with it. If they're not motivated, then you get all kinds of problems.Where I have used these techniques is largely on the basis of dream diagnosis. The dream puts the finger on the pulse of where the patient's at on a deep structural level. If the dream is showing some fear and anxiety, some resistance or denial, I might suggest that a patient, on the basis of specificity in a particular group, take a risk in action in the group.

TS: Could you give me an example?

ZL: For instance, patients express fears of abandonment, that they are going to be kicked out of the group, they are going to be rejected or ostracized. This is the preoedipal abandoning mother. The other part of the bad mother· is the oppressive annihilating mother who is much more of the witch that will destroy you and eat you up. But both of them represent early panic, terror experiences that are projected onto the group or onto the leader or particular individuals or subgroupings. Many patients come to treatment but they can't "undergo" it. Such patients can't regress—regression in the service of the ego to get down to the transferential level. In analytic work you have to get down to the transferential level; that's the key concept of all analytic work. But there are patients who have such rigid character structures and character armor. Therefore, you use any kind of regressive exercises that might be pertinent; the whole thing is specificity. For example, you know about the cradling that is often used with patients. The group members may set up a cradling situation and the patient is rocked. Some patients would never allow themselves to get into that.

TS: How do you deal with it when a patient resists the suggestion?

ZL: I would encourage them to allow their fantasies to emerge. I would ask what is the worst thought that you could think of, what is the worst fear? Usually something like this comes up, "I am afraid that if I lie down and let myself be cradled or rocked I will love it so much that I wouldn't want to get up" or "I won't be able to stand up on my own two feet." The regressive pleasures would be so great that I wouldn't want to leave the therapy, it's this kind of thing. It's the fear such patients have of uncontrollable regression, and what we want to help them reach is a point of regulated depression. Also, there is the pervasive terror of being dropped.

TS: If a patient actually told you something like that, as it seems to have happened, how would you follow that up, what would you do?

ZL: I would say we are trying to trace the origins of it and how the whole life style has been a way of avoiding any kind of regression at all because it's all or none thinking. In the cognitive structure there are all or none ideas. There is no feeling of easy and regulated regression, regression in the service of progression. These patients are terrified of it. What happens if they get down on that infantile level is that the transferential wishes become so powerful they are afraid they won't be able to control themselves. It's an ambivalent search for the idealized "good mother," who will hold them and take care of them. Or, on the other hand, if the transference is negative they'll be vulnerable and the witch mother will kill them. They can't believe that this is a good experience. I have a patient in a group who tells me "bad is real, good is unreal." Anything that happens that is bad she can believe. It's familiar. She knows she can trust it. She relates to it. Anything that happens that's good is suspect. She can't believe it. She won't trust it. She won't go with it. It can't be true. The group can become a most potent change agent because it symbolizes the early mother collectively and the early family.

TS: Has any technique ever evolved spontaneously from the group? In other words, you were sitting there without any intention of introducing anything, when all of a sudden something happened?

ZL: Oh sure, I think this happens all the time with creative therapists who are really interested in working through. They are always thinking of new ways to work through resistances, the defensive part of the resistances and working through the transferential part of the resistances.

TS: How do you work differently with the defensive aspect as opposed to the transference aspect of resistance?

ZL: Working through the defensive part is to try to get down to the deeper experiential layers, the transferential layers, the infantile level. Good psychoanalytic therapy has to overcome the defenses, the irrational inappropriate defenses and it has to overcome or rather have the patient relinquish the irrational infantile. The first stage is to move through the defenses down to the infantile levels. Then, the whole working through process is to work through the infantile to get them to grow up to be adults. This, of course, is done in a healing, caring matrix.

TS: Do you feel that the games and techniques could be of particular help in that first stage?

ZL: I think they're helpful either in the first or the second, if the group therapist knows what he is doing. If he knows what he is doing and he's zeroing in specifically and precisely to where the patient is at, whether it's the defensive part or working through the transference part. He can utilize these action techniques either in stage one of the working through or in stage two of the working through, either to break down the defenses and get down to the transferential level or to get through the transferential level in terms of adult responsible behavior, including the regressive. It depends on the skill and interpretive ability of the therapist.

TS: Are you familiar with such techniques as Directed Day Dream?

ZL: I heard about it. I can't say I've used it. I sometimes encourage patients to go with their fantasies to its absurd limits. In other words, I've used experiences like, "Imagine youself going back in time and getting smaller and smaller" a kind of hypnotic regression on a fantasy level, and getting back into the womb before birth and then working yourself back up. You have a timed regression, timed progression. With patients who are very tight and very rigid, you can help them experience their deep phobias.

TS: Have you ever done that in a total group?

ZL: As a total group experience, no, but I know it's done. I am sure it can have meaning. You see what I object to, in the total approach, is that if I'm working with specific individuals who are at different points, it may be relevant for one patient and not relevant for another.

TS: That's an interesting point because many of the techniques that are described in the literature are collective techniques. So you are saying they are not appropriately or accurately described.

ZL: They may be appropriately relevant for one particular patient, and another patient may get some by-product, but it's not necessarily relevant for another patient. There is a trend to utilizing more of the group as a whole in working with everybody in terms of the group transference and the collective life experience. I think there is some merit to that but I would use psychoanalytic theory, which is highly individualized, utilizing the group modality. It is still doing individual analysis in the group, but linking two, three, four people. Sometimes a patient might bring up a dream and the group spontaneously starts associating, or I could encourage association, but their associations are very unique and specific and individualized. Their associations are their projected fantasies. Sometimes you get fairly consistent consensual themes where everybody can get to something, more or less. But often what you have is that somebody comes in and starts working on something, somebody links on to it, or may not link on to it, or may say "I have to change the subject with something that's bothering me."

TS: Do you believe that the subject that is finally chosen for the group to rally around is the focal conflict?

ZL: It depends. The focal conflict idea has to be broken down in terms of its degree of involvement or degree of relevance. It's not relevant equally because it's not a homogenized situation. You are working with eight, nine, or ten different individuals. It is true there are human beings and there are universals, and you can work on a similarity level, but I still stay more on a difference level, on a uniqueness level. There are, of course, common themes which everone can relate to.

TS: That's a universal theme.

ZL: But even there you have differences. Last night in a group, for example, they were talking about death and someone said, "If you had two years to live how would you live," a common projection, and the group got into this and then it got more specific and closer to "What if this was the last group and after the group we all died?" Obviously, this was a focalized thing, but everyone went around and shared very different responses from, "I would sit quietly by myself and think about myself," to "I would want to hold everybody and be physically close to everybody," to "I would like to take off my clothes and have an orgy with everybody," to "I would like to send you all out." This patient couldn't accept death. His omnipotence was too strong to find an antidote.

TS: So you are saying there is a diversity of reactions and you have to investigate each one individually.

ZL: Yes, each one very specifically.

TS: Do you ever have any reaction to these theories on group development, the sequential analysis of groups, the different stages? The problem that I always find when I read them is that they always talk about close-ended groups.

ZL: These are time-limited groups. I had that experience here at the Center. I once conducted a fifteen session laboratory experience without saying a word, and there were definite sequences of stage one, stage two, stage three. Stage two was the expectational set that I would be the teacher and teach them. The good mother feeding. Stage one was the uncertainty, the anxiety, the ambiguity and a lot of anxiety and with the phony expectations. I became the bad depriving mother. So stage two was the getting out of all the rage, the fury and the hatred: "You son of a bitch, what the hell are you doing here." Then, stage three was the working through of the transference, and almost gratitude that I didn't say anything. By not saying anything it helped them get down to such deep levels of rage and fury.

TS: What was the rationale behind that technique?

ZL: The rationale was to really show them this was an anticipated evolution. You can't do this with all patients and you can't do this with any borderline patients. This was an experiment. It was very difficult. I worked very hard at being silent.

TS: Is this designed to show the stages that the patients go through?

ZL: Yes.

TS: Learning from that experience, have you ever tried that technique in your ongoing groups?

ZL: I try sometimes to be quiet. Generally, I am more quiet than not quiet, although I can be very active. I find that if you are doing any kind of analytic work, the less you say, the more ambiguity and the more projections will come about, but it is not so when you are dealing with sick people When you are dealing with borderlines you're talking about patients who need some measure of gratification. If they don't get that, they won't come back. I have had many good individual sessions where I haven't said a word.

TS: How do you feel about preparatory techniques to orient patients toward group therapy, like asking them to do drawings about their fantasies about groups? Or spelling out for them in great detail what does happen in group, prior to group.

ZL: I think it serves an important purpose. I think also if you have a family model, a family theoretical rationale, the more information diagnostically the therapist has, specifically in terms of the worst experience of a patient's life, the traumas, the historical and evolved difficulties with mother, with father, with siblings, the better you will work precisely and specifically. If you don't know that, you are working collectively.

TS: Some analysts are beginning to feels that perhaps at the cost of curbing some of the patient's projective tendencies, you can also cut down on his anxieties, which is one of the primary obstacles toward group. So many people drop out of group in the early sessions, I would say, as opposed to the later ones.

ZL: In the early sessions there has to some education to be a patient.

TS: You agree with that?

ZL: I think there also has to be a therapeutic allicance with a patient. The therapeutic alliance is to establish a partnership with the observable ego; to show the rational observable ego that we have a common enemy, the transferential. We want to work through the transferential. That is causing all the troubles. Patients have to understand this. This is the infantile, derivative level. I find that most therapists who do not have a substantive analytic model are dabbling. They help a little bit here, they help a little bit there, but they're not doing a systematic restructuring and reconstructive work. Some patients are very difficult to work with, but at least I thing I have a pretty good model that I am comfortable with. The fact that you know what you're doing doesn't mean you succeed. But I find that a lot of people seem to be doing everything under the sun with no plan.

TS: What are some of the things that you found distasteful?

ZL: I think that many people are working with superficial levels, and they're not working through the transferential. I think in my mind that that represents a bad approach. I think we have to differentiate the surface structures and the deeper structures. I think most therapy, in general, deals with surface structures, which is okay and people feel better but it's not a reconstructive approach, It's not getting down to the transferential, historical derivative level. With a lot of the patients you do superimposing work, reality work, reassuring, encouragement, supportive therapy, you get temporary results. They come back and they go here, and if the environment is okay they function quite well and they improve, but if they have a crisis or a trauma they revert back. There is a fade out effect that usually takes place.

TS: What do you think the effect is then of people who use the sort of "seat of the pants" approach with these techniques and games and interventions, in terms of what they do accomplish with patients?

ZL: I think what they accomplish is that they do crack defenses. I thing they do break through defenses and usually people get more in touch with themselves and people start getting euphoric and exhilarated but I think most of these people do not have a psychoanalytic model. They don't deal with transference, the concept is absent from their thinking. So, a lot of these pateints are left with open defenses. They may come in touch with more energy levels.

TS: So they may feel better...

ZL: The question They feel better but do they get better? is whether they can themselves utilize these energy levels for adult, productive, mature function. Sometimes they do, often they don't. In other words you crack the defenses and they start acting out more on an infantile level. They quit their jobs. They are more in touch with themselves. Your know, you hear in the counter-culture two words, "hassling" and "kicks." "I don't want any hassling" and "I want my kicks." This happens as a result of the cracking of the defenses. You get down to this infantile level and playing out this infantile level. But where does it go?

TS: To change the subject, a thought that reoccurs to me is that if I am the same agent who is trying to minimize the distortions that are projected on to me, the transference, as I am the person who is introducing the games, is there a necessary conflict there?

ZL: It's a conflict, if you don't deal with it. You have to deal with it, because it's transference inducing. You have to elicit from the patient, "what are the fantasies," if you're a game master, who you become transferentially. You are an introducer of games or tasks or exercises. This puts you in a certain role. It puts you in a more powerful omnipotent role. I think you have to look for all kinds of subtle signs, subtleties of reactivity; transferential reactivity, to you as the introducer of these games.

TS: But you have to keep your eyes open.

ZL: Yes, you have to aware of that. Something to think about is that patients take twenty, thiry, forty years to build up a defensive posture, and the therapist feels that with the use of these games he can magically plunge or penetrate right down to the core, center, gut level and there ought to be a kind of transformation. They do penetrate very quickly and deeply but then what happens? This is the great challenge; then what happens? There is no real longitudinal follow up with much of the innovative approaches.

TS: They don't do it.

ZL: To really be open to learning, a good clinician will use whatever he can find, so long as he has a clear conceptual and developmental model. Another thing, is that a lot of people are challenging the developmental model on moral grounds.

TS: What do you mean?

ZL: There is a moral challenge to it.

TS: What is the moral challenge?

ZL: The moral challenge means that if you're my therapist and you break through my defenses, and I'm in touch with all kinds of energy levels and emotional levels, that's all I want. I don't want to grow up. I don't want to work through transferences, and if I want to have my kicks, if I don't want any hassling, you can't tell me that I have to be a responsible adult. You can't tell me that I have to get married, or I have to have children, or I have to work. I just want to go out and have a good time. I just want to go out and travel and bum around and have my kicks wherever I can get it. I don't want this analytic nonsense to go through oral, anal, genital, narcissistic, post-narcissistic and be object-related. So you have a lot of that, that people are saying, "I want to be narcissistic," and they start using analytic language.

TS: How does the analyst deal with this new kind of patient?

ZL: Just by dealing with the anxiety levels; not by challenging it. They can only try to get behind; they see it as a kind of expelling, staying with the anxiety, the pain, the suffering and the distress. Assuming that both will agree that this is bad.

TS: Do you think group is a good approach for working with patients with that kind of orientation?

ZL: Sometimes you may get some collusion if you have a younger, more counter-cultural group of patients and it depends on the therapist too, where he's at with his values.

5

A Theory of
Group Development

The recent mushrooming of prescribed games, nonverbal exercises, and various action techniques dramatically reflects the impatience of many group therapists with the traditional approaches. Getting patients to express intimate feelings and anxieties solely through verbal communication in the setting of a slowly unfolding interchange is inadequate to the task of revealing the dynamic, paradoxical, holistic intricacies of real-life experience. The introduction of these new methods signifies a deepening awareness on the part of therapists that previously held assumptions which suggest that progress can only occur at the group's "natural" pace, is a damaging, outmoded concept. Therapists now have many methodologies at their disposal that can accelerate a group's learning. In the following pages, the author will try to describe how the therapist, by skillfully integrating new techniques with the more traditional group interventions, can accelerate patient change through the various phases of group development. But before we go on, it might be wise to consider which concepts best describe these changes and which developmental patterns are most desirable.

Many experienced therapists would probably agree that their groups move through specific developmental phases, with very few exceptions, yet this sequential process has not been used in any systematic fashion. This is most unfortunate since the use of a theoretical framework would help to clarify the meaning of seemingly random, discontinuous group events. The strangest part of this omission is that the various theoretical models that have been proposed to account for group development, have many identical elements and overlapping features (Culbert 1970). If so many different workers have come to the same conclusion, then certainly these findings should be of more than simply academic interest. The following outline summarizes the major within-and-between-phase trends suggested by the literature.

I keep these findings in mind during my sessions for, in general, I find the observations valid. However, I object to the passive quality of most descriptions. It is as though "the group happenings are inevitable and nothing can be done to change things, so let's just sit back and watch." In previous chapters I indicated how group process can be facilitated by setting contracts, establishing individual and group goals, teaching good communication skills, having better preparatory and orientation techniques and improved selection procedure. In the following chapter, I will describe how the use of games, structured exercises, and nonverbal techniques can also be helpful in working through the conflicts that different stages of group therapy present.

STAGE 1—TESTING AND DEPENDENCE

There is general agreement that the initial stage of group development is one characterized by minimal group involvement (Bach 1954, Corsini 1957). Members are busy attempting to discover what is to be accomplished and how much cooperation is to be expected. Everybody is feeling everyone else out. There is considerable discussion of irrelevent issues and peripheral problems, much "symptom" talk and good deal of intellectualization. Participants search for the meaning of therapy, attempt to define the situation, and to find out whether their suspiciousness and fearfulness is warranted or not.

A sense of "we-ness" is not present: the other members are not yet significant. According to Bennis and Shephard (1956, p. 95), "the only thing that is felt by every member present is the attempt to ward off anxiety. A group-shared search for a common goal, some unifying theme that will bring them together, often occurs." The ambiguity of the situation at this stage is likely to become very threatening, particularly when members consider that this lack of structure is going to continue. "The real cause for insecurity is not the absence of an agenda; it is the therapist. Patients secretly assume that the therapist should establish the rules of the game, tell what the goals are and what procedures have to be followed in order to achieve them" (Bennis and Shephard, p. 96). Members look for signals that will guide their behavior correctly. The therapist's role is often viewed as a put-on, a technique—the implication being that he is playing "hard to get" and that if he really wanted to, he could help more. The group's pretense of the fruitlessness of their search for goals is designed to demonstrate their helplessness without the therapist's guidance and their seeming receptivity to perform under proper direction for his approval and protection.

I am talking here about the dominant theme in group life during the first phase. Many variations are possible, according to the group composition, the therapist's style, the duration of individual therapy prior to group, etc. Individuals with a rebellious orientation, for example, may seek out signs in the leader's actions that will justify annoyance and irritation. For the most part, these critical and contrary tendencies do not manifest themselves overtly during the early weeks of treatment. Stage 1 continues until a majority of the group members have gotten tired of constantly repeating the same repertoire of behavior that has gained them favor in the past.

In describing this phase, Bach (1954) speaks of "initial situation testing," Bion (1961) identifies the "basic assumption of dependence," Corsini (1957) labels it "hesitant participation," while King (1959) refers to "acclimatization."

STAGE 2—NEGATIVE-AGGRESSIVE STAGE

The outstanding feature of this stage appears to be the expression of strong feelings by the group members as a way of resisting self-exposure, maintaining control over what happens, and challenging the validity and usefulness of therapy in general (Bach 1954; Martin and Hill 1951, Stoute 1950). Most writers see this stage as the most stressful and unpleasant in the life of the group. Suggestions of hostility toward the leader and toward one another are less strongly defended against. Interaction becomes uneven, certain key issues begin to polarize the group, and power struggles become an important concern. The competition increases as different individuals try to assume leadership by imposing their will on the rest. Much of the group's activities aim at punishing the therapist for his failure to fulfill needs and expectations and for abandoning the group in the middle of a very sticky situation. The failure to establish group unity creates a power gap and communicates a chaotic, helpless state of affairs to the therapist, who is then accused ("Look what you've got us into and you're not even helping us "). Some writers in this area have even suggested that no matter what the leader does, it will be ignored, misunderstood, or criticized. What really seems to be going on is that each patient has to establish his position in the group and gain some sense of security, group identity, and recognition in terms familiar to him (under his control), before he willingly plunges on to the "unknown" of further interpersonal relationships. The anger at the leader for not having a master plan can be seen as a projection by patients of their own phobic attitudes toward other people, as they see them in a new light, beyond their customary public image.

Abraham (1949) identified this stage as an interaction stage typified by defensiveness, competition, and jealousy. Parker (1958) talked about a "crisis period" where friction is increased, anxiety mounts, rules are broken, arguments ensue, and a general structural collapse occurs. Thorpe and Smith (1953) describe a stage full of feelings of group disintegration, withdrawal, tension, much defensiveness and emotionality, and faulty communication.

STAGE 3—GROUP COHESION

During this stage, the first strong sign of group solidarity and involvement begins to emerge. Individuals gradually come to realize that this is their group to do with as they please. Group generated norms begin to take hold as members become aware that if this group is going to continue to exist, then they have to work at creating a certain harmony. Thus the group becomes a viable entity as the members accept it as an important part of their lives. Greater self-acceptance and broader tolerance of the idiosyncracies of fellow members soon follow. The increased openness of exchanged interpretations, feedback, and self-disclosure increases the degree of involvement and the excitement characteristic of this period (Bennis and Shephard 1956).

But how does this turning point take place? It is quite remarkable that a group which seems to be on the verge of splintering and falling apart will suddenly find the strength from within its ranks to mobilize enough constructive force to make good things happen. Bennis and Shephard suggest that it is a shift in perspective and member orientation that changes the whole basis of group action. The group gradually becomes aware that libidinal ties toward other group members cannot be adequately developed until there is a resolution of the relationship to the therapist. Issues of intimacy and interdependence cannot be dealt with until other issues having to do with authority and depencence have been worked out. Many months are spent with the group focusing on how the member-to-therapist attachments affects member-to-member relationships.*

While this is transpiring, the group members begin to feel more autonomous, They take a greater share of responsibility for what is happening in the group, attribute less Godlike qualities to the therapist, and begin to evaluate contributions more by what is said rather than by who said it. Throughout this stage, the symbolic and actual lessening of the therapist's significance has the effect of freeing the group. Members become more aware of one another, pairing and subgrouping occurs on the basis of mutual interests and concerns, and important personality changes take place as members experiment with new ways of relating.

Coffey et al (1952), Corsini (1957), and Taylor (1958) charactarize this stage as the one with the greatest opportunity for common goal. . .group spirit. Shellow et al (1958) see the stage of crisis and factions (stage 2) being followed by one featuring consensual group action, cooperation and mutual support. Many writers view this stage as the one with the greatest opportunity for significant transference interpretations (Wolf 1949). The group comes to simulate the original family constellation at this point. Through group transference, members begin to react to one another as though they were members of a family. The therapist and the

---

*For example, a woman patient who felt guilty about a desire for closeness with the therapist compensated by being ingratiating and overprotective toward other women members while she repeatedly attacked the therapist for his aloofness.

other group members by now know enough about the person's history so that they can spot these projections and give useful reality testing.

STAGE 4—THE CREATIVE ENCOUNTER

By this time the group is like a finely tuned instrument. Little time is wasted, superficial resistances are dropped, open and direct communication frequently takes place, and the task orientation (problem solving) is both efficient and effective. Insights of a deep and genuine nature are common. The group as an entity serves a therapeutic function in providing a sense of mutuality, support, and common purpose. Members tend not to be passive when an individual is bull-shitting, real needs and insecurities are given strong doses of understanding, and task processes are facilitated by each member assuming a function-oriented role (giving the other person what they have and he needs).

During this stage the therapist should be aware both of his own separation anxiety and that of his patients. This phase is so difficult to get to that patients and therapist alike sometimes cling to each other because it's such a good feeling. Each therapist likes to have advanced patients in his group because now that the hard work is over there is a considerable ego investment in having before him living proof of his competency, and it's reassuring to have someone to see eye to eye with. The feeling is something like the loving father who finds it hard to face the fact that his kids are old enough to leave and so becomes possessive. Patients often show their ambivalence by either going through self-inflicted regression to justify their remaining, as it were waiting around till something happens so that they can say "boy, it's a good thing I didn't have to face that by myself," or becoming assistant therapists in the form of "the oldest member." There is a certain delicate period where a good group member who has gotten a lot and given a lot and has now overstayed his leave, simply becomes "a smart ass." By this I mean, newer patients soon tire of the patient who "has been through it all and knows what it's all about." Up to a certain point, long successful experience lends itself to empathy, optimism, and encouragement. Beyond that point, it can cause smugness, a patronizing tone, impatience, and can assume a certain repetitive, shopworn quality.

In effect, this phase–progression model is a way of making action-oriented statements which represent hypotheses the therapist has formulated about the sequence of issues which the group will probably have to face as the members strive toward their common goals. The conceptualization of specified stages of progression provides a rough outline with which to measure the group's activities and is a safeguard against getting derailed by the omission of an important issue. In chapter 7, for example, I tell the story of marathon group members who become so frightened of dependency feelings aroused during the forty-eight hours that, upon return to their regular ongoing groups, they became impossibly defensive and began acting out all over the place. If the therapist had used a phase–progression model for understanding the impasse, a number of alternative interventions might have been employed (eg., group members working though threatening dependency feelings instead of beligerently proclaiming their shaky autonomy and substituting elusive resistance for true interdependence).

As I see it, several practical considerations have to be taken into account in the formulation and working through of the various phase-specific tasks:

There must be a commitment at the outset of the group to a set of goals that will provide a framework for understanding and assessing group events. Explicit statements of group goals provide a face validity which allows participants to share in the responsibility for their group's outcome.

The therapist's own set of hypotheses gives him a frame of reference for evaluating spontaneous group behavior and provides a cognitive map for understanding whether the group's activities will service its original objective.

One useful way for the therapist to conceptualize a progression of phases is for him to formulate a set of tasks (or behavior dilemmas) which the group must acknowledge and work on before moving on to the tasks of the next phase.* The adequacy and thoroughness of the understanding at an earlier stage has important repercussions on

*This is in keeping with Erikson's (1959) notion of developmental tasks. Erickson suggests that the child's relative success or failure in finding solutions to the typical problems of the experiential areas occuring during any given age span, determines his level of effectiveness, and hence, his self-esteem. Thus, one's ego strength in dealing with current and future problems is directly a function of how well one has solved and integrated earlier developmental tasks.

the group's capacity to learn at a later one. The leader who works with the phase–progression model must (a) be capable of identifying the tasks emerging from the group process within any given session; (b) be sensitive to where the optimal level of learning is before encouraging the group to move on to another substantative area; (c) be aware of the fine line between giving direction and overcontrolling the group process.

The therapist should try to be cognizant of the typical countertransferential traps specific to the various phases of group development.

1. During the testing and dependence stage, therapists tend to experience a good deal of anxiety. They fear that patients will become dissatisfied and drop out and they are concerned about the dissolution of the group. The therapist's estimation of his own adequacy becomes a function of how well the group is working out. In insecure therapists, this can lead to overcontrol, an inclination to please everyone and be a good mother, and to defensively avert any hint of contagious group denigration.

2. During the negative–agressive phase, the therapist is often made to feel like a bad person. His prolonged suffering of projected attacks from group members frequently leads to depressive reactions or manic defenses. During this phase, therapists often get testy, sarcastic, martyrish, and grandiose. They must struggle with strong impulses to overcome their victimized state of helplessness by acting in. It is at this time in particular that therapists become vulnerable to the anxious introduction of games, overinterpretations, and other anxiety-reducing interventions. The unconscious mechanism behind these maneuvers is to demonstrate to the group that they do need him and to shore up against the varied threats to his self-esteem.

3. During the group cohesiveness stage, the therapist generally has a good feeling. The warm climate of belongingness and commitment that has been established tends to reassure him that he has done a good job. Two main countertransferential reactions emerge during this phase. (a) A narcissistic identification with the group. It feels good to belong to an elitist family. A "we're all wonderful people—Yes, you're the best group I have" syndrome

can take hold. This attitude, if it becomes too polarized, makes little allowance for deviance. The therapist whose need it is to bask in this feeling for narcissistic gains, may himself become insensitive to potential sources of trouble. Who wants to be a party pooper when everyone's having such a good time? (b) The opposite tencency can also develop. The therapist whose leadership style tends toward problem solving and who likes his patients dependent on and needing him, may be threatened by the group members' growing sense of autonomy. This anxiety may manifest itself though reaction formation in an exaggerated distrust of good feelings. The therapist, instead of enjoying the group's pleasure, will deal with the positive feelings simply as resistance.

   4. The most basic countertransferential danger during the creative encounter phase is separation anxiety. The average therapist finds it quite difficult to part with improved patients whose very presence are proof of his therapeutic capacity. By keeping such patients in treatment too long, the therapist is unconsciously reminding less advanced patients that he is an effective therapist, just in case they ever doubted this. If he is to grow, a therapist with this type of predilection has to ultimately learn to take greater responsibility for himself and sever parasitic symbiotic ties.

6

Group Exercises

STAGE 1 EXERCISES—TESTING AND DEPENDENCE

Who else is here? Who can I be in relation to them? What will it cost to join? How much am I willing to pay? Can I trust my real self to them? Will they hold me up if I am falling?

The first stage in the life of a group involves the process of formation (people must decide whether they do or don't want to belong to a group). Issues having to do with inclusion, membership, the need for attention, and the establishment of a unique identity are of primary concern. The techniques included in the Stage 1 section are organized around getting members to experience their basic feelings and to face the developmental tasks specific to the beginning group.

Introductions*

The first few moments of the first therapy session is often an awkward time for all concerned. Invariably, a few patients trickle in

---

*There are literally hundreds of games and structured exercises that have been developed for various purposes. What follows is a representative sample of these procedures, roughly

late and the members who are already present either sit in uneasy silence or make faltering stabs at small talk. One way that I have found helpful in breaking the ice is to ask the person on my right to tell his own name and then repeat the previous member's name. Each person in turn goes through this procedure, and by the time the sixth or seventh person introduces himself, the group is enjoying seeing if the last few members will remember all of the names. Members are asked to correct any mistakes in their own names and this is generally done in a friendly, supportive manner. People kid each other, the air of mild levity helps to unlimber them, and the group is ready to get on to more serious matters.

A follow-up approach that I have used to reduce the anxiety that comes from ambiguity is to restructure the group task so that it is placed in a meaningful framework. I go around the group asking each to say one word that they identify with themselves (e.g., strong, quiet, lawyer). I then instruct them to do this again and again and again (perhaps five or six times), and I encourage a discussion of what was experienced internally as they revealed these facets of themselves and what they felt toward one another.

Impressions

About a half an hour into the first group session, have each group member give a one-word summary impression of the leader; the leader gives one-word feedback (his reaction to the one-word impression) to each member. Members then turn to the person on their left and discuss how the word that they used to describe the leader might actually apply to themselves. The specific instructions are, "Discuss the personal meaning of your word." Next, members are told to turn to the person on their right. "Tell your new partner your one-word summary impression of the partner you just left; then elaborate with your observations and reactions." Then return to your original partners. "Close your eyes. Try to imagine that you are asking your previous partner to tell you what one word he used to summarize his impression of you. Hear in your imagination what

---

categorized according to the prevailing stage of group development. The operating rule is to suggest games only in accordance with the emerging character and needs of the group.

Some of the games described have been created by the writer, others borrowed or adapted from colleagues. Particular indebtedness is due to pioneers such as Moreno, Mintz, Perls, Shutz, Malamud, and Machover, all of whom led the way by inventing whole clusters of experiential approaches that are highly applicable to group psychotherapy.

this word is. Ask him to tell you more. Listen and hear what he says he reported about you. Now open your eyes and check out your fantasy with the reality of what your partner actually said about you." Discussion can be encouraged along lines of the discrepancy between self-concepts and the actual impression others have of you.

Mutual Interview

After the early introductions, I have sometimes broken the group up into pairs. The members are asked to learn as much as they can about each other in ten minutes. Next, the members are asked to introduce their partner to the group, relating what they've learned about him. The group is then encouraged to discuss whether really important information has been divulged about each person. They are prompted to ask questions of anyone in the group that would help them to fill in curiosity or interest gaps. I urge each member to tell those things that would help the group to know and understand him better.

During this exercise, the members are feeling each other out, sizing each other up, establishing permissible lines of communication, and setting the stage for subsequent transference reactions. The utility of this particular approach is that it uses the format of a factual, informational orientation that most people are familiar with to evoke a completely different but potentially useful source of comprehension, namely, subjective, emotional reactions.

First Impressions

Other workers have described a first impression game that I have experimented with but found to be too threatening to people who don't really know one another. Schutz (1967), for example, suggests beginning a new group by having members stand in turn in front of the whole group.

The group is instructed to give a first impression, based entirely on appearance, preferably even before the person speaks. Watch the structure of the body, the way the body is held, look carefully at the expression on the face, at the way he moves, at the tension and relaxation reflected in movement and positioning. Then go up and touch him, note the feel of his skin—the firmness or softness; the size, firmness, and tension of the muscles; the quality of the hair. Now push him or have him push you and see the resistance or compliance. Then add more adjectives or reinforce or amend the first ones. Now smell him.

In this exercise, each person is asked to give a first impression of every other group member and to continue to give his reactions and impressions as he faces him directly, looks him straight in the eye, and touches him. My objection to this exercise is its poor sense of timing and its inappropriateness. It is irrational to expect that a group of relative strangers would be receptive to touch experiences at this stage unless they are a bunch of group cultists. We should not pretend that premature physical contact is a substitute for slowly cultivated genuine intimacy. Another point worth noting is that it is unfair to put anybody on the griddle in front of the entire group, before a climate of trust and support is firmly established.

Awareness Expansion

"What is the way to truth?" asked the disciple.

"Your everyday mind," replied the master. "When I am hungry, I eat. When I am tired, I sleep."

The disciple was confused. "Isn't this what everybody does?"

"No," the master replied. "Most people are never wholly in what they are doing. While eating, their minds are on something else. When they go to the bathroom, they like to read. They cannot sleep because they are restless."

Most of us intellectualize our existence, rather than experience it. We react to new situations by interpreting them according to old, preestablished patterns. The actual is colored by the past. We see what is in terms of what was or how things should be. Seldom do we allow ourselves to experience the unique, evolving differences in each event. In effect, we have lost the natural marveling at himself and the world that a child senses. Our consciousness has been clouded by learned responses to other people's expectations.

The early group sessions are the best time for helping patients to get more in touch with their actual experiences of the moment. There is a liberating, joyful feeling that accompanies awareness expansion. To be able to see and feel more than you were ever able to before raises the distinct possibility that many things that you didn't think could change, can. If we can create this sense of growth and discovery from the beginning, then we are getting the group off to a good start.

Now I Am Aware

This game consists of stating explicitly what you are at this moment aware of. To concretize your contact with the present, begin each sentence with the words, "Now I am aware of. . ." The group leader can explain this procedure and then ask for a volunteer. This person is requested to let his eyes roam about the room, settling on things at random. "State specifically what you see." Notice how special an object is when you see it as a unique thing of the immediate moment. If the patient wanders from the present the therapist brings him back to "Now I see. . ." Each patient is then asked in turn to focus on the room and to give two minutes worth of "Now I see. . ." Next the group is asked to close their eyes and concentrate on their bodily sensations. Perhaps they can start with their thumbs. "Sense the size, the skin, the space between it and the next finger, the nail." This exercise can be repeated for different parts of the body. Members are requested to volunteer their awarenesses in the now. If a mind wanders off, bring the person back to what he is physically experiencing that is interfering with the now.

Words vs Things

Pass oranges out. Have each patient hold the orange in his hand and experience it with his eyes closed. "Sense its texture. Try to get to know what is different about it. See if you can really get to know it so that if it were mixed up with many others, you can pick it out. Is it perfectly rounded? Touch it to your face, your arms. Get to know the smell. Now open your eyes. Does the orange correspond with what you smelled and felt? What do you see of its shape, color, the markings on its skin? How is your orange unique? Can you pretend to be your orange? What would you like to do with the orange? Now rub your tongue across the orange. Break the skin and begin to peel it. Keep listening to the sounds. Watch the juice come out and see the peel tear away from the flesh. As slowly as you can, break the orange in half. Take one section and eat it. Savor the juice and flesh. Now turn to the person to your right and feed him a section of your orange. Watch as he eats it. Then, slowly have him feed you. Now discuss your experience with the group."

Sharing Games

When all members of the group can share common experiences with one another a giant step has been taken toward creating a sense of togetherness. Sometimes structured suggestions can quicken this move. The instructions are simply to share with the group the most painful incident in your childhood, your happiest moment, your most embarrassing experience, a personal secret (something you've never told anyone), your feelings about the part of your body you like the most and that you like the least.

When I Grow Up

"What were your thoughts when you were younger about what you wanted to be when you grew up?" Follow this up with what you would like to do in the future. This task is nonstressful and brings out valuable data concerning the fate of childhood dreams and ambitions. Group discussion frequently addresses itself to parental expectations and identifications and their relationship to career choice and personal goals. I have found that this puts participants directly in touch with forgotten feelings and memories.

Self-Description

Ask each participant to write down three descriptive adjectives of himself. Scramble the slips of paper, then draw one, read it aloud, and let the group speculate about what kind of person is described. Each participant can compare his self-image with the conjectures of the group. The exercise is helpful in focusing participants' attention on themselves, getting them to think about themselves, and encouraging them to voluntarily decide to share their inner thoughts with the other members. In addition, it facilitates the desired norm of readily sharing one's perceived impressions of the other group members.

Secrets

The group members are asked to think of their most shameful and embarrassing experience or feeling. "Don't speak, let's just sit in silence and imagine what the reaction of the group would be if the secret was disclosed." Participants seem to go through a number of emotional stages. At first, the members imagine reactions of disgust, contempt, and shock. As the silent fantasies continue, they usually become less disturbing. "Terrible secrets" tend to lose their valence if we concentrate on what the other person's reaction is likely to be. The magic of this technique probably has to do with the leniency and forgiveness of the externalized conscience as personified by friendly others, as opposed to the internalized skeletons in the closet. Group members are not asked to reveal their secret, but often members insist on sharing their "ghastly" thoughts. In practically every instance, there is a sense of relief and loss of shame, even when deeply traumatic feelings are brought out in the open.

Mary, a married woman of thirty-five, spoke with a stony expression, keeping herself in perfect control. "I slept with my father while my mother was in a mental hospital. I must have done it ten or fifteen times from the time I was nine till thirteen." The group was stunned and didn't know how to respond. But as Mary went on, it was evident that she blamed herself for the "seduction of the innocent." She remembered the terrible fear that betraying her father's perverted behavior would result in her being sent to an orphan asylum. The loneliness that made her enjoy incest as a way of getting attention, revealed the hidden sources of her guilt. At this point, she broke down in tears and the entire group swarmed around her and cradled her in their arms. That night, she went home and told her husband and he told her he loved her more than ever and that he understood how she must feel. The following week, she had her first orgasm.

What's In A Name?*

There is my name, my representative force in the hearing of those who make up my world, my sound effect, my story and my theme song, my personal share in the moving history that has made this land. (Evelyn Wells 1953)

There is a common belief that people tend to become like what their names suggest. Even if this is an exaggeration, we do of course become the person who has our name. The name becomes a symbol

*These exercises were developed by Lois Timmins and are described in her book *Understanding Through Communication.* Springfield, Ill., Charles Thomas, 1972.

of the person, the symbol of the self, and the symbol of identity.

Write your name on the paper. Experiment with some different ways of writing it. Print it, make it very small, try making it very large. Deliberately misspell it. Change it by adding or leaving out a letter. What color crayon would you like to write your name with? How do you feel about your first name as opposed to your last name? Say your name loudly; whisper it. Sing it. Tell the other group members your name. Ask them to tell you their names. Now talk about your names. Some Useful Guidelines:

1. What does your name mean to you? What does it suggest?
2. How do you sign your name? Compare signatures. What does your signature reflect about you? How do you feel about your middle name?
3. What do you think your parents had in mind when they named you? How do you feel about that? Did you live up to their expectations?
4. Is the sex of your name the same as yours?
5. Do you wear monograms (house, stationery, cigarette lighter)? Why?
6. How do you feel when you sign your name on a check, application, letter, etc?
7. How would you prefer to have yourself referred to when you die?
8. Have you ever changed your name? What was it before you changed it? Why did you change it? Has your family changed its name?
9. If you are a married woman, did you have any feelings about taking your husband's name? How about the married men; did you feel anything special when your wife took your name?
10. If you could change your name to anything you wanted, what name would you give to yourself?
11. Do you have a nickname? Who gave it to you? Do you like it? How do you feel about your being called pet names or calling other people by these?
12. How do you feel when someone forgets your name, misspells it, mispronounces it?
13. How well do you remember the names of others?
14. Is there anything embarrassing about your name, your initials? Do you pronouce it a certain way to avoid bad connotations?

Birth Order

The members are asked to divide themselves in different parts of the room according to their order of birth in their respective families (oldest children in one group; youngest in another, etc.). These subgroups try to explore the specific experiences they had by virture of their birth order and then get together with everyone present and share feelings. What did each patient's position in the family mean to him as he was growing up? "How did that original experience color your current attitudes, values, and coping mechanisms?" As the members begin to understand their past relationship with siblings resulting from their age placement, they can start exploring possible parallels with their behavior in the therapy group.

One patient was frequently angry with the therapist for not coming up with gimmicks to make more things happen. She felt the therapist wasn't taking enough responsibility for doing something about lulls in the conversation, impasses, and problem solving. The birth-order game was introduced during the tenth session. It turned out that the patient was the youngest of two sisters, the older sister having always been problem-ridden and sickly. The mother looked up to the patient for her maturity during adolesence, and relied upon her to look after the sister, take care of the household chores, and run errands. In the group, the patient revealed a strong need to please, covering over a basic shallowness and underlying hostility. She always asked concerned questions, gave pat answers and superficial interpretations, and seemed to shy away from deep involvment in what the other person was saying.

Family Photographs

This experiment is of value to patients in conveying the subtle climate and flavor of their early family life. Sometime during the first three months of treatment, after the group has a general idea of each other's background, I invite everyone to bring in five photographs of themselves as young children. I specify that the pictures should include the parents and other significant family figures. The photos are passed around so that the group can study such features as physical closeness to others, facial expression, stance, people omitted, the location of family members in relation to each other, etc. Then, the presenting individual gives his reaction to the group's speculations. I find that fellow patients get a better sense of what parents and siblings might be like by seeing pictures of them. In addition, early memories get revived and "incidental" aspects of family life take on new meaning.

> One patient brought in a picture of her brother who had a deformed leg. The patient had never thought to mention this in group, and yet the patient herself was married to someone with a severe handicap. The new information revealed an interesting lead to explore in terms of brother transference onto the husband.

Family Sayings

Every family has its own favorite expressions, slogans, and sayings. These recurring statements usually reflect characteristic attitudes that are deeply influential in determining value orientations within the family structure. The group might be asked to make up a list of family sayings, as a homework assignment, to be brought in the following week. The ensuing discussion helps patients to become more aware of the prevailing attitudes which might have permeated the atmosphere of their homes and significantly entered into the development of their own personalities. One group came up with the following collection: "SPS (self-praise stinks)" "The best school is the college of hard knocks," "Do you think money grows on trees?" "The only people you should trust in this world are your own flesh and blood," etc.

Death

The preciousness of life is something that most people take for granted. Many people continually postpone what they really want to do with their lives and act as though they were immortal. One way of confronting secret wishes and desires that are curtailed in everyday living is to face a group with the prospect of imminent death. "Imagine that a doctor tells you that you have an incurable illness and can expect to live only a few more months. What thoughts come to mind? Do you feel like telling anybody what you just heard? Whom? What are you going to do?" The group is asked to close their eyes, immerse themselves in fantasy, imagine their thoughts in action, and then open up the discussion.

Mirror Image

Each member is asked to bring in a pocket mirror. The mirror is kept face down until the following questions have been discussed: what memories did you have about looking in the mirror as a child, as an adolescent, and have now as an adult? Has your reflected image ever reminded you of one of your parents? What do you usually notice when you look in the mirror?

The group members are then instructed to look at the left side of their faces. "What features, expressions, traits do you see?" A similar procedure is followed for the right side of the face. The discussion which follows brings into focus the self-concept, conflicting attitudes toward the self, body image, and the connection between self-esteem and relationship with one's parents.

Inside Your Pocketbook (Wallet)

Group members are invited to share the contents and arrangement of items in their pocketbooks. They are asked to explain the personal meaning to them of the different things that the pocketbook holds. Then the group is invited to guess how much money each person has on him, together with an explanation for their estimate. (The leader should be included to elicit transferential attitudes.) This experiment helps patients to reveal undiscovered aspects of themselves more quickly (through their possessions) and also facilitates awareness of the variety of feelings, attitudes, and symbolic values that society attaches to money.

Changing Seats

After awhile group members seem to assume fixed seating positions week after week. The seating arrangement often reflects role behavior, and bringing the members' attention to this largely unconscious habit sharpens and emphasizes the different modes of relating to peers and authority. The prestige value often turns on one's closeness to the leader. Members who frequently drift off to the outer perimeter of the group may be indicating their feeling of being outsiders. Sometimes patients surround themselves with allies they can count on for emotional support in a pinch. Chairs turned in a certain direction tend to cut off the person on the other side.

The leader can get at the emotional dynamics that underlie these seating patterns by asking the members to pick a place as different as possible from the present one. The group is then asked what they observed and experienced as they went about the task. The following issues can be considered: Was there any person you did or did not want to sit next to? Was there indecision, competitiveness, or placation involved in where you chose a seat? How does the group feel in their new positions? Why did you choose the leader's seat? How do you feel with me (leader) sitting next to you? Why do you think these seating arrangements never occurred to you?

Balloons

Each member is asked to bring in a balloon. The therapist inquires about where people bought their balloons, who forgot to get one, or who brought more than one in, and how the group felt about the assignment. The members are then asked to blow up their balloons, tie a knot at the end, and to notice how they are feeling while doing this. "Rub the balloon gently against your cheek with your eyes closed. See what image comes to mind." Next, members are encouraged to make noises with the balloons any way they like. "What do the noises remind you of and how about the shapes?" The group is then invited to break the balloons in any way they wish. The novelty of this experience and such factors as noise, playfulness, physical aggression, and involvement in motor tasks seems to stimulate a wide variety of highly revealing emotional reactions.

Special Holidays

During the session immediately preceding a holiday (Christmas, Mother's Day, Father's Day, Brithday, Anniversary), the leader can inquire about member's subjective attitudes toward these events. For example, "What kind of birthday experiences have you had? How do you feel about giving gifts or accepting them? Do people have trouble giving you what you want? Why?"

Choosing a Family

"Who from amongst this group would you choose to be your father, mother, brother, sister, son, or daughter?" Have the members go around reporting their choices for each category together with some explanation. "How did you feel about being chosen or not being chosen for each category?"; "What dictated your own choices?"; "What role did most people see you in and how do you feel about that?"

Earliest Memory Test

Alfred Adler (1927) claimed that the major task of therapy was to understand the patient's style of life. "We must gather hints," he wrote, "from a multitude of small signs—in the way a man enters a room, the way he greets us and shakes hands, the way he smiles, the way he walks." But Adler believed that the most revealing indicator of all was the patient's memory. In keeping with the theoretical position that earliest memories represent the individual's current frame of reference, Mosak (1958) has suggested that earliest memories should change if progress is made in treatment. Either new memories will occur, old memories will be forgotten, the same memory will have a different emotional flavor, or the original memory will be changed somewhat in detail, so that while the recollected incident remains the same, the message it provides the patient with is different.

I find discussions in group of earliest memories are much more economical and fruitful than talking about dreams. The material is closer to consciousness, less symbolic and disguised, and easier for nonprofessionals to relate to. As a group exercise, I ask the patients to close their eyes and go back to childhood as early as they can remember. "Now I want you to think of your earliest memories, when you were four, five, or six—or even earlier. And now I want you to write down a brief description of each memory that comes to you—write what happened and how you felt. Keep writing until you can't remember any more. Write about specific instances, not general situations." Once everyone is finished, the therapist can make a brief statement about the general significance of earliest memories and then ask for a volunteer to read what he wrote. The group is then invited to join in and tell what they think it means.

When trying to understand earliest memories, here is a list of things to consider:

1. Is the child active or passive?
2. If passive, is he an observer?
3. What senses are used—auditory, visual, olfactory, taste?

4. Is the child alone or in a group?
5. Is the earliest memory pleasant or unpleasant?
6. Does it portray dependence or independence?
7. What emotions are evoked?
8. What significant person is present? Is any significant person that you would expect to be present, absent?

Earliest memories provide clues and hints about the individual's present style of life. I sometimes request one from a patient when I feel confused about where we are and want to get my bearings. It often gives me a fresh perspective.

One patient remembered putting his hand through the French doors in his living room (age five) and cutting his wrist. His next memory was recoiling in fear and running behind his mother when a dog started barking at him (age six). These memories were related to the patient's negative experiences in testing out his aggression. In the first instance, the exercising of his muscles gets him in trouble; in the second, he retreats from further exploration of his world because of potential danger. The reactions that group members came up with were very much related to the patient's present difficulties (fear of self-assertion, dependence, acting like a hermit).

Another patient came up with the following memory:

"I'm in a room that's very shadowy and very quiet. There's another bed next to mine but it's empty. There are no closets but I am sure we had to have closets in my bedroom when I was a kid."

Cindy, who told this recollection, is a forty-two-year-old married woman who had grown fat and lazy in recent years. She doesn't move out of the house, is overwhelmed by household responsibilities and has developed a rash of physical symptoms. Cindy plays the role of the martyr, collecting injustices, constantly complaining about what others haven't done for her, rarely examining her own role, hardly ever acting differently so as to get more for herself. The earliest memory represents the great emptiness that exists within herself and in her life. Cindy feels boxed in, separated from those around her (no one in the other bed), and deprived. Her association to the absence of closets was, "I had lots of clothes when I was young so I needed lots of closet space. We were rich.

My parents gave me everything." Another patient said, "But maybe they didn't. No closets sounds as though the things they gave you were not waht you needed." A second patient in the group said, "Things are so damn passive. Closets are for holding things, keeping them somewhere in case you want them and need them. No closets could be the fact that nothing they gave you meant anything; whatever they gave you didn't stick with you."

At this point it was clear Cindy was no longer listening to the group's reactions to her memories. "None of this is helpful. What does it all have to do with what's bothering me now?" Another patient in the group suggested that by complaining instead of listening, Cindy was preventing anything new from happening. "Maybe this is why you have that kind of memory. You feel all alone because you won't let anybody make real contact with you. By insisting only on what you want and on your own terms, you stop us from giving you what we can. Is that what your husband feels—maybe that's why he withdraws from you!" During the remainder of this session, Cindy continued to be resistant. The next week however, she returned with an interest in what had transpired. "Nobody ever called me demanding and impossible before except my husband. I always discounted him—he's my husband and I don't respect him so why should I listen? But I never realized that other people can see me this same way. Also I thought about my childhood. It wasn't so dreamy and wonderful. My parents were good with material things but otherwise I don't remember much about them. I don't remember them being around much."

Mirroring Position

Face a partner, make eye contact, stay silent, and then freeze. Stand perfectly still and try to become aware of your own and your partner's physical position. How are you standing? Where are your arms? What are you doing with your legs? How are you holding your head, etc.? How does this stance express how you feel right now in this situation? Now notice your partner's physical position. What is your impression of what his body expresses about himself and how he feels? Then share with each other what you are aware of in your own body position. For example, "My legs are spread apart, sort of defiantly. My hands are on my hips in order to create a very cool appearance. I have a smile on my face to look relaxed. The total image is to make you feel that I'm more at ease than I really am."

Now tell each other what you notice about your partner's body position. Try to be precise about what you actually see and then express your guesses and impressions about the other person's position.

Mirroring Identification

Many years ago, one of my instructors in projective techniques suggested that the best way to understand what the drawing of a person might mean to him is for the psychologist to imitate the position and appearance of the drawing. The kinesthetic identification with the person in the picture is designed to create an empathic understanding of what the patient's inner experience is like. The following exercise is based on the same rationale.

Divide the group into dyads. Have partner A mirror the physical position and movement of partner B. "If your partner changes position, you do the same; if he puts his left foot forward, the mirror image would be your right foot forward. Be aware of how you feel while you mirror him; how does the position he is assuming feel to you? What does it express?"

How does partner A feel as he sees his position reflected? "What do you do when you see some aspect of your mirrored image that you don't like? Try to become more aware of movements you don't like to see coming from yourself. Maybe if you exaggerate them, you will discover what the movement expresses about you." Continue this mirroring and at the same time, tell each other what you are aware of while you do this. Express all the details of your awareness of yourself and the other person. Now switch, so that partner B mirrors the position and movements of partner A. Again begin with silent mirroring, and then in a minute or two also tell each other what you are aware of as you do this.

Mirroring Speech

Now I want you to mirror speech and facial expressions by having partner A say anything he wants, while partner B immediately repeats whatever he says as quickly and as accurately as he can (same loudness, pauses, tone, etc.). "While you do this try to mirror all the expressive movements of the speaker's face and head. Try to really get the feel of being this other person. Do this for a couple of minutes."

Now switch, so that partner B speaks while partner A immediately mirrors everything he says and all his facial expressions and movements. Do this for a couple of minutes . . . now take time out to share your experience of doing this. What did you become aware of in yourself and your partner as you mirrored each other's speech and facial expressions?

Communication Games*

The exercises that follow are helpful in getting patients to recognize certain basic but subtle aspects of communication. As the patients pair off and go through these assignments, they are asked to keep the following questions in mind: To what extent are you making the other person aware of something that you are aware of; and to what extent are you able to understand what the other person is experiencing? Do you feel connected with this person and involved in his experience? Did you maintain eye contact or did you rather avoid looking at one another? Did the two of you really "talk" or was it mostly scattered bullshit?

"It" Statements
Talk to your partner for a couple of minutes using only sentences that start with the word "it." Now discuss the experience in terms of how you felt making "it" statements and how you felt as you listened to such statements.

"You" Statements
Repeat exercise A using only statements that begin with the word "you." No questions are permitted, only "you" statements. Compare this experience of "you" statements with how you experience sending and receiving "it" statements.

"We" Statements
Now talk to each other using only statements that begin with "we." No questions are permitted, only "we" statements. Compare your experience of making "we" statements with how you experienced sending and receiving "it" and "you" statements.

*These communication techniques draw on exercises developed by John Stevens and described in his book, *Awareness*, Moab, Utah: Real People Press, 1971.

"I" Statements

Now talk to each other using only "I" statements. No questions are permitted, only "I" statements. Compare your experience of making "I" statements with how you experienced sending and receiving "it," "you," and "we" statements.

Questions

Now I want you to do nothing but ask questions. Ask each other any question you wish, but don't answer these questions. Every sentence must be a question. Focus on your feelings about asking and being asked questions.

Changing Questions to "I" Statements

Now try to remember some of the questions you asked in the previous exercise and trasform them into "I" statements. Carry on a dialogue of these "I" statements (e.g., instead of, "Why do you have a beard?", your statement could be, "I see you wear a beard." or "I don't like how shaggy your beard is").

Why–Because vs How–Thus

Now talk to each other by only using statements that begin with the words "why" or "because. . ." Every sentence must either be a question about something here and now that begins with "why" or an answer that begins with "because . . ." Then, discuss with your partner your experience with these "why" and "because" sentences.

In contrast to this interchange, try out the following exercise and notice the difference: Each sentence must now either be a question about something here and now that begins with the words "how" or "what," or an answer to one of these questions. An answer to a "how" or "what" question cannot begin with "because." Which kind of question and answer really communicates information and helps you to make good contact with the other person?

But vs And

Make any statements you like as long as the word "but" is somewhere in each sentence. Do this for two minutes. Then make any statements you like as long as the word "and" appears at least once somewhere. Try repeating some of the sentences you just made with "but," substituting "and" for "but" and noticing what effect this has on the message. What does the word "and" do that "but" doesn't?

I-You Statements

Now use only statements with "I" and that have to do with your partner in some way. For instance, "I like the crinkles around your eyes; they give me a feeling of warmth about you." No questions are permitted. Discuss your experience regarding this kind of communication with your partner; compare it with the other types of communication that you have previously experimented with.

Summary and Consolidation of Communication Experiences

Sentences beginning with "it" externalize the subject; they make things neither part of me nor part of you.

"You" statements tend to disown the speaker's feelings, experiences, and opinions. They don't openly reveal or commit the speaker and often put the other person on the defense.

Most "you" statements are "I" statements in disguise. They hide the speaker's responsibility for what is going on and puts the necessity for changing on the listener. If I say, "I am irritated by you; I want you to stop getting to the session late," this clearly identifies the dislike as my internal experience, and shows that I want you to change in order to make me feel better (about how I feel inside myself and about how I feel about you). This sort of statement is much less distant and manipulative than, "You should stop coming late to the session!" Why? For whom?

Questions that begin with "Why" often reflect a veiled criticism. They tend to result in intellectualized, distance-taking, defensive reactions.

If the group acclimates itself through these gradual exercises to making mostly "I" statements, the members will begin to take greater responsibility for their positions, dislikes, opinions, and demands. Straighter communication breaks down the vicious cycles of nothingness that prevail in so many groups (why-because). Rationalizations and explanations take members further and further away from the essence of what they are experiencing. By eliminating useless verbiage and training the group to strive toward curbing endless exchange of futile questions and fruitless answers, the therapist moves the group in the direction of richer sessions.

The question "how" and "what" are real requests to know about the quality and process of what is occurring now. It is useless to guess about the past (the cause of the cause of the cause). The need for explanations and justifications in group often represents demands that drive feelings underground. Patients begin to feel that if they can't account for why they feel depressed, then they have no right to talk about being depressed or even to look bad. "How do you feel upset?" Or, "Exactly what is it that you do feel now?" are genuine requests for information, and resulting answers tell us more about the speaker.

One of the favorite devices that patients use to cancel or negate their feelings is to stick the word "but" in the middle of a sentence. The meaning of the first part of the sentence is often wiped out when "but" follows it. Some people cannot make a statement about another person without using such a qualifier (e.g., "I like the way you look but you should do something with your hair."). The "but" splits your experience. It alienates and disowns parts of you by acting as though the "like" is on one side of the room and "hair," for example, is on the other side. If you substitute "and" for "but," there is a more balanced awareness of both sides of you. Both sides can be simultaneously true because both are part of my total experiencing of you.

"I–You" statements represent the most direct form of expressing my awareness to you. By presenting myself in this way, I take responsibility for what I say, I say it straight out to you, and by saying something about you, I reach out to and tell you something about how I see you. It is really remarkable how much communication can be upgraded in group and how understanding can be deepened by changing familiar, stylized patterns of self-expression.

Some Guidelines to the Use of Nonverbal Expression

The purpose of the games in this next section is to settle the group down to a physical, nonverbal level. I want to sharpen the patients' sensory equipment, shake loose and free their preconceptions, interpretations, and assumptions, and help them to make direct and fresh contact with one another. Physicalization provides the opportunity for new, personal, concrete experiences.

People act as unified organisms. The whole body from head to toe (including the psyche) functions as one unit in a life response. An isomorphism exists between that part of the self outwardly displayed and what is happening within the individual. Body work is designed to harness the wisdom of the body so that it can be used as a sensitive instrument for perceiving, making contact, and communicating. By introducing the group to these exercises, I try to set the tone for the work to follow—adventuresome, natural, flowing, spontaneous, intuitive, and involved.

Traditional teaching–learning relationships have certain implicit rules and assumptions that strongly direct and control everyday behavior. We shall sit. We shall face one another. We shall talk, We shall not touch one another. We shall not yodel, yell, jump in the air, flap our arms. We shall bring people together in such a way that they will expect to obey certain rules. In some situations, these standards may be useful and necessary; under other circumstances these behavioral constraints rob us of an opportunity to know the rest of the person and perhaps to understand him better.

A crayon picture, a finger painting, or a collage may be a more useful vehicle than words for expressing what a person is feeling internally as a member of the group. When a group is at an impasse, a nonverbal way of expressing "where it is" (e.g., the members mingling until a group shape takes form) can be quite freeing and may open the doors for diagnosing the blockage and moving on to more productive work. Nonverbal forms of expression can also free an inarticulate person to participate better and express feelings less self-consciously (e.g., throwing a ball of clay against the wall). Sometimes the existing forces and/or relationships in the group aren't clear. One of the advantages of using a collective collage or choosing sides for a tug-of-war is that the group members can then immediately speak to the data and say what it is that they see in the expression of the group. Another point would be that exercises that involve the whole body or mild touching exercises (holding hands) seem to build trust more readily than just sitting around and talking. Finally, the use of different media in an attitude of exploration, without pressure to produce, often releases untapped resources, expands imagination, and can start a free flow of thinking.

A few precautionary notes are in order.

1. Try to reduce the likelihood of their misuse by providing adequate safeguards. In effect, this is an issue that has to do with the competency, sound judgment, diagnostic skills, and clinical experience of the leader. If the therapist has sampled these exercises himself, recognizes the strength of the emotions that can be aroused, and is sensitive to the specific level of integration of each participant, then I would feel secure if he chose to experiment with these methods.

2. Set limits to prevent physical and psychic injuries. Don't permit members to be coerced into involuntary participation. Interpret pressures toward group conformity.

3. Don't have an antiverbal bias. "Real experience" should not only take the form of screaming and emoting. The processing of an event is as important as the event itself. In my experience, catharsis has to be integrated with verbal discussion in order to extract significant personal meaning.

4. Identify to yourself what is going on in the group. Verbalize for and to yourself the stage or group issue that you want to explore. Frame a question mentally as if you were going to ask the group to face whatever is going on and talk about it. Translate the request for verbal articulation into asking for some nonverbal behavior from group members that expresses what's going on. An example might clarify what I mean. Let's say the therapist believes that withdrawal and uninvolvement are going on. He might frame the question, "I wonder how we're responding to one another," in his mind. He then translates this into a nonverbal activity that he requests that the group carry out. He might say, "let's place our chairs in such a way that they show how we have been responding to one another during this session." When the members find their spatial places relative to one another, the arrangements are attended to and processed.

5. Don't use an exercise without a clearly defined purpose in your own mind. If the leader finds himself turning to these exercises too readily, he might want to examine whether it is a sign of counterresistance (e.g., the leader may be avoiding dealing with an issue that is more threatening).

Bouncing Balls

Play the music of Simon and Garfunkel's "Sounds of Silence" in background. Spread out in a random pattern and stand. Imagine having a ball in each hand. Feel the weight, size, and texture of each ball. Throw one ball up in the air and catch it; keep it going. Then the same with the other ball. Now swallow one of the balls and when it hits the pit of your stomach start bouncing with your whole body. Swallow the other ball, too. Move, freely bouncing, jumping, and hopping, all over the floor. As you are moving let your head go; let your neck flop freely; let your arms flop. Fall loose as the ball keeps moving; give into it; move with it. Stop. Spit the balls out and relax.

Milling

Spread out and start walking. Walk, walk, walk, finding your natural gait. Become aware of your steps, your arms, your breathing, etc. Now change your pace and walk in slow motion, with very sustained, slow movements. Experience the change; center into yourself; become aware of every muscle as you move slowly. Sustain the slow motion and begin to play tag, reaching out to touch a person near you. Don't cheat and jerk into quick movements when you see someone aiming at tagging you. Keeping the slow pace, move yourself away, always being aware of yourself in relationship to others. Change your pace back to your natural gait and mill around some more. When you feel like stopping, sit on the floor and reflect.

Some variations might include:

1. Start walking and make hand contact with every person you pass.
2. Walk, feeling very closed, and avoid any contact with people.
3. Walk; be aware of people; look at each person you meet.
4. Walk and greet each person you meet in nonconventional ways.
5. Close your eyes and walk. As you bump into a person, take time to meet him. Be aware of your feelings.

Stretching

Imagine yourself getting up in the morning; yawn and stretch. Let all your tiredness out; stretch every muscle and let go.

Nonverbal Greeting

Get on hands and knees and bump into other people. Be aware of your feelings as you make contact. Be aware of interaction that develops, show with your while body what your responses are.

A variation might be: center into yourself and see what kind of an animal or bird you can be now. Gradually start moving as that animal or bird. When you make contact with others, show in your body what you are experiencing and be aware of the interchange taking place.

Walking Fantasy

With shoes off mill around the room clockwise, centering into yourself. Find your natural pace and keep walking, being aware of yourself—your body, your feelings.

As I describe some things to you, let yourself respond in any way that feels right. Show in your body and movement what your responses are to whatever I say.

It is a beautiful spring day. The sun is out. You are walking in the green fields. It's getting a bid cloudy now and you are beginning to feel a sprinkling of rain drops. You continue to walk and you find yourself stepping into a very muddy area. Your shoes and feet drag in the mud. Ugh! It's very mucky and each step you take you get more and more sucked into the mud. Now you see a path with stones and pebbles and sticks and grass. You get on this path. Wow, what a change. The path leads to the base of a mountain. The weather is changing, too. It is getting colder and colder. There is snow all over and the air is crisp and clear. The sun is shining. You are climbing up the side of a snow-covered mountain. The snow is glistening in the sun. You can smell the rays of the sun and taste the whiteness of the snow. Ahh! There is a slope to slide down or roll round and round. Wheee! As you come tumbling down, you find yourself in the middle of July on hot sand at the beach. The sun is blazing and your feet are burning with each step on the sand. Your arms and legs and torso and head—are growing more and more. You are now thirty feet tall! You are taking gigantic steps and leaps. You are moving and looking around, towering over everything. And now you plunge into the ocean, swimming in the brisk, cool water, moving your long legs and arms on top of the ocean waves, splashing about. Gradually you turn toward shore and swim back. With each stroke, you begin to shrink smaller and smaller. Your legs, your whole body is shrinking, even your finger and toenails. As you get closer to shore you find yourself transformed into a cork, bobbing on the surface of the water. With each wave hitting the beach you get closer to the wet sand and now you find yourself resting on the shore as only a cork can. Gradually you are coming out of your "corkness," growing your normal arms and legs and head and face and body. You are yourself.

(Note to leader; It is important to speak very slowly, allowing your voice to reflect changes in the flow of the fantasy, but do not overdo it.)

Walking In Different Environments

Walk through heavy space, light space, heat and humidity, heavy fog, rainstorm, etc.

Experiencing Different Environments

Experience driving a car through heavy fog, crossing a very busy city street at lunchtime, walking on pebbles in bare feet, being on Main Street in a small town, walking on thick carpet in a beautiful bedroom, walking through snow and slush in a dirty city, walking through a blizzard, walking through a field of fresh grass.

Reflecting Through Sounds

Here is a quick pulse-taking exercise for the group. Stand where you are; tune into your feelings now. As I point to you, make a sound that reflects what you are feeling right now. Whole group make a sound.

Hello

As a total group say "Hello" softly. Keep saying "Hello" and each time get a little louder—louder—louder. End with shouting "Hello!"

Chuckle Belly

One person begins by lying down on the floor on his back. A second person does the same, resting his head on the first person's stomach. Each person in the group does the same in turn, resting his head on the previous person's stomach. (If no one starts laughing, which is virtually unheard of, encourage laughter.) The exercise has run its course when the laughter dies out and is stilled. It can be done with eyes open or eyes closed.

This can be effectively used when a group of people first get together, to break down initial hesitation, embarrassment, and image protection. It seems to work best if not completely described and cooperation asked for, but rather if it is done with the instructions immediately carried out. Its advantages are that it lightens the group climate and provides for safe but fairly intimate physical contact with several members of the group.

Exploring Myself in Space

Music: Villa-Lobos, "Bachianas Brasileiras #5" or Dave Brubeck, "Time Further Out." Close your eyes, sitting easily and comfortably on the floor so that your hands are free and can move easily about you. Center into yourself. Focus on your breathing. Pay attention to the rhythm of your breathing. Begin to explore with your fingertips: explore your hands, your palms, each finger, the back of your hand. Are your hands rough? Are they dry or moist? Warm or cold? Now, let your fingers move up your arms. Are your arms uncovered? or do you have clothes covering them? What is the feeling of your arms, as you explore your shoulders? Are they rounded or straight, sloping or boney? Now as your fingers explore your neck what is the difference between the back of your neck and the front? Can you feel your Adam's Apple? Now let your fingers explore your face, carefully, feeling your skin. Are your features soft and rounded or sharp? Are your cheeks smooth? Is there a beard? Feel your eyebrows: feel your hair. How does your hair feel? And your ears? Now slowly as your hands move down let them move over your chest and breasts. Your fingers are very sensitive to the differences of the textures in your clothes—coarse and fine, smooth and rough, hard and soft, delicate and durable. As your fingers move over your body explore your genital area. Now feel your hips and buttocks. What is their contour like? Move along to your thighs and legs. Are they tense or relaxed, hard or supple? Feel your feet. Let your fingers be sensitive to each of your toes. Now with your fingers feel the space around you on the floor? Is there a rug? Or is it hard? Is it cold or warm? Coarse or fine? Can you feel grains of dust and dirt under your fingertips? Explore the floor around you as far as you can. Now slowly let your hands return to your center. Return to yourself. With

your hands reach out into the space around you. Touch the outer
boundaries of your space and press against your walls. Are they
resisting? Do they give and expand when you press out? Now break
through; push though the walls. Want to move out further and
further. Remove the wall, pull them back from over your head; pull
them away at your sides. How far does your space extend now?
What is the feel of your space as you move your arms about? What
are your limits? What are your possibilities? When you feel ready,
slowly let your arms return to your center, to yourself.

Exploring the Space of Others
   Music: Villa-Lobos, "Bachianas Brasileiras #5." The focus of this
exercise is on the experience of moving into the space of others, and
having them move into your space. It may be done by a pair sitting
back to back, two or three feet apart, or in clusters bunched together
so that everyone can touch each other.
   Arrange your hands comfortably and close your eyes, With your
hands begin to move slowly, moving slowly up; explore your own
space and body, keeping close to yourself. Explore the space
immediately around you, very slowly, the side before you, over your
head. Now reach out into your space and begin to explore it more
widely, and as you do, perhaps you will come into touch with
someone else. You will feel someone entering your space, feel
yourself moving into theirs. What happens? Is it frightening or
reassuring? Is it comfortable or curious? Do you play or struggle?
Explore or retreat? Continue moving into the space of others. When
you come in touch, let it happen. (Long pauses to allow the action to
occur are important in this exercise. The music is helpful in allowing
people to have sufficient time to try a variety of contacts and
encounters. It is important that this not be harried nor yet unduly
prolonged.) Now, slowly drawing back, let your hands come back to
yourself. Return to your center. Once again, back into your own
space, let your hands quietly come to rest.

Searching In Space
   Music: Hovhaness "Symphony #4," andante. This exercise is
similar to Exploring the Space of Others, except that it involves
moving about the room. It takes greater risk to do it. With music
going, ask the group to move around the room greeting one another.
Then ask them to stop and close their eyes. With the music

continuing, and with the group still standing, center down on yourself. Let your arms and head relax. Let the string that runs through your spine and up through your neck hold you erect, but let your head fall freely, as you move into yourself. Slowly your head comes up and you begin to move in your own way, moving forward or to the side freely, in your own way, searching for others, searching in your own space, searching in the space of others, coming into contact with others. What happens? (Sufficient time should be allowed during this exercise for interaction and encounters to develop.)

Experiencing the Totality of Myself

This exercise can help people to get in touch with their feelings, become related to their surroundings, develop some capacity to tune into themselves, and prepare them to get in touch with their fantasies. There should be sufficient room for everybody to lie down on the floor, fully extended, without interfering with others. Eyes are to be closed. You may be very aware that your body is tense and that it is difficult to lie on the floor. Perhaps your head hurts at the point where it's lying. Turn it so you are more comfortable. Try to relax the muscles and let the floor carry more of the weight of your body. Turn your feet in such a way as to make them most comfortable, so that the floor can carry their weight. Place your hands so that the palms are down, touching the floor.

(The presenter may wish to participate in this exercise, speaking from the floor himself, and using his own participation as a guide to assisting others. Attention should be directed to each part of the body, in an effort to have people relax.)

How do your toes feel? Partly tense and clenched? Or are they relaxed? Can you relax them even further? Let them go; let all the resistance drain from your toes. (This process should be continued over the whole body. Attention should then be directed to breathing, temperature, sounds in the space around, being careful not to cue feelings but to help people begin to reflect on what their feelings are.) Again use polarities: do you find yourself resisting or cooperating? Do you feel afraid or secure? Are you angry or joyful? How do you feel about yourself? (After each question, time should be allowed for the person to get in touch with the particular point to which attention is directed. Some preliminary exploration of fantasy may be possible by suggesting that people allow their minds to wander and as feelings and thoughts come, trying to put them into pictures. What did they look like? As pictures come to you how do you feel about them? As you are aware of sensations coming to you from yourself and your surroundings, what associations do they evoke?

Doorways

You are standing in a very narrow doorway, pressed in and squeezed, centered in upon yourself. Imagine that you are standing in a doorway where the sides are very close to you, in a narrow doorway. Your hands reach up and feel the sides of the doorway on either side of you and the lintel post over your head. Is it an arch or is it a squared door? Imagine now that you are in a doorway that is very wide as one between a living room and dining room. Standing in the middle of the doorway, you have to stand with your feet wide apart to touch the side posts. Lean over to reach them although you are not able to touch both at the same time. Now your world is very wide. Return to yourself. Stand in your own doorway. What's your own doorway like? Is it wide or narrow? Is it confining or freeing? Is it closing upon you or opening to you?

Instant Images

Experience internally and express through your body what it feels like to be: an ice cube, a stick of chewing gum, a conservative house, a piece of machinery, an old cottage, a dripping faucet, an old dollar bill.

Feeling Self with Self

Beginning with the bottom of your feet, feel what is against your body at each point. Feet may feel your socks, your shoes, the floor underneath; your legs may feel your slacks or socks; waist feels your belt, finger may feel your ring; your lips may feel your teeth, etc.

Silent Scream

Group is seated. Ask the group to scream without making sound. Scream with your toes. Your eyes. Your back. Your stomach. Your legs, Your whole body.

When they are responding physically and muscularly as they would for a vocal scream, call, "Scream out loud!" The sound should be deafening.

Inner Explorations

Find a comfortable spot on the floor; lie down and close your eyes.

In your mind's eye see each person in your group. Pick one person you feel closest to at this moment. Produce a movie (in color, black and white, wide screen) in which you and this person are the two principle characters. In the course of the story something dangerous happens to the person you have chosen. What is it that you do when you discover this?

Variations

Choose someone in the group who turns you off or who bugs you. At this moment you feel distant or angry or hostile toward him. In your fantasy make up a story in which you and he go someplace or do something. What happens? How do you end up?

Think of times when you do things alone. What kinds of activities do you most enjoy doing alone? What kinds of things do you find yourself doing by yourself, but dislike doing them alone?

What is your favorite tree? Imagine that tree growing from the pit of your stomach. Fantasize every inch of growth. How much does it grow? What are its roots like? Its trunk? Branches? Leaves? Stems? Fruit, if any? Flowers? Seeds? Pods? The environment around?

What Am I?

Sit comfortably with your group. Tune into yourself and get in touch with what your feelings and attitudes are about yourself now. Think of an item of furniture which would express who you are at the moment.

Variations: it could be done with animal or bird or plant or cars, etc. Could also be done with textures, smells, sounds, tastes, instruments, etc.

Looking and Seeing Another Person As——

Sit in a circle. Look at each person and see him. In your mind's eye associate a smell or sound or taste or color or art form that best expresses the person you see at the moment.

Space Box

Find a box or tube (shoebox, hatbox, carton, large tube, etc.) Using string, ribbon, paper, beads, gauze, etc., design within the space of the box. Create a setting in which something wonderful could happen.

Stand back and look. Does it lead your eye in? What effect does it have on you? What do you experience?

Collages

Take a large piece of paper (newsprint or a large-size construction paper). Using paper, textured objects or material, crayons, paints, magazine pictures or any combination, try out various shapes until you have found what you want to say. Then paste, pin, or secure together all your pieces on the large background sheet.

The following are other possibilities:

Tearing construction paper for shape and color relationships
Magazine picture cutouts plus word cutouts
Arrangement of nature objects (leaves, twigs, pine needles, shells, etc.)
Using "colorless" materials (sand, grass, newspapers, typewriter papers, etc.) against a gray background

Mobiles

With a wire clipper, clip wire coathangers into various lengths for the arms of the mobile. Bend each piece of wire into an arc for easy balancing. Make objects to hang from various arms of the mobile, using thread. When entire mobile is balanced, secure each object in place with a drop of rubber cement. Be sure objects don't bump into each other when moving. This medium may be very natural for expressing different facets of one's personality.

Exploring Media

Prepare a table with a large variety of art media: paints, clay, fingerpaints, stuff for collages, stuff for mobiles, stuff for sculptures, etc. See "Materials for Art and Rhythm Activities."

Ask each person to walk about the room and see what's around, including the stuff on the art table. After taking in the eye what is available, choose a medium or a combination of media you have never worked with before. Explore its characteristics. Let them medium massage you; let it get under your skin; into your blood; let it absorb you. Become at one with the medium. See where it takes you. Speak through the medium (media). For example, take a ball of nonhardening clay and knead it in your hands. Close your eyes and let your thoughts wander. See what your medium creates.

Mirroring

Music: Dave Brubeck, "Time Out." Select a partner and face him or her. One partner starts to move or gesture while the other mirrors your movements exactly. Reverse roles. In final phase, let initiating and following flow back and forth between you.

Crosscut Saw

Select a partner and imagine that together you are working with a crosscut saw. Is the saw moving easily? As you work together can you feel each other pulling? Are you aware of the saw as it bites deeper into the wood? Are you aware of the motion of each as he pulls back and gives to the other? How does it feel as your work becomes labored and heavy and difficult? How does it feel as your saw breaks through to the other side?

Tug-of-War

Two people play tug-of-war with an imaginary rope between them. Give the imaginary rope reality! Feel the rope; feel its texture, thickness, strength.

When ended, players should leave this exercise with all the physical effects of having actually played tug-of-war (i.e., warm, out of breath, pink cheeks, etc.).

Opposition

Sit facing one another. One person says, "I will"; the other person says, "You won't," repeatedly. Upon reaching a climax, each gets on hands and knees; one hisses like a cat; the other growls like a dog.

Eye Conversation

Two people sit in chairs about three feet apart, and look into each other's eyes. Gradually move closer and closer until faces are about ten inches apart. Try to carry on a conversation with eyes. Exercise should last about ten minutes.

Communication Through Hands

Face one another, standing. Close eyes and hold hands. Tune in on whatever comes through. Become aware of the pressure, texture, temperature of your joint hands. Associate colors with what is being expressed. Associate sounds, tastes, smells.

Back Talk

Sit back to back about two feet apart. Explore your own space. Explore your own body. Enter into each other's space. Express feelings through back, head, neck, arms, hands. Without breaking apart, press palms against floor to stand up. Eyes still closed, face one another. Bring foreheads together. Nonverbally decide whose forehead is a magnet; whose forehead is steel. Sustain the contact and move.

Pole Conversation

Two people put their hands on a pole (dowel about 4 feet long, 1½ inches diameter). Nonverbally decide whose pole it is.

Looking and Seeing

Sitting on the floor, face your partner. Look at one another and associate an art form with what you see in your partner's face. For example, colors in a painting, a modern dance, a marble sculpure, a wood carving, a mobile, etc. Tell one another what you fantasized.

Who Are You?

Pick a partner. One person asks, "Who are you?" The other person using verbal imagery expresses who he feels he is at the moment. Partner keeps asking "Who are you?" to explore what range his partner is experiencing himself to be. For example, "I am an orange bird swooping down over the trees." Reverse.

Paper-Pencil Conversation

When two people are in conflict, engage them in a written "conversation" on a sheet of paper which is passed back and forth between them.

Levitation Cradle

One person lies on the floor; six or seven others lift him up as high as possible, walk him around, rock him back and forth, gradually lower him to the floor.

Depending on the mood, the group may want to touch the person's arms, legs, fingers, neck, face, torso, etc., in massage-like fashion, tenderly. The group may want to pile on top of him and feel the warmth and closeness, etc. Follow through as spontaneously as possible.

Feet Conversation

Groups of three to six or seven sit in a circle with feet in the center touching. Look at one another; then engage in foot conversation. Tune into feelings and let the whole body follow through with total expression. Stop. Look at one another.

Involvement

Form a group of three or four people. Group agrees on an object which cannot be used without involving all. They are to participate in a joint action in which all move the same thing, (e.g., pulling a fishnet, pushing a stalled car, pulling taffy).

Group Shape

Ask one person to stand someplace. One by one each person places himself in such a way that he indicates what person or persons he feels closest to. Hands and arms may be used to indicate closeness. When done, hold the shape and look around and see who is alligned with whom and who feels isolated (if any).

Animals

Ask each member of the group to think of an animal that reflects his mood at the moment. Then move around as that animal, greeting others or bumping into one another, being aware of the feelings and interaction taking place amongst you.

Playing Ball

The group first decides on the size of the imaginary ball; then the members toss the ball to each other. Once the game is in motion, the leader calls out that the ball is becoming various weights; the ball is one hundred times lighter! The ball is fifty times heavier! The ball is normal again! The leader may also change the kind of ball being tossed: beach ball, golf ball, football, hard ball, etc.

Spokes of a Wheel

Each person lies down on the floor like a spoke of a wheel with his head in the center touching other heads. Get comfortable. Say what you are feeling now. Tell one another things you feel confident about. Offer your strengths to one another.

Variation: Make up a story as a group. Each person adding and helping to tell this yarn.

Power Chairs

Line up chairs in a row (one for each person in the group). The first chair in the row is for the person who sees himself as the most powerful one in the group; the last chair is for the person who sees himself as the least powerful. Each person in the group picks the chair which best reflects where he feels he is in terms of his power in the group.

I Have a Secret

The purpose of "I Have a Secret" is to see if individual participants can have empathy for another (i.e., feel the other's situation). The method also provides some opportunity for alternative solutions to problems. The method is explained, and then the group decides whether to proceed. Each person has to write a short paragraph describing some secret he has about himself. No names are signed. The "secrets" are put into a bowl, and the bowl put in the center of the circle. Then the persons who are participating, write their own name on a slip of paper and that is placed in another bowl. A name is drawn from the "names" bowl, and that person then will draw a slip from the "secrets" bowl and read the secret aloud. The person is then asked to put himself in the other person's shoes and describe the feeling. The group responds with how they might have felt, and what others might do in similar circumstances. There should be group interaction, as participants contribute any additional feelings the person with the secret may have about the situation, and as other possibilities or alternatives are suggested for the person who has the secret. This often helps the person with the secret gain valuable insights into his situation.

A Human Machine

One person takes a stance (standing, kneeling, lying down, etc.) and moves one part of his body in a steady rhythmic movement (e.g., head turning from left to right). Another person moves in with a complementary movement. Each person in the group joins in and together a human machine is formed. Keep it moving for a while;

then gradually transform it into another machine, and then another. Sound effects may be utilized.

Spontaneous Playing
(Letting a Happening Emerge, Group Process Flow)

When a group has evolved far enough to be able to enjoy free play, each individual may want to "do his thing" or choose someone to do something with. Or, a subgroup of three or four people may find some spontaneous activity emerging amongst themselves or the whole group may move as an organic unit—a happening!

Have a table full of "things" available which may be utilized in the following ways:

Mood music as background (Makeba or Santana, etc.)

Blowing Soap Bubbles

Finger painting with someone

Tying a spoon to the end of a ball of yarn, and stringing it through shirt and slacks, throwing it to someone else for "stringing" until a subgroup or the whole group are "strung" together, then moving to music as one person

Blowing balloons and making a balloon sculpture

Face and body painting with finger paints

Everyone lighting a joss stick (Indian stick incense) end dancing in the dark, letting the red glow of the burning tips of the joss stick form flowing movements and enjoying the fragrance of the joss stick incense, etc.

Peak Experience

This is especially useful for persons who are doing some life reassessment and planning. Persons are asked to lie on the floor with heads together like the spokes of a wheel. With eyes closed (minimum light) and allowing an unhurried period of time, the staff member suggests: "Imagine yourself into a setting and experience that fulfills your wildest dreams; where are you? What are you doing? Who is with you? What is it like? How do you feel in it? Is it one year from now? Five years? Ten years? Take lots of time to feel your way into it. Do this in silence."

After adequate time has elapsed, encourage group members to share their fantasies in as much detail as each is comfortable in doing. Other group members may ask questions—particularly the kind that fills out and enriches the total imagined "wish."

A Trip Into the Body

It is very useful to translate abstractions into physical terms whenever possible. When a patient uses a metaphor (I have a knot in my stomach") to describe his present feeling state, we can take him literally, and ask him to enter his stomach and take a good look at the knot. By contronting the difficult-to-work-with psychophysiological symptom, we can gain access to the hidden fantasy of the surface complaint.

Mintz (1971) for example, describes a woman who saw herself as being emotionally unresponsive. She sadly described these feelings with the expression, "I have a cold heart." Mintz asked her to take a trip through her body by entering her heart. She did so, eyes closed, speaking aloud to the group as she progressed down her throat, through her arteries, and into the left ventricle, where she sat in fantasy for a long time. Then it seemed to her that one spot in her heart was warm. She began to cry, and relive the memory of childhood episodes in which she had felt warm and loving, but had been rebuked. The group reenacted this episode with her, playing various family roles with a sympathy she had not experienced in childhood. She wept unrestrainedly. During the remaining hour of the group, she expressed her feelings more freely and related more affectionately to the other group members.

The Directed Daydream Technique

The Directed Daydream Technique (also known as Guided Affective Imagery) is a therapeutic device that until recently was used almost exclusively in Europe. The procedure is very simple. The therapist suggests a typical scene to the patient (climbing a mountain, in a meadow), asks him to visualize himself in such a scene, and then to tell a story about what follows. The worker whose name is most associated with this technique is Leuner (1966). Desoille (1965), and Assagioli (1965), have used it only in individual treatment. In the following paragraphs I will describe how this highly imaginative approach can be applied to group therapy.

The Directed Daydream approach is based on the premise that since many psychological maladjustments derive from a preconscious level of experiencing, and the language of these conflicts is highly symbolic, they must be treated in symbolic terms. The underlying assumption is that spontaneous healing can be achieved if we can alter the dynamic equilibrium of various symbols. For example, if we put a patient in a scene with a dragon and his first impulse is to run, Leuner et al. suggest that we should put a sword in his hand and encourage him to slay the dragon. Theoretically this will significantly transform his symbol arrangement, create a better feeling of self-confidence, make him feel better, and provide positive closure. I haven't done complete justice to the traditional application of this approach for there are other principles that are systematically employed besides symbolic confrontation with archaic figures.

1. The Principle of Feeding.   Suppose a huge giant comes out of a cave. Let's say he's angry and wants to harm the patient. What can be done? We may suggest to the patient that he feed the creature. The therapist can recommend how much food and the kind of food it should be. Instruct the patient to feed the giant as much as possible. This overfeeding is important since what typically happens is that the giant gets lazy, loses his rage, becomes drowsy, and lies down to sleep.

2. The Principle of Reconciliation.   The purpose of this technique is to make friends with hostile symbolic figures by addressing them, touching them physically (petting and stroking them), and showing tenderness toward them in differenct ways. The feared symbolic figure in the patient's visualization usually represents a part of the patient himself in the sense of a derivative of an introjected parent. Being nice to this symbolic figure means assimilating this introject which has been rejected, split off, and projected onto the symbolically visualized creature.

3. The Principle of Magic Fluids.   With neurotic patients, the imagined brook never gets to the ocean without some obstruction. The water can be dammed up, peter out, get sidetracked, or get absorbed into the ground. Finding one's way back to the original spring is a healthy regression to the sources of psychic energy. Patients may benefit by rubbing the imaginary water on hurting parts of the body, they can conquer fears of being drowned, they can take a bath in it, or they can splash it around. Other magic fluid experiences that the patients can get involved in are cow's milk, mother's milk, blood, spit, and urine.

4. The Principle of Exhausting and Killing.   Leuner (1966) offers the following example of how it can be used.

As a consequence of an automobile accident, a thirty-four-year-old woman suffered from a hypochondria which made her feel she would soon die. Although free from any organic trouble, she remained weak and would not leave her bed. In her imagery, she saw Death emerge out of the trunk of the tree against which her husband had driven his car. Death was brought forth into the daydream, and now was forced (by suggestion) to run into the countryside in order to exhaust him. When he wanted to sit down for a rest, he was pushed on. . . . At last he arrived at a stream and fell into it. The waters dissolved his bones which fell away from each other. The next day, the patient's fear of death had vanished. She got up and for the first time since becoming ill, she began to do some housework.

As far as possible, we should try to hand over responsibility for the therapeutic process to the patient's own spontaneous inner psychic pace maker. The patient can be asked to let himself be guided by one of his own symbolic figures such as a horse or a dog. One can then wait for the chosen animal to lead the patient. Sometimes good fairies or other types of nourishing mother figures (cook, nurse) are brought up. These positive feminine images can provide patients with better access to repressed childhood memories of the good mother. When these dissociated images can be reintegrated by reducing the anxiety associated with them, the improvement will be manifested both on a feeling level and in the transformed content of imagery.

While the previous workers who have experimented with this technique have reported truly startling results, I think that by neglecting to anchor the application of the technique to historical reality and by not working the emergence content through, many therapeutic possibilities beyond temporary catharsis have been overlooked. Let me provide a case illustration to indicate how I have used this approach in a group setting.

Suppose the group as a whole or an individual member is grappling with a problem such as unrealistic self-expectations that cannot go beyond clichéd truisms ("Maybe I'm trying to punish myself!"). This might be a good time for the therapist to introduce the procedure for the Directed Daydream Technique. The group is advised to close their eyes, put out the lights, and try to relax. After a short period of silence, the therapist suggests a scene that he asks the group members to visualize in their mind's eye. The therapist doesn't suggest the entire fantasy; he only sets the stage and the patients are asked to relate the events that follow. In this instance the group was asked to imagine themselves climbing a mountain and to fantasize about all the obstacles they meet and all the things that happen to them during the course of this experience. After about ten minutes the lights were put back on, and the group was encouraged to swap experiences.

One patient reported himself awed by the sight of the big mountain facing him. "I feel like a baby in diapers—crawling and groveling. Now I feel as though I am in water up to my eyes and the mountain peak is rising out of the water and crumbling. Could that have anything to do with my impotence problem? And now the water is receding." (Therapist—"Can you imagine a way to get to the top of the mountain?") "Yes, now I suddenly feel stronger. I am on a great white stallion. It is streaking up the mountainside with incredible speed. It gets to the top and now its feet are firmly planted on the peak. The peak doesn't seem so formidable now—it's more like a plateau. Suddenly the wind is blowing with great force trying to push me and the horse off the top. I know this sounds nuts but there is a face in the wind. It reminds me of my grandfather. (Therapist—"Can you think of a way to cope with the wind?") "Yes, I face directly into the wind till it finally subsides. I feel strangely relieved."

This fantasy trip led the group to productive inquiry concerning the grandfather (who turned out to be the patient's ego ideal), the relationship between impotence and unrealistic aspirations, and the connection between the achievement of career ambitions and early childhood experiences. Two other members then disclosed their stories and the rest of the group involved themselves in trying to understand the personalized meanings of these fantasy identifications. I have discovered that group participation can be intensified if the speaker is advised to express himself in the first person and the present tense, as if it were happening now. Also, I suggest that "it is best to express yourself to someone—don't just talk to the ceiling or to the middle of the room. By hearing in detail what you experience and how you experience it, other members can share your experience and begin to understand your life as you live it."

Among the typical scenes that can be used for Directed Daydreams are:

1. A meadow. This can represent a fresh start or a screen for one's current moods.
2. Climbing a mountain. This can represent one's level of aspirations; a check on the progress of therapy.
3. Following a brook upstream to its source or down to the ocean. Patients often have difficulty in imagining that the brook flows freely to the ocean without obvious signs of obstruction. The stream may get lost in a big hole in the ground, the water may be dammed up by a wall or it may simply peter out. These various interpretations can be viewed as signs of resistance. If the patient can be helped to focus on them, then unpleasant but useful feelings may be aroused.
4. Describing and exploring a house. Freud considered a house to be a symbol of one's personality. Dynamically important parts of the house are explored after the patient has stepped in; the storage and kinds of foods in the refrigerator, a description of toilet and bathtub experiences, the bedroom, the content of the closets, the basement and the attic, the soundness of the superstructure and how clean or dirty it is.
5. Visualizing a close relative. The patient is asked to observe this person from a distance, to describe his behavior and especially to note his attitude toward the patient when the person approaches.
6. Visualizing situations which are designed to evoke patterns of sexual feelings and behavior. To the female patient the following situation can be offered. She is to imagine that she has taken a long walk by herself in the countryside, or perhaps that her car broke down on a lonely road far from home. In either event, another car comes along, stops next to her, and the driver offers her a lift. For male patients the suggestion is that they see a rose bush in the corner of the meadow, describe it—have them pick a rose to bring home.
7. Visualizing a lion in a cage, in a jungle, or on a desert. This test is useful for showing patients how they typically deal with their aggressive tendencies. To do this, I ask the patient to visualize a person whom he dislikes face to face with the lion, and then to describe the lion's behavior.
8. Looking into a dark forest from the meadow; or, for deeper material, looking into the dark opening of a cave. Certain imaginary

situations foster the appearance of symbolic figures representing deeply repressed material. A witch, a giant, or other such fearsome creatures, usually of the same sex of the patient may come out. These images symbolize introjects with their neurotic patterns and associated affects.

There are innumerable possibilities for fantasy trips and directed daydreams. Following are additional fantasies which I have used that have yielded the best results:

1. You are standing in front of a cave by the mountain. Go in.

2. Place yourself someplace at a certain time (present, past, future). Listen, someone is calling your name.

3. You're with someone from this group and the two of you are walking through a park (going on vacation, having dinner, fixing something together, having sex, etc.).

4. You are walking down a long, dark road. Off to the side, there is a high brick wall. Walking toward it, you spy a heavy iron gate slightly ajar. Go through the gate.

5. Imagine you're in a very dark building. You know it's some kind of art museum or art gallery. Directly in front of you there is a statue or sculpting of yourself. It can be realistic, or abstract, but in any case, the statue shows you as you really are. Go closer. Discover more about this statue. Go close to it and touch it. How does it feel? Now, try to become the statue. Change your posture to fit the form of the statue. Describe yourself as the statue. "I am . . ." What is your life like as this statue? What must you do to bring this statue to life?

6. Imagine that you are in a quiet place, alone by yourself. Close your eyes and really get in touch with what is going on inside your body. Take some time to really contact your inner physical sensations and feelings, and discover what you're experiencing within yourself. Now imagine you have a companion there with you. What is the companion like (clothes, posture, body, facial expressions, movements)? Keep trying to discover more about the companion. Ask questions and listen and watch for replies. Now become this fantasy companion. As this person, what are you like? How do you feel physically—what is your body position like, and how do you move? Try to get more and more into the feel of this

companion. What kind of things do you do and how do you interact with others? What parts of you are revealed through this extended ego?

7. Imagine you are a motorcycle. How do you feel as this motorcycle? What's your life like? What kinds of sounds do you make when you're running? Where do you go? Who rides you? What kind of relationship do you have with your rider? Have a dialogue with the rider.

8. Imagine that you are walking in the city at night in the rain. You turn down a neglected side street and soon you come across an abandoned store. The display window is dirty, foggy, and splattered, but if you look closely, you can make out some dim shapes. What was left abandoned in this store window? Wipe away some of the mist and moisture so that you can see more clearly. Examine the abandoned thing closely. Try to become this thing in the abandoned store. What is your existence like as this abandoned object? Why were you left here? How do you feel as this thing?

9. You're walking down a strange side street in a strange city and you come across a swap shop. In the store window, you see a variety of things—some old, some new, some very ancient. There's junk and there's also the kind of treasure you'd never expect to find there. A friendly little old man comes out of the front door and invites you into the store. He explains that this is no ordinary store. Anybody who finds his way to this shop can choose any one thing from the shop and take it with him. Take some time and look around the shop. There's lots of nooks and crannies and many side rooms. Try to decide the one thing you want to take from this store. When you have made up your mind, take some time to get to know the thing better. Look at it carefully and notice all the details about it. Touch it with your hands, smell it, handle it. How do you feel about this thing? As you start to leave with your prize, the storekeeper speaks to you again and says: "There is only one condition to your having the object of your choice. You must give me something in return. It can be absolutely anything you have." What will you give the old man? Take time to decide. Tell the old man what you will give him. Then slowly say goodbye and leave the shop. Now return to this room and bring with you whatever you decided to take from the shop. Now become this thing that you found in the shop. As this thing, what are you like? What is your life like? What happens to

you? What is your functional use? Now become yourself again. Look at the object. You understand it better now? Slowly say goodbye to this object and put it away somewhere in your memory.

10. Imagine yourself at a younger age walking up the street, approaching you as you are now. Have a dialogue with this younger you.

11. Imagine you are cleaning a closet or attic full of old things from the house you once lived in. Rediscover things that were once important to you. Find an old photograph album and look through the pictures.

12. You are looking at a blank TV screen. Some image appears that is not a commercial or part of the regular programming. It is some representation of your inner feeling that will appear on the screen. Become that image and see where it takes you.

13. You have just crash-landed on another planet. Explore this new planet and meet one of its inhabitants. Interact with this person, conduct a dialogue, identify with him.

14. Imagine it's a very dark night and you're running away from something or someone. Discover what it is that's chasing you. Then turn around and face this thing. What happens? Reach out and discuss this situation with your pursuer.

15. Imagine yourself to be somewhere and the rest of the group is coming toward you.

16. Make yourself tiny and enter your own body. Be as aware as you can of what you see, of how you feel, of each of your senses as you move about within your body.

17. Imagine yourself to be inside a cocoon. Feel the inside of the cocoon. Slowly explore your space inside the cocoon. How do you feel? Now slowly get out of the cocoon and be aware of your senses.

18. Think of yourself as a puppet with strings attached to all the parts of your body. The puppeteer slowly raises your left hand—up, up, up, and holds it there. Then he lets it suddenly drop! Then he lifts your right hand—up, up, up, and holds it there. Then he lets it drop! He slowly lifts your left leg, etc.

19. You're sitting alone in your living room in the middle of an autumn afternoon. Someone is knocking at the door.

20. You are all alone on a deserted ocean beach. It is dark and beginning to become chilly. You're digging for clams, and you have a bucketfull of them which you are taking home.

21. Desert island fantasy. You're stranded on a barren island with no hope of rescue. A year passes. A ship appears on the horizon. A small boat comes toward you. One person is in the boat.

22. Wise old man. You're talking to the wisest man in the world. You can ask him one question. He gives you a gift. Become that gift.

23. Approach of an important person. Someone's coming toward you down the road. You're just beginning to make the person out. The face is familiar. It's someone who has been very important to you.

Psychodrama

With creativity and sensitivity in its application, the psychodramatic method developed by Moreno (1956) can make a major contribution to ongoing group therapy. This approach integrates the modes of cognitive analysis with the dimensions of experiential and participatory involvement. By using action methods in the exploration of the psychological aspects of human experience, psychodrama cuts through overintellectualization, brings the component of nonverbal cues to the attention of the participant, and converts the urge toward "acting out" into the construction channel of "acting in." Through psychodramatic reenactment, impulses and their associated fantasies, memories, and projections are made consciously explicit, thereby getting unexpressed unconscious and preconscious feelings out in the open and simultaneously developing the individual's self-awareness. If the reader is unfamiliar with this method, it is strongly recommended that he introduce himself to the basic principles and concepts described by Corsini 1966, Moreno 1956, and Sturm 1965. The following account is only intended to illustrate how psychodrama can be used in group therapy.

Over a hundred psychodramatic techniques exist, along with many variations and modifications. Let me give you a brief outline of how these methods can be used for a variety of purposes and then I'll get into the specifics of the major techniques.

Techniques of Psychodrama

In order to clarify a patient's feelings, the techniques of soliloquy, the double, and multiple selves are used.

For intensifying and facilitating the expression of emotion, the therapist can use amplification, asides, and the exaggeration of the dimensions of height, space, and position.

The patient can be helped to become more aware of his own behavior through the use of such self-confrontation devices as video tape playback, role-reversal, behind-your-back, chorus, and nonverbal interaction exercises.

Issues of group process can be crystalized through the techniques of the spectogram and sociometry.

Through the skillful use of the above-mentioned techniques, the group therapist can help the patient to reenact a broad range of experiences and scenes from everyday life (actual occurrences, dreams, memories, fears, fantasies, physical symptoms).*

The Auxiliary Ego

Members of the group other than the target patient can play the role of significant others in his life. This auxiliary ego helps the protagonist to explore his situation by acting toward him in the way his real-life adversary does (employer, wife, student, brother, etc.). By speaking in the here and now and acting in a way complementary to the protagonist, the auxiliary ego tends to pull the target patient into a genuine encounter. Once he gets involved more deeply, when actual transactions begin to take place that resemble real life interaction, core conflicts and suppressions come out more rapidly and completely than they normally would in a therapy group. There are a number of ways to choose the auxiliary ego. The therapist can assign one according to the degree to which he thinks a group member can identify with a target patient's situation. He can also allow the patient to select his own auxiliary ego. (Here, it may be useful to later ask the patient to examine the reasons for his choice.) Sometimes, the therapist might himself want to play the auxiliary ego role. After an enactment, I often find it useful to ask the auxiliary person to comment on his own experience "in role." This provides the protagonist with good feedback regarding his impact on others and how it in turn causes them to treat him. The protagonist should be checked with occasionally to see that the auxiliary ego is playing the scene accurately.

*I often demonstrate psychodrama during the first stage so that patients can use it as a model for self-initiated intervention later on.

In a couples group, a husband and wife had been engaged in a bitter quarrel for the past two months. The wife's father was a widower, lived right above them, and ate supper in their apartment every night. The husband experienced his father-in-law as superior, condescending, and unfriendly. About three months earlier the husband had stopped coming home for supper, and began eating out; and coming home late at night. No mention was made of this peculiar arrangement in the group until the husband blew up and threatened to forbid his father-in-law to ever enter his house. The wife realized that in some way she was provoking the husband but she kept rationalizing this away by emphasizing her father's age and his loneliness. The group members and the therapist were generally unsuccessful in getting her to see that her protectiveness and need to appease her father were exaggerated. Reactions of members to the effect that she was giving greater priority to the father–daughter bond than to the marital relationship were agreed to with a shrug of the shoulders. Interpretations along the lines of compensatory behavior to assuage some hidden guilt felt toward the father were wasted on her.

Here was a complex situation with many possible interventions. I decided to use the wife as the protagonist and I chose a sensitive, verbal group member to represent the husband. The reason for this choice was that the husband was a passive, unexpressive man who kept things in and then exploded, without really conveying how he felt as a result of his wife's attitude. I thought the auxiliary ego could read the wife better than the husband could, and that his performance would provide a constructive role model for the husband to identify with.

The gist of what happened is that the auxiliary said: "I love you. I care for you. Why do you push me away? Your father bothers me but I really wouldn't mind him if you didn't stick him on me. Why are you putting him between us? I like to be alone with you." The wife kept bringing up the father's hurt. The husband persisted in attacking her attachment to the father. The auxiliary ego cut in at this point and asked "Why can't we talk about us? After a while, the wife became somewhat less defensive and began to be aware of her difficulty in talking about her own feelings toward the husband without bringing her father in as sort of a package deal. The husband raised an interesting point: "You know what I just thought? You must be more fed up with him than I am. Maybe you want me to fight your battles with him. I know it sounds crazy but I always feel you're so careful and uncomfortable with him." Shortly after the session, the ugliness of the arguments started to diminish, the husband had much less tendency to get sucked into attacking his father-in-law, and the wife became more contemplative and analytic about the displacements from father to husband.

The Double

The double technique (also called the alter ego) involves active empathy. The therapist appoints a group member to stand behind a protagonist and portray what the protagonist 1) might be experiencing inwardly but not expressing or 2) provide support for what the protagonist is saying, thereby helping him to take more risks and enter the interaction more completely. Throughout the enactment the double continues to speak in the first person ("I think . . ."; I feel . . .").

There are many different kinds of doubling:

1. The double can emphasize or amplify statements made by the protagonist. If the protagonist is feeling something strongly, but is not expressing those affects, the double may speak out and ventilate anger, love, or whatever is experienced.

2. The double can maximize and dramatize the emotional content of an attitude. Thus, if the protagonist says, "I like you," the double can say , "I need you"; "I am irritated" becomes "I hate you."

3. The double can verbalize nonverbal communication. For example, if the target patient smiles ingratiatingly, the double responds, "Why must I smile when I speak to him?" If another person's actions are annoying the protagonist but he only grits his teeth, this may be verbalized as "this is really getting me angry!"

4. The double can reinforce the protagonist's right to his feelings.

5. The double can question the protagonist's attitude: "Maybe I'm fooling myself," or "Could that be the way I really feel?"

6. The double can contradict the protagonist if he believes there are inconsistencies emerging.

7. The double can actively state the paradigms of the protagonist's character defenses. Denying: "This isn't happening!"; Isolation: "It's not affecting me at all!"; Displacement: "I want you to take the blame!", etc.

8. The double can interject a self-observation for the protagonist. "I'm getting more tense"; "Here I go intellectualizing again."

9. The double can do some low-level interpretations. "I used to

feel this way when I was younger"; "I become dependent on all women just like this."

10. Humor, satire, opposition, and provocation can also be very effective. "I'm happy you're mad at me because I don't need anybody"; "Of course you didn't hurt me; I like getting shit on"; "I can be nice to people no matter what they do to me. I love everybody. I'm just a big, wonderful, loving person."

Sometimes I do the doubling in my groups myself and, at other times, I either ask for a volunteer who can identify or appoint an advanced, sensitive person. Doubling is made easier if the person imitates the protagonist's posture, expression, gesture and voice tone. If this is done properly, the somesthetic cues can provide a wealth of intuitive information about how the subject feels. He should notice how the protagonist uses words—get a feeling from his self-system, the kinds of language he uses, the connotations, the level of abstraction, at first, just trying to paraphrase what the protagonist is most consciously trying to express. Any discrepancy between voice tone and content should be observed. If the protagonist has a very depressing date with a boyfriend but comes into the group full of charm and buoyancy, the double might reflect: "I'm upset and agitated but I'm trying to entertain you." He should identify with the feelings a person would ordinarily go through in certain common life situations (going through a secret abortion, discovering his wife is cheating, losing his job, getting married, falling in love). The double can express for the protagonist what he hasn't mentioned out loud up to this point. It is then up to the protagonist to question the absence, distortion, or minimization of typical reactions to these life roles.

Soliloquy
If an impasse is reached during an interaction and the protagonist seems to be spinning his wheels, the protagonist is instructed to walk up and down and talk to himself out loud, in order to clarify his feelings. He is then encouraged to reenter the interaction with whatever new insights he has gained.

Focusing on the Nonverbal
Often what is said in a discussion (the content) is less significant than how it was said (dramatization of the expression, posture, tone

of voice, angle of the body, gesture). Many of the ingredients crucial to the Gestalt emphasis on explicitly portraying nonverbal communications were originated by Moreno in his use of such psychodramatic techniques as role reversal, group feedback, amplification of gesture, and the mirror technique.*

Presenting the Basic Attitudes

Everybody has dozens of internal commands ("lies we live by") that direct our behavior according to "shoulds" and "oughts." These basic assumptions are usually implicit in the attitudes we assume and the decisions we make. An important step in the psychodramatic exploration of the problem is the explicit portrayal of the protagonist's attitudes and basic beliefs about himself, others, and the nature of human relationships. In group therapy I try to get patients to state these superego values and internalized sentences in the form of explicit pronouncements. Many of these irrational attitudes have been described by Ellis (1958). They include:

1. It is absolutely necessary for an adult to be loved and approved by everyone.
2. It is necessary to be completely competent, adequate, and achieving in every possible way if one is to be considered worthwhile.
3. We are made unhappy and frustrated by external events beyond our personal responsibility.
4. We have no choice of restructuring our life circumstances to more closely align them with our needs.
5. It is catastrophic when things don't go the way we would like them to.
6. Men shouldn't cry.
7. I should be able to handle this myself.

---

*In mirror technique, someone from the group acts the same way as the protagonist in order to provide feedback about unconscious pieces of behavior, e.g., a woman in one group had a very imperious, scathing manner. Even when she was involved only slightly in a transaction, she would behave as if she were gravely offended and the other person were "beyond the pale." When someone imitated her behavior, she burst out laughing and said, "My God! Is that me?" When everyone in the group said yes, she began to loosen up and to examine the reasons for her overreaction. Another tool that I have found helpful in getting patients to deal better with unresolved authority conflicts is to have the auxiliary ego (acting as the parent) stand on a chair (so that the patient may feel small and at a disadvantage). Conversely, the protagonist can stand on a chair to equalize the status and encourage self-assertion.

8. Being emotional is a sign of weakness.
9. To express anger is tantamount to losing control.
10. If I try to love someone, he should be happy and appreciative.
11. If I'm not happy, it's because you don't really love me.
12. A person should be able to resolve his conflicts.
13. I should have gotten a certain way by now.
14. If I haven't lived up to my expectations, I must be a failure.

Once these truisms are articulated ("I shouldn't upset my mother—she's an old woman"), the double can move with the resistance by saying something like "Right! I shouldn't upset the old lady no matter what happens—no matter what she does to me." By this exaggeration of the protagonist's defense, he is forced to a new explanation for his feelings ("I love her. How could I upset her deliberately?") To this the double might reply: "I can't love and hate at the same time." This sort of interplay frequently leads to a greater awareness of the contradictions and paradoxes in our self-systems. In this case, the patient realized that his inablility to get his feelings out and his oversolicitude for his mother made their relationship very shallow and as a result he did not want to see her frequently but always wanted to avoid her. The patient ended up making a statement that had a much healthier ring to it than in his earlier black-and-white attitude. He said, "If I can't get mad at my mother, if I can't get her upset, if I can't let her feel what I'm feeling, then how much can I love her, how much of a feeling can I have?"

Act Hunger
Blatner (1973) defines act hunger as "the drive toward the fulfillment of the desires and impulses at the core of the self." The group therapist has to be creative in finding symbolic fulfillments so that patients can satisfy and finally let go of their unrequited feelings toward significant others.

During one group session, Jack, a man of forty-one, mentioned that he was thinking of his foster mother who now lived in Florida. He speculated about what her reaction would be if he told her he was sorry for all the aggravation that he caused her when he was an adolescent. In the subsequent discussion, it developed that whereas he originally sought her forgiveness as his goal (if you accept my apology then I'll feel loved), he now saw that it was equally true that his capacity to forgive his foster mother for her mistakes would open him up to loving her without underlying resentments. The group urged him to call her up from the therapist's office while he was still in touch with these new feelings. The ensuing conversation was quite remarkable considering that these two people hadn't spoken to each other in seventeen years.

This technique of "doing things on the spur of the moment" can be applied to

1. Writing letters that should have been written years ago (They don't necessarily have to be mailed.)
2. Giving a valedictory address to an audience of loving "parents" (In this case, the patient's father hadn't taken time off from work to go to her graduation even though she was the valedictorian.)
3. Visualizing one's own death (Who would you want there, what would your final words be, what were you sorry you didn't accomplish, what do you think they'll say about you?)
4. Spending five minutes with a loved one who has died (Express your honest resentments and appreciations, don't try to change them, say goodbye, ask your final questions, have the double say what the patient might really be experiencing, have your auxiliary ego respond as a very human, flawed, but well-intentioned person. Working through to a feeling of atonement [at-one-ment] and a saying of goodbye in a self-supportive way ["It hurts but I can let go"] are important for reinforcing a patient's sense of identity.)

In a countertransference workshop, Ruth Cohen once demonstrated a technique that illustrated act hunger and act completion. A student analyst was experiencing good feelings about his professional growth in general and his work with one patient in particular. Excessive modesty and a fear that he was going to sound too boastful prevented this man from describing the real extent of his work satisfaction. Ruth Cohen had the therapist brag a little bit about how good a therapist he was. Once he warmed up to the task, the therapist began to see, through exaggeration and playacting, that what he referred to as bragging was actually self-confidence. Apparently this man's background taught him to play down his strengths and take a guise of humility (the family motto was "self-praise stinks"). The bragging game was a good experience in "feeling his oats." Similarly, I have encouraged mousy women to slink around like seductive sex pots; have gotten men who always thought they were physically weak and unmanly to challenge other men to arm wrestling (it's surprising how well these men seem to hold their own); I have urged patients who constantly claim that what they have to say is not important enough, to demand attention and to insist that others listen to them; I have initiated healthy regression with stuffed-up obsessives, in the service of the ego, by making my favorite animal noise and asking everyone to join in and do the same (we even gave a name to this noisy festival—The Barnyard Symphony). If the patients demur on the grounds that the proposed actions don't seem natural, I tell them to fake it. "Make believe. I (the therapist) won't let anything bad happen."

By reinforcing an acceptance, enjoyment, and eventually an integration of previously rejected and suppressed dimensions of the personality, we can validate a patient's inner experiencing and help him to redefine himself as someone who, as a vital living being, possesses many different sides. The presence of the therapist in the group sustains the patient's "observing ego" so that he doesn't feel that he is going to lose self-control. This external support also enables the patient to go further than he ordinarily would in testing out undeveloped desires.

The Gestalt Approach

Rules

Many of the concepts that I try to filter into my group during the early sessions came from the writing of the Gestalt therapists. In contrast to psychoanalysis, the Gestalt approach emphasizes the "how" and the "now" of behavior (as opposed to the "why" and the "then"). It contends that patients hold onto past behavior and roles by obtaining environmental support through manipulation rather than by utilizing self-support. For example, a man constantly complained that his wife's criticality was ruining his romantic feelings and prevented them from having the right climate for sex. When the wife's hostility appreciably diminished, it was revealed that the husband was still terribly anxious and suffered from strong feelings of inadequacy. Thus, it would seem that he welcomed her criticism as an excuse. The Gestaltists believe that only by making him directly experience this fear within himself in the present, can this kind of patient be helped.

The Gestalt approach offers two sets of guidelines that are designed to dig out resistances, promote heightened awareness, and demonstrate to the patient the many subtle ways he stops himself from fully feeling himself. First, there are the "rules," then there are the "games."

The Principle of the Now

Focus on the immediate moment, on the present experience. Communicate in the present tense. "What is your present awareness?" "What is happening now?" "What do you feel at this moment?" The most effective means of integrating past material into the personality is to bring it into the present. Try to avoid bland, intellectualized "aboutisms"; give all material the impact of immediacy. In this regard, a technique that I have employed in early history-taking sessions, is to have the patient play each of the members of his family, and have each of them tell the story of the patient's life from their viewpoint. The rule is that when the patient refers to events of last week or of his fifth year, we must direct him to "be there" in fantasy and to enact a vignette in present terms.

Keep pointing out to the patient his difficulty in staying with the now. When patients talk about absent individuals, reminiscences, or gets preoccupied with the fears and fantasies of the future, Gestalt workers identify this as resistance to remaining in the context of present awareness.

I and Thou

True communication always involves both sender and receiver. If patients are talking out to the group, try to ask them, "To whom are you saying this?" Make the message as direct and unequivocal as possible. People listen more carefully when they are addressed by name. Have there been any social-psychological studies exploring the relationship between level of involvement and the number of times you used other group members' names and they've used yours? Make patients aware of the distinction between "talking to" and "talking at" the listener. Is the patient's speech too fast so that others cannot follow, too low so that other give up from the strain of concentrating, too dramatic so that others lose concern for the "boy who cried wolf." Is his verbal behavior intended to make contact or to ensure avoidance?

It Language and I Language

This rule deals with degrees of responsibility and involvement. People usually refer to their bodies and actions in third person language. "What is your hand doing?" "It is trembling." "What do you hear in your voice?" "It is trembling." By means of changing It language into I language, we can identify with the particular behavior in question and to assume greater responsibility for it. As we get the patient to repeat this excercise over and over he is more likely to participate in the group as an active agent who does things rather than allowing things to happen to him. For example, if the patient says "I can't do that," the therapist will ask, "Can you say, I won't do that?"

The Use of How Instead of Why

"How do you experience the anxiety?" Focusing on awareness of body feelings, sensations, and perceptions constitutes our most certain knowledge. It takes us away from endless verbalizations, explanations, and interpretations.

No Gossiping

Gossiping is talking about an individual when he is actually present and could just as well be addressed directly.

Changing Questions Into Statements

Group members often initially express their feelings in the form of questions instead of statements, as if they had a rule against the open expression of feelings. Questions beginning with "Why . . ." (e.g., "Why did you do a stupid thing like that?") illustrate the functions this rule performs. These questions lend themselves well to being employed as double binds, since it is impossible to pin down what the asker intends by his communication. Consider the question (asked tensely) "Why are you so angry with him?" Responding to the affect by saying something like "You seem to object to my being angry with him" can evoke the reply, "Oh no, I was just curious."

Responding to the question as if it were indeed a request for information is likely to evoke further angry questioning or accusations, since not dealing with the affect leaves unfinished business. "Why . . ." questions, then, are very well suited to evasion of responsibility for one's own "negative" reactions. Their appearance is therefore likely to signify that people are operating as if there were a rule against expressing negative affect directly or "unreasonably" and are seeking to avoid being blamed for such expresssion. Such a rule may, of course, be an internal one; a person may feel guilty if he allows himself to express anger directly "without a good reason."

In order to help group members become aware of the consequences of such a rule, the leader might focus their attention on their communication pattern by saying: "We seem to be expressing our feelings in the form of questions instead of statements; perhaps we are developing a norm against the open expression of (negative) feelings. In this strategy of caricature, the essence is to ask group members to behave deliberately in accordance with a rule they were already following implicitly, now under conditions which allow its experiential impact to be heightened. To foster this heightening, the leader may ask members to exaggerate behavior already existing. For example, in a situation in which members seem to be expressing their feelings only in the form of questions, the leader might prescribe a game where the members may only communicate for the next five minutes by asking questions. "Once you have asked a question, you may ask someone else in the group another, but no one may answer any questions during the game. You may not question the person who questions you more than twice in succession" (so that the interaction will not focus on two people for very long). This exercise very rapidly elevates the tension level and may reveal many content issues previously hidden as it becomes obvious to participants that questions are also statements. In addition, members become attuned to the affect-laden nature of questions in general and particularly to the accusatory quality of "Why . . ." questions.

Splits

Gestalt therapists seek out whatever divisions or splits that appear in the personality (topdog [superego] vs underdog). The topdog specializes in shoulds, and is bossy and comdemning; the underdog is passive, resistant, makes excuses, finds reasons to delay. The patient is asked to have a dialogue between these two components of the self. This can be applied with various parts of the body participating (the right hand vs the left hand).

Making Rounds
This need not be confined to verbal interaction. We can ask the patient to touch everybody, observe everybody, frighten everybody.

Unfinished Business
We can have patients role-play any unfinished business they have.

Responsibility
With each phrase, we can ask the patient to say "and I take responsibility for it." What at first seems mechanical and foolish then becomes heavily laden with meaning.

Terrible Secrets
Each person thinks of a well-guarded personal secret. He is instructed not to share the secret itself but to imagine how others would react to it. Or we could have the patient boast about what a terrible secret he nurses (then the unconscious attachment to the secret as a precious achievement begins to come to life).

Playing the Projection
If the patient says, "I can't trust you," he may be asked to play the role of an untrustworthy person. If the patient says, "You are not interested in me—you just do this for a living," he will be told to enact this attitude.

Role Reversal
We can ask the person to use a role-reversal technique (symptoms commonly represent the reversal of underlying latent impulses). If the person is timid, we ask him to play an exhibitionist; if he's touch to criticism, he is asked to listen very carefully to everything that is said to him.

The Rhythm of Contact and Withdrawal
Gestalt therapy emphasizes the polar nature of vital functioning. Withdrawal is not dealt with as resistance, but as a rhythmic

response to be respected. Consequently when a patient withdraws, we ask him to close his eyes and withdraw in fantasy to any place or situation in which he feels secure. He describes a scene and his feelings there, and then he is asked to come back to the group and share his experiences. Usually the patient returns with restored energies, new feelings, and fresh insights.

Rehearsal
People share their internal rehearsals and preparations for playing their accustomed roles out loud in front of the group.

Movement Exaggeration
Patients are asked to exaggerate by repeating a movement, gesture, or piece of verbal behavior. "There are many times when the patient's unwitting movement or gesture appears to be a significant communication. The gestures, however, may be abortive, undeveloped, or incomplete—perhaps a wave of the arm or a tap of the leg. The patient is asked to exaggerate the movement, repeatedly, at which time the inner meaning will frequently be more apparent" (Levitsky and Perls 1969).

Cynthia was sitting in group, withdrawn and seemingly distinterested, while some of the female members discussed their feelings toward the leader (a male). Cynthia was compulsively playing with her hair by grabbing loose ends and putting them under her nose and smelling them. The leader drew her attention to this mannerism and asked her to leave the room and continue this behavior until a fantasy or forgotten memory occurred to her. After about ten minutes, she returned and reported her father used to braid her hair until she was nine and then stopped for no apparent reason. "The only thing that comes to my mind is something having to do with sex. I used to hear sex noises; I smelled the bedsheets and was afraid my mother would find out." At this moment, Cynthia reported that Alice (another group member) was probably mad at her for getting so much attention. She started getting into a whole obsessive rap about why Alice might be jealous. The leader said, "Screw Alice; what do you want to do?" Cynthia replied, "I like your attention but I'm scared to take you away from her." The group started rooting and cheering, "Do it—wrestle her for him—fuck her." They wrestled with Cynthia, winning. Cynthia agreed to share the leader with Alice but only if she

(Cynthia) could "have a lot of him." At this point, she got a little timid and insecure. She mentioned as an aside that her husband had a standing joke regarding her five-second embraces. The leader encouraged Cynthia to go around the room and show how she embraces men. She balked, acted very timorous, and finally blurted out, "The women will be jealous." The men in the group urged her on. She broke down and sobbed, "I wanted them both to love me (martyrish mother and passive father); I love them. I have never been able to express anger to them. While I was fighting Alice I felt close to her, looser. I was feeling trembly and good at the same time." Alice came over and embraced her while she cried. Different men in the group surrounded her and stroked her. She reached out to one of them and cried on his shoulder while clinging to him.

Following this session Cynthia had her first confrontation with her mother and told her to stop feeling sorry for herself. She brought up the subject of her father's death, talked about her feelings about him and had the first honest conversation with the mother in her life. Two weeks later, Cynthia had her first orgasm after five years of marriage.

The reader should take notice of how the therapist integrated the Gestalt approach and certain Encounter techniques together with his understanding of psychoanalytic theory to work through the patient's resistance to dealing with the fear of competition and the resulting self-abnegation.

Circle Voicing

Elliot (1971) reports on an interesting game invented by Stanley Russell of Elysium Institute. I have applied this technique in groups where the participants are already somewhat loosened up and know each other fairly well. It is particularly effective for creating greater feelings of openness, spontaneity, and a sense of mutual acceptance.

Ask the group to sit in a circle holding hands. "Each person, starting with me, will make a sound and all the others will imitate it and the position I put my body in. When I'm through I'll tap the person to my right on the shoulder and it will be his turn to vocalize while the group copies him." After you tell them this, give forth with some sound you enjoy making. (I personally like whooping like a cowboy waving his hat while he rides a bucking bronco.) Make whatever sounds you like. The patients that follow may start out copying you but, in a short time, they're off on their own trips—laughing, giggling, mooing like a cow, shrieking, screaming, grunting, making baby talk. The rest of the group imitates the sound as it is made. Bodies start to move, there's swaying and rocking, arms go up and down, there's lots of dancing and jumping around and a general feeling of freedom and expansiveness breaks out. A second go-round carries this process even further and brings out whatever else was left inside.

When I have presented this technique at various workshops, I have been criticized on the grounds that it has no place in therapy. "There's too much merrymaking and fooling around. It's acting out with no special purpose in mind." My own experience, after I have introduced this game a number of times during, let's say, the tenth to twentieth session, is that the group becomes much more relaxed. Members become looser, they say things to one another that are uncharacteristic of them, fixed cognitive sets get fractured, and the unexpected is more likely to happen.

STAGE 2 EXERCISES—NEGATIVE AND AGGRESSIVE BEHAVIOR

Who is calling the shots here? How much can I push for? Must I do what they require of me? Do I have the confidence to say what I really think? Will they let me? Can I take it if they say what they really think?

Once a group is fairly well formed, new problems begin to take precedence. Power struggles, competition, and influence become central concerns. The whole decision-making process in the group is subject to much scrutiny. Some members want to be controlled and have others take the responsibility, while others want to dominate and have the power in their hands. Themes having to do with strivings for independence, rebelliousness, compliance, activity-passivity, male-female roles, homosexuality, and learning to share responsibility are prevalent. Members seem particularly interested in leadership behavior, rules of procedure, proper orientation to the task, reevaluating their own competence and strongly questioning the authority of others.

What Do You Want?

Divide the group into pairs. Each partner alternately asks one question, "What do you want?" Say this with many different gestures and inflections as your partner tries to answer the question. Keep the answers in the "now." Then reverse roles. This experiment helps to put patients in touch with their ever-changing flow of wants and desires and also helps them to express these feelings openly to another person.

One man's list of responses to the question "what do you want?" was as follows:

Her tits
The window open
More freedom
More time with friends
I want to feel close
I want to stop bullshitting
I want to cry
I want to kiss you on the cheek

Guilt-Resentment-Demands

Working through feelings of guilt is a very tricky business. Many patients have learned to use catchwords like "guilt" manipulatively, in order to evoke reassurance that they can then reject.

If a patient in your group gets stuck with guilty feelings, try the following exercises: "Think about the situation that you feel guilty about. Recall the situation with all the details. Is there someone else in the picture? Describe exactly what you did that makes you feel guilty. Then think of the one person in the world who would be most angry or upset if he or she knew about your guilty action. Imagine this person here right now. What kind of facial expression does he (or she) have? Pretend that you are talking to the person and tell him exactly what you feel guilty about. Express yourself (out loud) as if you were this other person. What do you feel as you answer the guilty party? Continue this dialogue for a while . . .

"Now become yourself again, and really try to get out the anger and resentment that is hidden behind the guilt. For example, if you feel guilty about not visiting your mother enough, the resentment might be, 'I resent your expecting me to be there more often than I want to go.' Say this directly to the person you feel guiltily beholden to. How do you feel while you are doing this? Again, change places and respond to what you have said as if you were this other person. Get into the mood of how this person would respond to this state of resentment. What do you say back? How do you feel physically as you respond to these resentments? Continue this dialogue for a while longer.

"Now express the demand that lies behind the resentment. For instance, if the resentment is "I resent you for expecting me to be at your house more often than I want to go," then the demand might be something like, "I am me, treat me like an adult!" Express you demand clearly and strongly, as if you were giving orders. Keep in touch with your physical experiences as you do this. Again change places and respond to the demands that have just been expressed. How do you feel as this other person? Try to develop some honest communication between yourself and this other person."

A very productive technique that can be used in conjuction with this procedure is to ask the target patient to play the role of the party he feels most guilty toward (e.g., mother). Then the therapist and the other group members can interview the "mother,"sounding her out on how she feels about her son. With the proper handling, the mother's collective grievances and resentments give way to softer things. As one man play-acting his mother put it: "You were my sun and stars put together. I didn't have any life with your father. I needed you. I felt lonely. I know I ask too much, but who else am I going to ask?" . . . cries.

Give It To Me

Here's a game for bringing out the characteristic ways that you behave when you want something from somebody or when someone wants something from you. Are you a placater? Unnecessarily stubborn? What approach do you respond to best? When you want something, how do you ask for it?

Break the group into pairs; in each pair decide which person is A and which is B. How do you decide who is A and who is B? Did one person take greater responsibility and decide? If so, did he decide for himself, "I'll be A," or did he decide for his partner, "You be A"? Did one of you try to pass the buck and force the others to decide by waiting passively, shrugging, or saying, "What do you want me to do?" Discuss this briefly and think about how this expresses what you do when a decision has to be made.

Now I want you to play a game called: "You got it; I want it." Try to imagine that A has and wants very much to hold on to something that B wants very much. Pretend you both know what this something is but don't discuss this with each other. Just begin talking to one another. B might start off with, "I want it," and A answers, "No, I won't give it to you." B then could say, "Why not—give it to me" (reaching out with his hands). A might answer, "No" (pulling away). Continue this dialogue for five minutes, Then switch roles so that B has it and A wants it. Again have a dialogue for five minutes.

Now discuss all the details of the interaction with your partner. What did you become aware of in yourself while playing both roles? What feedback can you give your partner about his behavior? Can you get in touch with how your present role behavior might parallel the role you played in your original family? Were you the person who tried to get other people to open up and give or the person from whom other people tried to get things? Did you complain, beg, or try to make your partner feel guilty? Did you use logic to convince him he didn't need it? How did you rebuff the other person's attempt to get it? Did you feel good about refusing to give up that which you wanted to keep or did you want to give in and please the other person even at you own expense?

Primal Connectors

Welch (1973) has described a technique which he calls "Primal Connection," to help people get in touch with and recreate the experiences and feeling of early childhood.

The Womb

The therapist asked the group members to lie on the floor, close their eyes and breathe deeply, hold it for a count of three, and then relax. He asked the group to feel the tightness and tension in their muscles, and then again to relax. ("Feel the tightness and tension leave your body.") The group is led through this exercise three times. Then the leader asks the group to tighten up and feel the strength in their arms. Then again they are told to relax and let be. Next the shoulders, face, legs, feet—each time feeling the tension, then relaxing, until progressively the whole body is experienced as if it's suspended or floating.

While this floating, drifting mood is setting in, the leader gently asks the group to recall a pleasant experience, one that has warm, loving, secure associations. Slowly, the leader guides the group back to childhood. "Try to remember some pleasant scenes from high school—where were you, what were you wearing, how was it out, who were you with?" Then the group is successively led back to junior high school, public school, kindergarten, and nursery school. Then the therapist asks that everyone imagine drifting back to their mother's breast. "You're at your mother's breasts—she's softly cuddling and caressing you." About three minutes are allowed for the mood to be established. "Now you are going even further back. You're in your mother's womb." Enough time is allowed for the group to immerse themselves in this experience, then the therapist calls for the journey back to the present. "Count very slowly from zero up to that number which corresponds to your present age." This is designed to ease the reentry problem. When everyone's eyes are open, the therapist asks if anyone would like to share his experience with the rest of the group.

This experiment is used to recapture the original world of harmony and bliss before "it all happened." It helps set the stage for the following exercises where less pleasant feelings are unearthed, by providing a before-and-after basis for comparison. Moreover, it highlights the ongoing developmental process whereby life gradually becomes more complicated and less balanced.

Birth

The birth process involves leaving the warmth, security, and serenity of the womb for the sharp penetrating pandemonium of the outside world and the coldness (78 degrees) of the delivery room. To recreate the experience of birth, we need to simulate the womb with its darkness, warmth, and quiet. Then we need the lights, coldness, and noise of the delivery room. The womb can be approximated with a sleeping bag and an electric blanket. The "feel" of the delivery room can be recreated by using ice water, a high-intensity lamp, and a tape recording of a baby's crying and screaming. The staff of the delivery room consists of a doctor (the therapist), "mother," and three assistants. After the "baby" gets inside the sleeping bag in a prenatal position, it is zipped up and an elastic band is placed around the sleeping bag. Keep the lights dim. Have the "staff" (patient volunteers) gently rock the artificial womb. Have the delivery doctor say, "slowly, gently, quietly, relax. Don't think of anything. Just relax. Quietly, very quietly," The doctor (therapist) is in charge of watching the birth and seeing to it that his assistants do not make any undue noise, giggle, rock too fast, or in any way break the atmosphere of calm.

The "mother" places herself at the closed end of the sleeping bag so that the feet of the baby press against her legs. When the birth begins, she moves with the baby so that the subject can always push against something solid. The assistants busy themselves with sprinkling water on the emerging baby's head, turning on the high-intensity lamp so the light shines in the baby's eyes, and pulling the elastic band over the head and body of the baby in order to make the exit from the womb a little difficult and so that the infant has to push in order to enter his new world.

The doctor signals the start of birth by gesturing to the mother and assistants to unfold the electric blanket and increase the tempo of rocking. Gently, he takes the baby out of the womb. "Easy—here we go—slowly—easy now." He reaches into the sleeping bag to grasp the head of the baby to assist in the birth. As the head begins to emerge, one assistant sprinkles ice water, another put the lamp on, another starts the tape recorder supplying the baby's cry and the loud and confusing noise of the delivery room. This continues until the baby has come completely out of the artificial womb.

After the delivery, the therapist begins the discussion by asking such questions as "What were you feeling while in the womb?"; "How did you react to the doctor's noise?"; "How did you feel about leaving the womb and emerging?" The "mother," assistants, and therapist also share their responses to the experience. Then the rest of the group can share their own personal reactions.

The Crib

After the arrival of the new baby at home, an endless line of adults come to visit and gaze admiringly upon the new baby. The father, mother, uncles, aunts, grandparents, and friends gather around the crib to mimic faces, utter sounds, and make all sorts of crazy gestures to evoke some response from the child. To construct this scene, we can line three tables on their sides, put the baby on a blanket between the tables, and receive his visitors. The admirers (group members) appear at the side of the crib and talk and gesture to the baby in the same way they would talk to actual babies. Then the participants stop and discuss what they have been doing and how they feel about it. The "infant" is given an opportunity to dialogue with various of his admierers to tell them how he responded to their particular attempt to entertain or amuse him.

This exercise causes the person playing the "infant" to thoughtfully consider what his crib experiences might have been like. If the visitors in the group are kinder than what the patient feels those of his own early experience were, for example, then feelings of indifference and deprivation are bound to emerge. If the visitors' behavior resembles the nostalgic recollection that the patient has to the past, then the patient is likely to focus on what has happened since to ruin the Garden of Eden.

Toilet-Training

Toilet-training often represents the power struggle between the parental wish for obedience ("Do your doody") vs the child's striving for independence and self-assertion (moving his bowels at his own choice of time, place, and quantity). This exercise is designed to get group participants in touch with the effects of excessive coersion and threats on the sensibilities of a young child. The leader brings a stool to a group meeting and places it on the side of the room. While the session is going on, he observes the members, searching for some mannerism or piece of behavior which is fairly obvious in each member. For example, several people may be observed brushing back their hair, frequently crossing thier legs, biting their lip, etc. After isolating some particular behavior, the leader jumps from his chair and grabs the person exhibiting the target behavior. He shouts, "Don't do that here! We have a place for that. If you have to do that, here is the place." The person is led to this stool and told to sit down. Then the discussion is continued. If the person upon the stool is observed repeating the behavior, the leader jumps up again and says, "Good boy! I'm proud of you." The "child" is then returned to his former seat. Like a mother talking with her friends in her living room, the leader continues at the same time to keep watch over the "children." If one of the participants exhibits the target behavior, he or she is immediately rushed to the stool! If the child sits on the stool for a long time without repeating the target behavior, he is returned to his seat. The leader may say something like, "Well, if you're not going to do that, then go back to your seat, but remember we have a place for that!" If anyone dares ask what that is, the leader does not respond except, perhaps, to say, "You know what that is." He may add a brief lecture about their being a proper time and place for doing such things.

After about fifteen, twenty minutes like this, the leader stops and inquires if anyone knows what's gone on. He may ask, "How do you feel about what's happening?", "How did you feel when I grabbed you," or "How did you feel sitting on a stool?" More often than not many of those present realize what is taking place. Most of us have, when children, experienced such a situation. As in all of the experiences, this one concludes with the patients sharing how they felt, especially those who, unaware of what was happening, were first grabbed and rushed to the stool!

Getting Dressed

Two- or three-year-old children don't have the kind of hands that can perform certain physical tasks well. Buttons are a nightmare, getting one's clothes on is a terribly frustrating task, tucking in a shirt is a major project. If it were possible to invent exercises where we could transform well coordinated, experienced-in-dressing-themselves adults' hands into chubby little toddlers' hands, then the patient could revive the forgotten feeling revolving around "getting dressed" experiences.

The leader brings in a large shirt, a big pair of pants, a pair of large shoes with laces, and the hands of a two-year-old in the form of very large rubber gloves. The experiment consists in putting on the gloves and then attempting to put on all the other clothes. The participants get a big kick out of their clumsy struggling effort to dress themselves. As they observe the futile, stumbling attempts of others, it helps them to loosen up and identify their feelings of respect and admiration for their own heroic efforts when younger to finally master these skills. All sorts of getting dressed memories crop up for further analysis including more current data in terms of husband-wife experiences.

One man who had struggled mightily, just couldn't get his shoes laced with the rubber gloves on. He remembered how awkward and uncoordinated he felt as a child. "My mother used to treat me like a real baby. She chose my clothes till I was fourteen or fifteen, would lay them out for me, would help me on with them—I know it sounds crazy. She even gave me a bath until I was eleven. Anyhow, my wife and I get into clothing hassles. I don't know whether this has anything to do with the exercise but often I can't make up my mind what color goes with what; you know, whether a yellow tie goes with a blue jacket. I like to ask my wife because she has a good color sense. But if she suggests that my jacket doesn't look well with my pants, I get so angry I could spit nails. I can't stand being controlled. But she says if you don't want me to tell you, then why do you ask me in the first place?" The exercise provided the group with a significant entré into the relationship between dependence needs and the fear of being controlled.

Learning to Write

Learning to write is damn difficult but most adults have forgotten just how hard it was for them when they were in first grade. I use this exercise in group to help patients experience the fustration of learning how to write all over again. This is a simple exercise. One simply takes a pencil and completes the following tasks. Using a drawing similar to the one below, one attempts to draw and complete a line between the parallel lines forming two starts, one inside the other. One then completes the human figure, draws a line to the center of the maze, and finally, draws a triangle or other figure in the empty space.

The catch in this exercise is that one must do it with the opposite hand one usually uses and at the same time looking in a mirror. It really isn't difficult. The participants know exactly what they want to do. The problem is one's hand won't do what it is told to do!

This exercise seems to bring out a burst of forgotten incidents ranging from painful memories concerning the attempts by well-meaning teachers to change a lefty to a righty, to recollections from someone who is a new college professor how because he had bad handwriting, his parents were informed that he was mentally deficient and advised to place him in a CRMD class. Someone else remembered that because his penmanship was neat and precise he used to get kidded about being a fairy. This caused him a lot of grief around eight, nine and ten.

Rejection Games

Sometimes people have a need to get everyone to accept them. This indiscrimiate appeal for love becomes particularly striking in a group situation where individualized responses are called for. Group members who respond to practically everybody in a homogenized way are probably fearful that if they act assertively and show special preferences, they will arouse jealousy, resentment, and experience rejection. One way over this hurdle is to have the group members invite or reject each other without talking. "You can shake your head, nod, smile, scowl, flirt, turn your back—you can encourage or push away anyone you want."

Another derivative exercise is called the High School Dance. Men line up on one side of the room, women on the other. All mentally choose a partner of the opposite sex from across the room. One at a time, the men cross the room and nonverbally invite the women to sit down with them. Those chosen are free to reject or accept. If the inviter is rejected, he walks back alone to his original position. The gender of the initiating member should be determined by the prevalent mood in the group (whether the men or the women are most fearful of an indifferent or rejecting attitude at this particular time). The participants then process their experiences.

Yes-No Games

In this exercise, the participants can only communicate by saying either yes or no, either of which can be said by each participant as often as he wants and in any order. It is an especially useful device for better understanding what the power dynamics are behind a deadlock of wills. Another way this exercise can be used is for assertiveness training. If someone is trying to work through difficulties in demanding something that they think they deserve, have them say yes, while the partner or the group in unison shouts no. If someone has difficulty in refusing demands placed upon him, have the other members say yes and have him say no. If this exercise is repeated with escalating voice volume and power, the individual gets a tremendous sense of his real capacity to be strong if he needs to be.

Breaking Through Blocks

The Outsider

If someone in the group talks about feeling left out or less close than the others, have him position himself physically on the outside.

He may sit out the door within earshot, in the corner of the room, or simply further away than the others. After awhile, process the feeling. Another variation of this technique is to ask the person to actually leave the room and close the door behind him. Discuss him while he is gone. Then tell him to come back, but don't tell him what you talked about. After awhile, inquire about his feelings.

Blind Man's Bluff

If a person in the group has difficulty in making contact with people because of a fear of rejection, supersaturate him with rejection. Tie a handkerchief over his eyes, put him in the center of the group, and then have him try to tag one of the other members. Meanwhile have the group badger him, tease him, and goad him. This may sound like a cruel sport but it does help to replicate inner experiences the patient may have in real situations. When the rejection and inability to make contact occurs in a laboratory situation, these experiences are ripe for examintion "hot off the griddle."

Opening the Fist

Divide the group into dyads and have the partner on the right close his fist very tightly. The other partner is told to open the fist by any means he chooses, verbal or physical, while the first partner can choose to resist or comply. Most people are much more responsive to softness, persuasion, or cajolery. After the game, start up the discussion of what it might show about their personal styles of dealing with others. Ask each partner to discuss first with each other and then with the group what they were experiencing during the exercise. For example, when the fist was closed, did he feel guilty about not complying earlier, did the other person's approach make him more obstinate or more yielding, did his attitudes toward opening or staying closed change as the game progressed, and why? An offshoot of this game is to ask the group the question, "Who were you in the family—the opener or the closed one? Which role best describes other members of the family?"

In answer to this question one member of the group replied as follows: "I was capable of resisting much longer. I gave up too easily because I wanted to please Sally. I feel anxious when I'm frustrating someone else.

I even feel nervous when they're frustrated and it's my fault. It is always my role to put everyone else at ease. If my mother was annoyed at my sister, I volunteered to wash the dishes. If my father came home from work grouchy, I drew him out and calmed him down. In another way, though, maybe I was the closed fist. Part of me I keep away from everybody. They never see that beneath my niceness and accommodating front I have a lot of hate and bitterness. I feel very selfish and hard inside." After this revelation, the group helped the patient to work through his feeling of unwarranted guilt whenever he wanted his feelings taken into consideration. Two sessions later he asked to go through the exercise again. This time, however, he kept his hand tightly closed for three or four minutes and then slowly opened it. "I wanted to prove that I could be independent and that I could open it when I wanted to—it feels great!"

Resentments

This exercise is a particularly useful tool in couples' groups, but it also has application between two group members who periodically got locked into a hostile interaction. Have them pair off, make eye contact, and hold hands. "I want you to take turns expressing your resentment toward one another. Begin each sentence with the words, "I resent . . ." and be specific about what you resent in your partner. When you are done with the resentments, be silent while your partner expresses a resentment of you. Continue alternately expressing these resentments for about five minutes. When you get stuck, just say, "I resent. . ." and see what words occur to you next."

Appreciate

Now substitute the word "appreciate" for all the resentments that you expressed. Say these new sentences to one another. How do you feel as you say it? Is there any truth in the new statement which at first might sound quite peculiar and on the surface might even seem to be saying the opposite of what you feel? For instance, one of my sentences might have been, "I resent your telling me when to get off the highway. I can read the signs." When I change this to, "I appreciate you telling me when to get off the highway. It makes it easier for me to relax and not have to concentrate on where the exit is." Here I realize that although I consciously resent "unnecessary" reminders, it does satisfy some dependency feelings. The new phrasing makes me aware of how I might cue my wife to remind me, without even realizing it.

When the paired-off group members have attained some realization of their real appreciation, have them repeat the sentence that begins, "I appreciate . . ." and then have them elaborate on their appreciation. The awareness of the appreciation that is often hidden in the resentment is a real eye-opener that gives the protagonist a much more balanced outlook. It is typical that the wives of alcoholics or gamblers are people who need to feel superior to someone. Their self-righteousness and martyrdom draw them to helpless, dependent men. The inconvenience and heartache involved are far outweighted by the neurotic gain. They always seem to be in the heroic, long-suffering, "nursing" role.

Trust Fall

If the time is ripe for patients to explore their feelings of suspiciousness and defenses against trust, then have each patient fall backwards into the arms of a partner. Feelings can be intensified by having the falling partner throw their arms up and yell as if they'd gone over a cliff. "Try not to catch yourself but trust the person in back to catch you. Do this several times." This experiment can point up feelings of competence (of incompetence) regarding responsibility, wariness about trusting oneself to others, inappropriate trust feelings, etc.

Trust Walk

This is an even more dramatic way of bringing out dependency dynamics. Divide the group into pairs, have one partner put a blindfold over his eyes, and have the other person lead him by the arm outside. Let the sighted partner expose his ward to varied experiences (touching a leaf, a rock, a lamppost, an unfamiliar object, skipping, running, crossing the gutter). Each person should be in touch with what they are experiencing. Is the sighted partner overprotective or underprotective (not enough anticipation and signaling of realistic dangers)? "Would you feel safer with another partner in the group? Who? Why? Now reverse roles.

The FBI and Repetition

Here are two games that I devised for the purpose of penetrating tough character defenses.

In many cases patients behave in highly defended ways that are very difficult to spell out. The more trouble the therapist has in articulating the ways in which the patient wards him off, the harder it is to reach the patient. Even if the therapist clearly discerns the pattern of neutralization that a patient employs, his interpretations and observations will be typically blunted by patients with character problems, by means of denial, rationalization, obsessional mechanism, and repression. One way I found of overcoming this was to play the game of FBI with such a patient: "Pretend you are a member of the FBI. You must listen to this tape recording of yourself, and read between the lines. What is this guy omitting, what is he really saying, how is he impeding justice—how is he stopping us from getting to the truth? Be very paranoid—suspect everything. Don't let anything pass by. Be a skeptic. Here, you run the machine and stop the tape whenever you have a question to raise. Talk back to the guy (himself). Argue, challenge, confront. Don't let the guy get away with anything." The reader will be amazed at how effective this tactic is with "unreachable" patients. They discover things the analyst wouldn't have thought of, say it in the kind of ways that are acceptable (after all, how can they deny it? They said it), and render ego alien what was previously ego syntonic.

One night in group, Donald was minimizing his reaction to the knowledge that his wife was having an affair. He never said anything to her, was getting progressively more and more depressed, but was staunchly maintaining her right to be independent and do what she felt like. I played parts of a fifteen-minute monologue back to him. The recording was dry, dull, and slow. Donald found it boring to talk about such an unimportant topic and launched into an overintellectualized dissertation on "open marriage." When I made him an FBI agent, he listened for three minutes and shrugged his shoulders, "Nothing." I played the same excerpts to him three more times. The fourth time around he yelled, "Bullshit! I sound like I'm dead. Is that the way I sound to you? Boy, I sound really depressed. I have been depressed, I guess, but I couldn't feel it. I just felt sort of empty. But on the tape, I come off as a real loser. I still don't feel her having an affair bothers me but listening to how my voice drops—I can hardly hear myself—maybe it's there and I don't know it. I tell you, I feel like I'm in a straightjacket right now, like I have claustrophobia. My body feels like it's right around me. (Someone in the group makes a comment regarding how the tension must build up terribly inside seeing how Donald keeps himself in so rigidly.) Yes, I wanna breathe. I sound like a fucking robot."

In the game of "Repetition," the therapist picks up on a key word. Instead of having a patient free-associate to the word, the following instructions are given: "Close you eyes and sit very relaxed. Take a deep breath and slowly let the air out. (Repeat the exhaling procedure three times.) Now I'd like you to repeat the word over and over to yourself. You can say the word out loud too. Try to say the word in different ways, with different intonations. Experiment out loud, then to yourself—any way that you want. Take about three minutes . . . now share your thoughts and feelings with the group." The choice of words to select and the timing for this experiment to be worthwhile require good clinical sense. When a patient appears upset or loses some composure as he mentions a particular word or phrase, this indicates that there is a "felt meaning" underneath that is dying to be uncovered.

Janet was describing how she was helping her husband fix up his new office. After spending several hours alphabetizing, filing things away and helping him to organize his papers, she was accused by the husband of having misplaced one folder. "Don't be so clumsy, if you want to help me do things right." While Janet was telling why the outburst hurt her feelings, it occurred to me that the word "clumsy" evoked her strongest emotional response (gulping, looking down, lowering her voice). I explained the exercises to her—here were her associations.

"It hurts to my bones. I can't stand that word. It's an accusation—like you're good for nothing. I thought of something I've never mentioned to you or the group before. When I was five, my mother had me dial the phone for her all the time. Sometimes she even expected me to ask people things on the other end (like telling her aunt that her mother would be over in half an hour, asking the operator the time, etc.). My mother thought it was cute that a little girl could use the phone like that. I couldn't stand it. I don't know how we got into that but she came to expect it. I used to dread making a mistake. My mother used to say 'Stop being so scared, nobody's going to bite you.' I was afraid she'd make fun of me if I got scared so I stopped acting scared. As I was mentioning the word 'clumsy' to myself I noticed I sounded angry. Well, I am. I'm sick and tired of carrying other people's responsibilities around. If my husband wanted me to straighten out his office, then he should be appreciative. I'm so busy worrying whether I'm doing things right that I don't give myself any time to think about what I want. Another thing I noticed is I sounded apologetic to myself. You know, 'Please forgive me. I'm just a poor little klutz. Don't expect more of me.' I act that way, I know. (Somebody in the group points out that it's a put-on. She's actually just as strong and efficient as her husband.) "I can't bear myself for being such a doughnut. . ."

The power of this exercise is impossible to translate onto paper. The breathing preliminaries serve to heighten anxiety and promote getting in deep touch with feelings. The repetition intensifies the emotional experience. Shutting the eyes makes the patient feel all alone with these upsetting inner feelings and magnifies the pressure within. The therapist's choice of the key word is very significant. The patient's associations with this charged word taps the deepest layers of his longitudinal and stratified consciousness. The kind of material that gets unearthed is truly remarkable.

The Name-Backwards Technique

These days an increasing number of patients are seen who do not present distinct symptoms. Rather, they complain of general and vague dissatisfactions relating to whom and what they are, where they fit in today's world, the purpose of their lives, and the emptiness of their daily relationships. This group of patients who have what might be called character disturbances or borderline personalities are among the most difficult to engage in treatment. After awhile, the ambiguity of their productions, the absence of detailed, concrete descriptions of significant instances, the frequent silences, and the underlying passivity mount up and become resistances that frustrate the therapist and defy his patience and understanding. He would like to do something but the primitive fixations of these fragmented patients frequently involve preverbal ego states that prevent clear articulation of feelings and personal experiences.

A wide variety of innovative techniques and approaches (Gestalt, paradigmatic, bioenergetic) have been proposed to work through and circumvent these different character resistances. I would like to share a game that I have been experimenting with recently, that is relatively nonthreatening, immediately involves the patient in interesting, relevant speculations about himself, and crystalizes the focal preconscious problem. The instructions to the patient are simply: "Write both your names backwards and then pretend that each letter in your name is the beginning of a word. Together these words will form a sentence or group of words that will have significance to you. Concentrate on each letter and see what it wants to say to you. Don't discard anything because it seems irrelevant or foolish." I use this intervention in one of two ways.

If an individual in the group is blocked, fuzzy, and generally unable to spell out what's troubling him, I'll ask him to write a sentence and share it for group discussion.

If the total group seems to be in a state of resistance and, despite different approaches, continues to baffle the therapist about what's really going on, the suggestion might be made for everyone to write a sentence. Often, the sentences have a common theme and provide good leads to the latent unresolved conflicts that might be operating. The reader is advised not to use this technique capriciously, at the earliest hint of group blockage or confusion. It is generally helpful to introduce it only after more conventional interpretations fall short and the group continues to flounder.

Some clinical illustrations follow:

aicirtaL   retsooM*:   An itinerant cryptologist is ready to attack Latricia: ready enough so that somebody oughta outlaw "mokies."

This was a very withdrawn patient who was detached, seemingly uninvolved, and offered little spontaneous emotional material to work with. The sentences conveyed her strong defensiveness, the intense experience of the analyst as the enemy, her tendency to depersonalize (referring to herself in the third person), and the crude nature of her underlying hostility to being put on the spot. The antisemitic innuendo was particularly valuable since on the surface, this was a very prim and proper, rational, well-bred woman who couldn't believe that she could harbor such outrageous feelings. The written statement provided a concrete confrontation, like a voice from the unconscious that was hard to deny. The following sessions were productively employed following

*Names and sentences have been altered to preserve anonymity.

up the implications of the sentence: (1) focusing on her tendency to view the analyst's interpretations as aggressive assaults rather than as concerned inquiries; (2) pinpointing her way of counteracting this by speaking in an undecipherable language; and if these avoidance mechanisms didn't work, (3) attempting to deny the analyst's existence by minimizing the transactional aspect of the interaction. Moveover, the group members saw a whole new side to her (the desperation and reactive ugliness and aggression well covered over by a civilized veneer), and they began inquiring about and successfully managed to get her to talk about it.

asorappaC   arrodnA: On the day I was married I had relations. No, I didn't like; another time I might. Roslyn is sick.

This patient was expecting a sister home from a mental hospital. She was bracing herself for the many extra responsibilities she would have to shoulder and was fearful that her husband would resent the time and attention she was diverting from him. This attitude seemed to be confirmed when the husband said, "If you let her get you upset, then I'm going to get upset." The patient took this to be a sign of the husband's insensitivity, selfishness, and lack of appreciation of her devotion to her sister. She went into a severely agitated depression that lasted several weeks with no relief. She discussed the episode with the group but the discussion that followed didn't ease her suffering. Then the name–backward technique was suggested.

The patient's associations to her sentences revealed that her mother had taught her that men see women as objects to be used. This led to a feeling that sex was a way of letting men control women and take advantage of them. The early years of this woman's marriage were marked by flight behavior that was designed to prevent the exploitation that she was sure accompanied intimacy. While this harsh conception of marital relationships underwent considerable mellowing through the years, the incident with the sister revived latent conflicts regarding letting oneself be manipulated. Her concern for the sick sister was sincere and genuine but the guilt that made her feel entirely responsible for the maintenance of her sister, led to the paranoid feelings that caused her to displace onto the husband her own resentments and misgivings. The husband's statement, while perhaps not the most tactful in the world, was his intuitive response to his wife's tendency to overdo her mothering, and at the same time asked for some reassurance that he would not be forgotten. The use of the name-backwards method in this case immediately relieved the severity of the patient's depressive episode and revealed the core dynamics that triggered her overreaction. The written sentences revealed to the group the unconscious meaning of the discussion with her husband, and gave them a better opportunity to understand the hidden issues that were causing the outbreak of depressive symptomatology.

Another game that can be used in group (Malamud 1965) is one where the target patient or the total group is asked to spell out his first name in reverse. (Eric would thus become Cire.) "Pretend that this is a word in the Martian language and define it as it would appear in the Martian dictionary." In one case a woman named Bernice defined Ecinreb as "a small household receptacle that is used for spitting in." This message reaffirmed her suspicion that she felt exploited, hated being a housewife, and ought to reevaluate her plans for herself. This is a light, relaxing exercise that helps to loosen the group up and get the members to explore their self-concepts from fresh perspectives.

Giving and Taking Coins

Everyone is told to sit on the floor and put all the coins in their possession out on the desk. The therapist then states that they can give as little or as much of the change as they wish to as few or as many of the people in the group as they choose. "What you give away is for keeps." When the change is all distributed, the patients can share their reactions and observations with regard to choice of recipients, amount distributed, how they themselves felt about being recipients, and the coin experiences with the leader (giving and receiving). In the second part of this experiment, the patients are told to keep all their coins out but this time to "feel free to take as little or as much money as you wish from as few or as many people in the group as you choose." The patients proceed to move around the room picking up change.

This exercise highlights members' relations to each other, the critical role of giving and receiving in the dynamics of inter-personal relations, in symbolizing personal worth, affectional needs, and the capacity to love and be loved.

Conflict Games

It is desirable for the therapist to have a repertoire of exercises by which anger, competition, and hostility can be fully experienced and safely expressed through physical means. If the participants are conscious of these feelings and have no difficulty in getting them out themselves, the games are unnecessary. If words are not enough, if the participants appear blocked, or if the member doesn't seem to understand the source of his own feelings, then conflict exercises can be helpful in meeting these needs and enhance self-understanding and self-acceptance.

Thumb Wrestling: The mildest of these games is most appropriate for anyone who would be dangerously threatened by the violence of more physical nature. The participants shake hands, interlock their fingers, keeping their thumbs upright, and each person tries to pin down the thumb of the other to the count of three.

Arm Wrestling: Opponents lie on the floor, belly down, head to head, hands clasped, with the right arms resting on their elbows. When the signal is given, each tries to push down the other's arm. (In order for the exercise to work, the participants must be instructed not to move their elbows.) Encounters between men and women can be equalized by allowing the woman to use both hands. The experience can be intensified by asking the opponents to keep looking into each other's eyes and making whatever sounds they wish.

Among the dynamics that come to light and become extraordinarily meaningful here are, the fear of succeeding, difficulties in total commitment or involvement, attitudes toward winning and losing, and feelings toward the expression of agression.

Mintz (1971) describes three techniques that are primarily useful in evoking and releasing stored-up feelings from the past and bringing them into the present. (This is in contrast to arm wrestling which engages two people in such a way as to change their actual feelings toward each other.) In these exercises, Mintz offers herself as a mother symbol to bring out buried feelings of rage. In arm squeezing, the group member squeezes the fleshy part of the therapist's forearm as hard as he can. In hand slapping, the therapist's hand rests on a rug (palm down) and the patient is encouraged to hit with full strength using an open palm. In hand pressing, the therapist's hands are clasped together and the patient presses them tightly.

In order to recapture the significant emotional climate, the group member is asked what his parent called him and what he called her. Get in the groove of this name exchange—try it our between yourselves (the therapist and the patient) a few times. Then say, "Now tell your mother whatever it was you always wanted to say and never did." If the therapist is not the same sex as the parent to whom the repressed anger is felt, ask a same-sex patient to volunteer to be a parent surrogate.

Sally was a strong, detached woman, who constantly complained that her husband was not protective enough. She saw herself as outside the mainstream of his life and felt that he never thought of her feelings in the relationship. Her history was a tragic one. Her father had sent her to live with a gentile family when the Nazis invaded Poland. The rest of the family died in a concentration camp because the grandmother refused to go and the mother wouldn't leave without her.

Sally had the following flow of associations to the hand-pressing exercise: *Sally:* (Long silence) This is foolish—(Presses Lightly)— *Therapist*: Press together, look in my eyes and let yourself go—what would you want to tell your mother? *Sally*: Ma—I can't do it; I'm sorry. *Therapist*: Don't apologize—try again. What are you sorry about toward your mother—tell her! *Sally:* I'm sorry I'm alive—no, I don't mean that. I'm glad I'm alive but I . . ." (Cries) . . . (Long pause) I can't understand why my father didn't make her go. *Therapist*: You're angry at your father for not being stronger. *Sally*: I'm . . . you can't say you're angry at dead parents . . . my whole family . . ." (Cries) *Therapist*: Say I won't get angry at my dead parents—repeat it a few times. *Sally*: (Repeats it three times). I won't, I won't, I won't (Screaming)—How can I complain—she did wrong but what can I say—she died and I didn't. (Crying) *Therapist*: Maybe if you can let your disappointment out, you could forgive your mother and she could forgive you. *Sally*: Forgive me for what? (Silence) It's true. I can't think bad thoughts about either of them because they're dead—but I do resent being left alone but I feel guilty at the same time. Oh, what's the use. I'll never feel better about that. *Therapist*: What's frightening you now? *Sally*: I see my husband sitting over there (Couples Group). It's the same with him as with my parents. I lost them and he's never there.

At this point, the other group members joined in, pointing out to Sally that her repressed and denied anger prevented her from feeling close to her parents even in memory. One member suggested that her self-righteous anger toward her husband kept him on the defensive and prevented him from feeling that he could offer her anything. The fact that an attempt was made to integrate dissociated, unmentionable topics, the possibility that tragedy need not permanently interfere with the good that was, and the way in which the past was affecting the marital relationship, were other aspects of the case that were dealt with in subsequent sessions.

Katherine was working for months in treatment on the problem of lacking a certain depth of feeling. She saw herself as shallow and superficial and was struggling to get past her narcissistic defenses. During one group session, she was describing how her parents discouraged dolls and frilly things but tended to reinforce tomboyish, rough-and-tumble activities. During the hand-pressing exercise, she was trying to ask for a doll from her mother. Since she had never done this in actuality but had pretended to be happy to be seen as a little spitfire, her involvement was very tentative and touching. In the middle of her associations, however, she broke off eye contact with a female whose hand she was holding, and instead started making seductive goo-goo eyes at the male therapist. The therapist and the other members helped her to see that the softness and pleasure of dependency must have been extremely threatening. The substitution of the sexual behavior was interpreted as an exhibitionistic defense against the fears and guilt that go with more genuine concern. The patient's poorly integrated use of her sexuality had been pointed out numerous times before. This was the first time, however, that she herself was able to experience the difference in how good she was feeling prior to her gyrations and the "as if" quality while she was going through her act.

Communication Games

Hand Dialogue

Two people who are at an impasse sit facing each other. One volunteers to be the leader, the other opts to be the follower. The leader is instructed to improvise a dance with his hands. The follower is advised to imitate the leader. After three minutes, they reverse roles. This game and the other nonverbal games on the following pages add a new dimension to dialogue by rising above a purely rational, intellectual level. We can add playfulness and a more spontaneous self-expression to the exchange. Wordiness and endless explanations often obscure the essence of what is transpiring.

Foot Dialogue

Tell the partners: "Remove your shoes and socks and stretch out your legs so that your feet just about touch. Now talk to one another with your feet." Transcending the conventional, ritualized forms of communication adds a different kind of directness and flexibility to the interaction.

Name Game

Here the two protagonists face each other and carry on a conversation consisting entirely of their two names, each to be used in any preferred order and any number of times. This exercise doesn't sound like much on paper, but it can significantly reveal nuances and depths of feeling about personal identity. It is surprising how many people have difficulty in uttering their own names clearly and affirmatively. Usually people tend to say the name of their partner submissively several times. A great deal of pleasure is gotten from uttering their names with different intonations and finally by being able to forcefully affirm their identity.

Language Usage

Words frequently serve to isolate us from real contact with others and from awareness of our own experienceing. The words we use are often poor substitutes for the way we feel about things; the difference between the felt experience and the way we express ourselves about it is enough to confuse anybody. Language is like a procrustean bed that arbitrarily forces our consciousness to take shape. It makes us label and dismiss our sensory environment instead of letting it replenish us. The significant message is often to be found in the voice itself: in the volume, the tone, the rate of speech, the hesitations, etc. Some workers have gone further and have experimented with the construction of a silent community. Weir, for example, runs week-long workshops where words are absolutely prohibited except for emergencies. He encourages the participants to use the silent time to take in and receive experiences that otherwise would have been disowned or pushed aside by words. One experiment the leader might want to try is to have a silent meal with someone else. See how much of the tastes, textures, and flavor of the food you have been losing as a result of continuous chatter, and see what else the silence allows you to become aware of. The following experiments are helpful in sensitizing patients to what is communicated by the voice itself, irrespective of words.

Voice listening

Have the group pair off and then ask everyone to close his eyes and be quiet. After about three minutes speak to each other about this experience of having your eyes closed, and while you do this, try to focus your attention on your own and your partner's voices. Pretend that the other person is speaking a foreign language that you can't understand. Only listen to the emphasis, the tone, the hesitations, etc. Do this for about five minutes and then express what you notice about your own and your partner's voice (what are you aware of and how do you feel about it). For instance: "I am very aware of how loud and heavy your voice is. You sound like a West Point cadet. Your voice seems still and you don't breathe at all while you talk. I keep feeling you're going to explode."

Gibberish

Gibberish is making noises that sound vaguely like a real language but the "words" don't make sense. For example: Ble Megaga Feely! The function of gibberish exercises is:

1. To help patients to see that feelings can be expressed without the conversations sounding meaningful
2. To overcome anxiety regarding feelings of silliness and childishness
3. To break through inhibitory attitudes regarding the expression of anger

"Maintain eye contact with your partner and just gibber away. Be aware of how you feel as you do this. Now discuss with your partner what you experienced as you talked gibberish to each other." Many people have some degree of unwillingness to go through with this exercise because they feel silly, self-conscious, etc. Have those in the group who report these feelings imagine the worst thing that could happen to them if they deliberately acted silly. "Now take a couple of minutes to share the repercussions of this sinful behavior with your partner.   Now again talk gibberish with each other. Try to enjoy it and really express whatever you are feeling. Tell your partner what you are experiencing in nonsense noises, while at the same time turning in to what impression the sounds are making on you." What is being expressed, what you are feeling physically, how you sound to yourself, etc. At this point tell you partner in *words* what you noticed.

I found this gibberish technique particularly useful with patients who are uptight and fearful of losing control. Anger doesn't seem so terrible when it takes place with a "foolish" structure. Shy people need a little encouragement and then they seem to get into the task. Feelings come out more easily when the individual doesn't get frightened off by the emotional charge associated with the use of certain words. Removing the need to use fear-inducing language results in the reduction of inhibitory tendencies.

Identifying with Your Own Voice

Let the target patient listen to his own voice, identify with it and then describe his voice and what it expresses as if he were his voice. For instance: "I am my voice. I am hoarse and weak but trying to be soft. I sound intelligent but I also try to make it seem that way. Sometimes I am modest and humble, other times I am strong and raucous." If the patient gets stuck tell him to just repeat "I am my voice"—listen to this phrase and see what else he can discover about himself.

Your Mother's/Father's Face

Sometimes therapists have difficulties in conveying to patients key concepts concerning internalization processes. For example, suppose a patient identifies with her masochistic mother to the extent that she cannot seek to improve her own life while her mother is suffering so. Interpretations along the more conventional lines of "you can't go out with that nice guy, Joe, because you have to appease that jealous, deprived mother inside of you," often fail. Patients require a good deal of sophistication in order to grasp such advanced concepts as identification, introjection, and incorporation. Anita Roggenbuch, a transactional analyst, has described a technique that concretizes the intervention. She believes that little children become very aware of the expressions on people's faces. It doesn't take long for the child to realize that if he is well-behaved (according to parental standards), he brings a smile to the face of significant others. If he behaves badly, their faces get worse-looking. If the child doesn't like the way their faces look he'll either have to change it before he can feel better or watch out how he behaves.

Roggenbuch suggests the following technique: "Imagine your mother (or father) were six feet behind you; then turn around and look and tell me what kind of expression she (or he) has on her (or his) face."

> For instance, a man finally acknowledged that his sexual problems with women probably had to do with hostility toward them. The group helped him to get to the point where he realized that prior to the anger, there was a period of wanting, enjoying, and then fearing the intimacy. I had the patient concentrate on that short span of time early in the sexual encounter when things were still pleasureable. Then I had him pick out a woman in the goup who reminded him most of his mother and asked him to imagine the expression on his "mother's" face while he was enjoying himself. "My mother has her back turned as if she couldn't stand the sight. My father's face is blank in my mind as though he wouldn't recognize it if he saw it right in front of him. Their sex life was probably so miserable; my father was never into it and my mother hated it. Maybe that's why she held onto me. She had to have something in life."

Parental Expectations

This is a game that I originally devised to eliminate the typical roles that patients play in group. After a while, however, it became clear that this can also be a very valuable tool for highlighting transference phenomena and resistance. Instructions are as follows, "Close your eyes and concentrate on what your parents expected of you—in what way they would want you to be in order for them to consider you a good boy (girl)." After about five minutes, "Now think about how this relates to your behavior—the roles you take, the way you act—in the group." Members are then requested to share their awarenesses and discuss them.

> During one group session, Sandy was looking very bored and annoyed. She manifested two basic attitudes in the group. (1) The first role was to be the most helpful, perceptive, responsible, mature group member or (2) to act disinterested, remote and dissatisfied. It was at this

point that I hit upon the idea that perhaps her boredom was a passive expression of resistance which reflected her resentment at having to be my favored daughter by acting out the role of my assistant. By denying her own needs and patient status, she was apparently fulfilling some implicit expectation that she transferred onto me ("I will love you if you act grownup, stand out above the rest, and are always bright"). Interpretations along these lines proved to be very helpful in breaking through her silent resistances and bringing her into the mainstream of the group as a fully participating member.

After this experience, it occurred to me that it might be profitable to formalize and make explicit the mechanism that worked in the case of Sandy. I judiciously began to ask patients to think about parental expectations and relate this to group functioning whenever I met up with a resistance pattern that defied routine analytic expectations. Let me give a few examples of what I am talking about. about.

Barry often played the role of a bullshit artist in the group. He would strain to make brilliant interpretations, to talk profoundly, and to grope for the wise-men role. Unfortunately this pressure to prove himself smart was doomed because his comments often had absolutely nothing to do with what was transpiring. At other times, he would sit in the group as though he was stupified. His face lacked expression, he seemed unable to grasp what was happening, and he generally presented himself as the slowest learner. Barry recollected his folks' expectations as follows, "My mother wanted me to be a help to mankind; some kind of inventor, supercreative. My father saw me as a nothing, a schmuck." His behavior in the group was interpreted as his attempts to lift up (or down) the two contrary perceptions, one of which overrated him and the other demeaned him. His sporadic attempts to be the resident genius in the group symbolically represented his wish to satisfy his mother's impossible dreams. The failure and frustration that we invariably experienced resulted in his acting out his father's expectations—the impotent moron. These concepts were helpful in getting Barry to accept himself more realistically, to set more manageable goals for himself, and to relate more relevantly and appropriately to fellow group members. The two polarized selves began to mellow and merge into a more stable, sold state of ego functioning.

Jack operated in the group as a silent, unemotional, withdrawn person. His constant refrain was, "I don't know what I feel so how can I tell you what it is." His memory of his parents' expectations were, "Be a good Jewish boy. Be someone who would not be so ashamed of what he is or what he did. Never cause embarrassment to us. Don't ever reveal yourself in any way that would jeopardize that position or state." The interpretation was made that these attitudes had nothing at all to do with Jack as a person. They were superimposed homilies which had the effect of objectifying him. The standard, the pose, the role, the morality, the status, were approved of—the person inside had to fit himself into that confining mold. Jack's behavior in the group becomes comprehensible in the following sense: his extreme passivity reflects a fear of commitment, avoidance of the controversial, a neutralizing of anything but the caricature of how a good person acts. In effect, he is being a good boy according to his parents' standards but he carries this out to an absurd degree (practically nonverbal). Perhaps his extreme passivity and withdrawal is a way of transferentially seeking revenge on his parents—"Okay, I'll carry out your wishes ad nauseum but you'll never get the real me—you'll get nothing from me. I'll only give you back the same hollow shell that you made me into." This line of approach provided the group with a toehold in Jack's case. With the aid of these concepts and the content that emerged, group members showed a greater interest in involvement with Jack's operations. Jack began to participate somewaht more actively and use the concepts as reference points to identify his behavior ("Is that what I'm doing now?").

Arthur came across as either very self-demeaning or rudely interrupting what other people were into, as though he was afraid he would never have a chance to get his two-cents worth in. Arthur's reminiscences were, "I was a foster child. The foster parents' motto was: Don't make trouble. Save the toilet paper. Don't ask for the biggest piece of pie. Don't resent the nicer treatment your younger brother gets—remember, you're not his age; you have to act grownup."

Interpretations were made along the line: "If you feel like a second-class citizen, one way of compensating is by asking for very little. Then you won't be disappointed by a turn-down and you'll be appreciated for your good behavior and modesty." Arthur's true elephantine interruptions ("Hey, what's the matter with you people? You didn't let me speak tonight") were now seen as hungry compensations for the many times when he asked for so little. The annoyance that he evoked in other people when he behaved like this only served to remind him that people don't really care. It never occurred to him that it was his manner rather than himself that was at fault. Interpretations like this had been made before but never rang a bell. The reason it seemed to work this time had to do with Arthur's response to the exercise—directly linking his past expierience with his present conduct and spontaneously seeing the obvious connections.

Body Sculpting

Sculpting is a therapeutic art form that was first introduced in a family therapy setting but now seems to be used with increasing frequency by group therapists (who like the way it blends the cognitive with the experiential).

The sculpturing intervention is appropriate when the therapist believes that a participant isn't clearly expressing his feelings and attitudes toward another member or toward the total group. The member is requested to create a tableau which physically symbolizes his emotional relationship with another person. The individual toward whom the feelings will be expressed is told to pretend he is a lump of clay and the target patient is asked to be the sculptor. This method cuts through intellectualization, obsessive defenses, and the projection of blame. With typical verbal smoke screens denied to them, members are compelled to observe behavioral phenomena on the basis of visual, sensory, and symbolic understanding. Triangles, alliances, and conflicts seem to be choreographed, revealing in a condensed form aspects of dynamic interaction that have ordinarily remained hidden from view (Papp et al. 1973).

On a night when a couples group was shrunken by the absence of two couples, one pair had just finished dealing with their problems. The leader happened to glance around the group to encourage someone else to speak, when he met Sam's eyes, and Sam broke out into a broad grin. When asked about his expression, he said he felt happy but when questioned added that he had nothing special to be happy about. Up to this point in the group's history (six months), Sam had been quiet, withdrawn, and uninvolved, and had managed to avoid being drawn out no matter what the approach. The leader suspected that the smile represented uneasiness at the smallness of the group, one couple had already spoken up, and now there was a good chance the spotlight might fall on him. When this interpretation was made (in the form of "I don't trust you smile..." Sam admitted experiencing some degree of discomfort. When other members pressed him to elaborate on this, he, as usual, was not able to produce any feeling adjectives. In the course of this fencing around, however, he did let slip the statement, "When you were accusing me . . ." Inquiries to get him to explain the implications of this "offensive" statement by the leader led nowhere.

At this time, the leader suggested the Body Sculpting technique. "Pretend I (the leader) am made of clay. Sculpt me—my body, my arms, my facial expression, so as to express my accusation. Then sculpt yourself the way you experienced the discomfort you said you felt." With some hesitation, Sam began sculpting the leader with frown and pointed finger and then postured himself with his arms across the chest in a defiant position. The other members present commented on the defensiveness of his posture, the strength of his opposition in contrast to his customary surface compliance, and the staring contest that seemed to be going on. When Sam was asked to share his feelings, he made reference to the leaders penetrating eyes that seemed to see right through him. He came back to the eyes over and over again and emphasized the intensity so much that it suggested this was a significant area to explore further. Sam associated the eyes with his mother's look that could stop anybody dead in their tracks. "If looks could kill then she had it." He went on to explain that this was her way of controlling everyone in the family—"It was like a giant TV monitor that surveyed and manipulated everything in the house." The patient then went on to describe how he hated to go to Hebrew School because he wanted to play ball. The principal of the school was a friend of his father, however, so he had to attend and keep up with his work. The group questioned him about what form his resentment took. Sam couldn't come up with an answer at first; then, with the group's help, made it increasingly clear that the shalllowness of his involvement, the "as if" quality of his good-boy appearance, and his disjointed, placating nature (e.g., the pasted-on smile mentioned earlier) were silent expression of resentment and defiance. The therapist suggested that his also seemed to be his style of operating in the group—present but not really there.

Throughout these happenings, the therapist in his overeagerness to capitalize on the unexpected opening up, was busy reminding the patient that the unpleasant feelings which were now emerging had never been mentioned before. In this way, the therapist hoped to imprint on Sam's mind the idea that now that the cat was out of the bag, he should remember it for next time and not seal over after he left. Around this time Sam got up, walked across the room to get his pipe, and took a seat far away from the therapist. When asked about this, Sam denied having any ulterior motive other than getting his pipe. It was interesting that several other members in the group noticed the therapist's "nagging" of Sam and suggested that this might have been the cause of his moving away. Sam slowly got in touch with feelings of resentment at the therapist's "hounding." For the first time, he spoke feelingly about how difficult it was for him to express even the mildest form of irritation and annoyance while he was growing up. "Here you were trying to help me and I knew you meant well; how could I tell you that you were beginning to piss me off?" This brought the group to focus on how it is possible to disagree and even get angry with somebody without necessarily driving them away and risking a loss of love.

Some Variations

At different times the group may be deadlocked or drifting and the therapist feels at a loss to understand why. He could have one or two members illustrate what seems to be happeing by sculpturing it (using the whole group as a piece of clay). The group can then affirm or deny whether this touches on their perception of the issue.

Another possibility would be to ask the total group to model the group mood, a group fantasy, or a group wish. One member is requested to stand in the middle of the room, and each of the participants modifies the evolving sculpture until there is a nonverbal consensus that the happening represents the group as it exists. Members can then process their experiences and observations.

The therapist might ask two members to sculpt each other as they would like their relationship to be.

If the leader wants to assist the members to become more aware of the existence of subgroups, the formation of coalitions, the degree of group cohesiveness, the feeling of belonging, etc., he can ask everyone to position themselves to form a group statue. The spatial positioning of individuals relative to one another gets members to think of their role in any dimension that we might wish to explore.

Visual Images, Sounds, and Metaphors
A poet patient of psychoanalyst Emanuel Hammer has written:

Extend to me a picture of almost things
Of things not quite expressed . . .
Abide with me awhile
to unlearn words.

Since visual images, sounds and metaphors are unfettered by convention or logic, I often use them to get patients to vividly project their inner picture of themselves and others.
One exercise is to have a patient go around the group assigning each person a sound that conveys how he feels about them.

Jerry came up to this one woman and hummed a tune, "St. Louis Woman," giving it a sultry rendition. The woman, who was quite sexy and attractive, at first expressed a great deal of hostility and resentment for being given this association. After about five minutes of renouncing Jerry's reaction, she broke down and started weeping bitterly. She went on to explain that she didn't like the seductive connotation; she would much rather be represented by something soft and nice like "Fleur de Lys." The group got on her for keeping this lovely, sensitive side of herself hidden under heavy makeup and for her Anna Lucasta disposition. At this point the patient's defensiveness melted and she got in touch with forgotten memories of beautiful, romantic music that she secretly listened to but never revealed open interest in. Valuable data was unearthed regarding early repressions of more feminine identifications. The session ended with the patient playing "Fleur de Lys" on the piano while the rest of the group crowded around her and cried.

Another technique is to go round the group giving each patient a nickname, revealing the nickname they always wanted to be called, or acting out the role of a great person whom they always admired.

One patient described how, when he moved into a new neighborhood at age nine, he went around telling everyone to call him "Blackie." He would invent stories about his being leader of a gang of about fifty kids in his old neighborhood. Looking back he realized how scared and insecure he really was, and how lies and fantasies that he really began to believe in became an important part of his life. The person he admired most was the first black ball player, Jackie Robinson. "He was an underdog—he beat the odds. He didn't have as much ability as a lot of others, but he did a lot with it. That's the way I always felt about myself—not so great but making the best of my potential." Subsequent questioning by the group brought out the fact that the patient's self-imposed persecutory feelings led to a compensatory chip-on-the-shoulder attitude with a "me-against-the-rest-of-the-world" outlook. This insight provided an important wedge with which to further reach the patient's projecting symptoms of loneliness and feelings of detachment.

The use of mental-imagery techniques and of metaphoric descriptions often hits the nail on the head and lets the patient see in a vivid manner how he is coming across.

Once in a couples group, a very obsessive, emotionally unrelated man, was busily denying his inaccessibility. The woman to his left said, "You remind me of a locked door with a little peephole and a welcome mat outside." The man across from him had the image of "a pillbox which you could see out of through the slits but nobody could see in." About three of four sessions later the patient reported feeling the impact of these reactions to him and he began to have his own metaphoric experiences. "I feel—I do feel like a glass pane is between us. I can walk around it and at the time I feel as though it doesn't have to be there if I don't want it to. But I really know that I can't get over it even if I want to and that's scary. I keep having the feeling that I'm going to fall off something. What does that mean?" Finally, the patient was starting to come out with emotionally meaningful material.

Harem King

Some individuals feel socially unpopular. Because they're so afraid they'll do the wrong thing, they inhibit many of their natural reactions. The essential strategy here is to help them to see that their impulses do far less damage than the defenses against them. Patients like this never get a chance to exercise their imagination or see what would really happen if they allowed their secret withheld feelings to emerge.

In such cases, I have experimented with having the patient choose a harem from amongst the female members. "Your every wish is their command." At first, there is usually considerable hesitation about entering into the spirit of the game. Once the choices are made, the patient feels awkward, oftentimes because he has some embarrassing sexual thought on his mind. When this fantasy is expressed it is usually revealed to be a defense, an excuse for not coming out with even more difficult thoughts. The desire for intimacy, the wish to be held, the fear of being in an assertive, masterful position, the spontaneous expression of pleasurable desires, the guilt that inhibits gratification even when it is freely available—all these come out in various degrees as a result of this exercise.

Akaret (1972) has described an approach that he calls "Acting through." According to Akaret the crucial condition for personality change and growth, is complete self-participation. Only if thought, feeling and behavioral movement are combined in the treatment experience can the patient break away from the past. The "Acting-through" process uses the group as an arena where "words, feelings, and problems are placed in movement in order to create an intensity of experiencing, in order for people to recall certain lost parts of themselves, and in order to provide patients with an opportunity for new behavior."

1. If a patient is fearful that her viciousness is a very destructive and ugly thing, let her become a vampire. "Imagine sucking people's blood—see youself with fangs and claws dripping blood." If the patient has trouble "getting with" the experience, turn off the lights. "Try and scare the hell out of the group." This not only encourages further action but it also puts other members in touch with feelings about the dark, death and terror.

2. If a member is at an impasse and is sick enough of being stuck to really get down to business, have him tell a fantasy about the group.

Jane begins: "When you (therapist) sit opposite me like this, I feel like you're my mother. My mouth feels like cotton, my head gets swirly, and I feel like a complete idiot. Everything I say is going to sound stupid to you." Someone in the group asks her to imagine where she would like the therapist to be so that she could feel freer. "I don't know but I just want to be on top of her (mother) for once." The group urges the therapist to lie on the floor with Jane sitting on him. After some initial giddiness, Jane says, "I can't believe this. I hope I'm not crushing you but it feels great. I feel suddenly stronger, not because I'm putting you down, but because I feel I could assert myself now if I wanted to." Three weeks later in the course of an argument with her very domineering mother, Jane started questioning the mother about her own background. In fifteen minutes, this formidable, overbearing woman was in tears, talking about the lack of love in her life, how bad she felt about not talking to her brother for the past ten years, and how she felt about the patient's deceased father.

3. Shirley shares her terror of going crazy. Her mother had a breakdown when the patient was ten. The therapist asked her to imagine what would happen if she allowed herself to go crazy. "Find out about the madness in you, Shirley. Let youself flip out. What are you like? What do you feel? What happens to your body, what happens to your mind? Think it over." When selected patients (nonborderline, or psychotics) are encouraged to act out this role, it is usually a very upsetting experience, but the windup is that chasing the bogeyman out of the dark closet tends to reduce fear.

4. If a patient is at the stage where he is trying to understand his fear of intimacy, let him be touched by each person in the room and have him try to identify them by the way they touch him. Which conveyed feelings was he able to pick up, and which intended feelings did he misinterpret? Is there a difference in terms of the sex of the toucher? What about the people whose touch he couldn't recognize as belonging to them? Why would this be? What does it mean historically?

5. Akaret gives an illustration of a girl who feels paralyzed and claustrophobic in the subway. If someone "feels her up," she becomes both terrified and speechless. The group becomes the people in the subway, the rug becomes the subway car. Everyone is packed together. "Try to feel flesh everywhere, smell the air, the sweat. Make you faces dull and silent. What are you? Where are you?" The patient finally screams and lets out all her held-in feelings.

Questions that emerge and get worked through include, "How does it make you feel as a woman? How do you feel when your body is invaded? What does it remind you of? What rights do you have? Why do you let yourself get treated like shit?"

6. If a patient complains about feeling all knotted up, make the other members his knots. With his permission, have the group hold him down and ask him to unbind himself. After he has broken loose, inquire into the preconscious fantasies that came out as he was struggling. This exercise usually results in a release of physical tension, but beyond that, it concretizes the internal experience and places it in an interpersonal context.

In keeping with the concept of trying to understand the real meaning of verbalizations by finding concrete representations for them in the group, let me give one last example with a patient who abhorred snoring:

Reyna was a divorcee who had a knack for pursuing ungiving men and for rejecting more available, decent prospects. One night in group, she told about her growing irritation with a nice guy whom she was dating for the past two months. In passing, she happened to mention that she is starting to get increasingly bothered by him and that the thing that annoys her most is that he snores. "That's the one thing I just can't stand." With that, I asked her to choose a man from the group, and then I instructed him to snore. After some initial kidding around, Reyna got into the swing of things and produced the following memories: "My mother always snored. After she came out of the hospital, she was always on medication. It used to embarrass me to bring friends home because she was always sleeping in the daytime. I could never ask her for anything. If I wanted money, I would have to take it from her purse." Reyna started trembling as she went on to describe her anger at her mother's unavailability and incompetence in understanding her needs. When the mother died, the patient felt guilty about her nasty behavior toward her. The group started her on the way toward working through this bad feeling by suggesting that the mother couldn't help herself and for that she must be forgiven, and that Reyna was but a child and for that *she* must be forgiven. The masochistic dynamics with men were revealed as punishment for the exaggerated notion that she was asking too much from her mother and had no right to her anger for being deprived.

STAGE 3 AND 4 EXERCISES—
GROUP COHESION AND THE CREATIVE SYNTHESIS

Am I willing to care? Can I show my caring? What will happen if I show I care for one person before caring for others? Can I show I care before the other person says that he cares for me? What if they do? What if I don't care for someone in the group? Would the group be able to bear it? What shall I do with all the love I feel for these people? How can I ever leave them? What will happen to me when I do?

The major task in these stages involves learning how to appropriately negotiate closeness and distance. At this point individuals begin to feel more comfortable in close emotional interaction as well as in situations requiring emotional distance. (We all want to be liked, but we can accept dislike as a function of the relationship with one other person; it does not mean that we are totally unlovable.) Patients slowly discover the value of expressing genuine, warm, affectionate feelings. They not only begin to accept this positive force within themselves but something even more basic seems to occur. The individual is able honestly to *be* his feelings, whatever they may be. He can be characterized as more transparent, authentic, candid, and thoroughly himself. He becomes responsive, interested, alive, and energetic. He starts noticing art, nature, music, and all the little things in life.

New ideas begin to emerge ... there is an element of excited surprise. The very act of creating brings with it great energy to work with. There is enough pride in the "new baby" to press the creator on to the work required to make the new concept into a social and workable communication. Doorways to the unconscious are opened up. Constructive daydreaming provides an upthrust of past feelings and experiences and wishes and hopes and fears. The art of fantasy is the best way to keep the personality flexible enough so that "good stuff" in the bowels of the mind can get into a usable position. Patients at this stage give themselves more time to think. They get into participant recreation, they have more spontaneous experiences and adventures, they pursue personal interests, they develop a broader circle of friends, and cultivate a few deep relationships, and they try like hell to break out of their particular treadmill. Under these circumstances, life becomes more exciting, alive, and joyous.

Strength Bombardment

Herbert Otto (1968) devised a method to develop an individual's latent strength and bring out his true potential. He suggested that very few patients ever undertook a systematic evaluation of their assets and resources, usually didn't appreciate them, and often tended to downgrade themselves by making unfavorable comparisons to some idealized standard. Taking inventory involves getting the target patient to sit in the middle of the group with a pad and list his strengths. The rest of the group is encouraged to participate and contribute any additional positive traits that they perceive. Problems and shortcomings are not brought up at this time, and any discussion of these is gently but firmly discouraged. When it becomes difficult to think of further strengths, the next step is discussing what additional strengths have to be developed. A separate list of these is made and forms the basis for *action programs*. Action programs are any planned activities or experiences that the individual undertakes to build or develop a particular strength. The program should be tailored to the specifications and needs of the target patient. A wide variety of assignments is possible, limited only by the imagination and perceptiveness of the other members. The patient should want to enter into the strength role assigned him and he should be able to get some satisfaction from successful completion of tasks.

Giving and Receiving Appreciation

In this experiment, I want you to express what you like about the others in the group and to become more aware of how you feel as you give and receive these messages of liking and appreciation. One person at a time will sit in the center, and as long as he is in the center he must remain silent. I'll give you time for discussion and feedback later. The person to the left of his former place in the circle begins, and tells the person in the center three or four things that he appreciates about him. I'm not asking you to be phony. You can find three or four things you like about anybody, even your worst enemy.

Be as superficial or as deep as you like, but be honest and express things that you really do like. Look at the person in the center, speak to him directly, and be very specific and detailed. Don't just say "I like you," or "I like your hair." Say exactly what you like about the person or his hair.

After the first person has said three or four things he likes, he says "pass," and then the person to his left says three or four things he likes about the person in the center—and so on around the circle, until everyone has expressed their appreciation. Then the person in the center returns to his place and the person to *his* left moves to the center. Continue in this way until everyone has sat in the center and received appreciation from all the others. When you have finished, sit as close as is comfortable, and share your experiences with each other. Say anything you wanted to earlier, but didn't.

I want you to be particularly aware of your physical sensations as you give and receive these messages of liking. Is it easy and enjoyable for you to express your liking, or do you feel a lot of discomfort and tend to avoid communicating directly with the other person? Can you really accept and enjoy what others say to you, or are you uncomfortable and tend to avoid, dismiss, or reject these messages of liking? Any questions? The leader then asks for a volunteer to be the first to sit in the center. "Okay go ahead. . . ."

Tom had told Iris that he liked her because she was sexy and vivacious. "When you drop your eyelids halfway down, the crinkles around your eyes give you a worldly look as though you're deep into your feelings. Then you have this bright-eyed, little-girl lilt to your voice. The combination of being innocent and having 'seen it all' really turns me on." During the subsequent discussion, Iris remembered having rebuffed Tom's compliment by thinking, "you're only saying that because it's safe for you. You know I'm engaged." When the group pressed Iris about why she had this cynical thought, she got in touch with the guilt she felt toward the other women in the group. One woman in particular, Ronnie, seemed very depressed and woebegone that day. "How can I take admiration when she's getting so little for herself?" The group recalled that she largely ignored her boyfriend's affectionate display but kept harping on his shortcomings. "Maybe there's a pattern there." Several sessions later, Iris had a dream which strongly suggested that her guilty protectiveness of Ronnie was a masochistic identification with a martyred mother. Iris was able to see that her style of warding off good things was an unconscious appeasement of a suddenly resentful, jealous mother (who had been widowed in her early thirties and had never remarried).

Animals

Close your eyes and picture a blackboard. Now try to imagine a hand drawing some kind of animal on the blackboard. Try to concentrate on the possibility that this animal could represent you. Look at the sketch very carefully. What kind of animal is this? What is it like? What is it going to do? Is there anything special or peculiar about this animal? Now become this animal. Try to identify with it. What is your life as the animal like? Describe yourself as this animal. Say to yourself, "I am—"; "I have—"; "I do—." How do you feel physically as this animal? What are your surroundings like? How do you relate to these surroundings?"

Keep your eyes closed and now actually take a physical posture that expresses your being this animal. If you were, what kind of position would you take? How do you feel as this animal? What are you about to do? Now stay pretty much in place but make small movements and actions of the kind this animal would make. Get more in touch with the feelings of being him. How do you exist as this animal? Now begin to make some small noises that he would make. What kind of noises do you make? Now make these noises louder. Now move around more, but stay with being him. Continue to be him and make these sounds and movements. In a moment I want you to open your eyes and interact physically with the other animals for several minutes. As you do this, be aware of how you feel, how you move, and how you relate to these other animals. Okay, open your eyes and interact.

Now sit quietly for a while and consider your existence as an animal. Don't try to analyze it, just stay with your experience and absorb it. What do you recognize in this experience? Do you see any connection between this experience and your everyday life?

Now gather together with the total group and each tell your experience of being this animal. Tell about your surroundings, and how you relate to these other animals. Do this in the first person, present tense, as if it were happening now. For instance, "I am a real tough dog, a street dog, and I feel very vicious and mean." Try to tell all the details of your experience of being this animal. Take his posture and become him as you tell about yourself. Take about five minutes for this.

Now close your eyes and become your animal again. Take a posture that he would take and again start to make whatever movements and noises he would make. In a moment I'm going to ask you to open your eyes and interact only with the other animals in the group for a few minutes. Okay, open your eyes and interact with these other animals.

Now discuss how you interacted with each other as these animals. Were you active, passive, aggressive, loving, etc? Which other animals did you interact with, which did you avoid, and how did you feel in these interactions?

Now take a little while to sit quietly and absorb more of your experience of your "animalness." Say to yourself silently, "I am a castaway, a dog of the alleys and gutters. I protect myself. I look for fights," or whatever your experience is of being this animal and interacting with these other animals.

Now discuss to what extent your fantasy of being this animal expresses the kind of person you are—how you act and how you relate to others. Can you at least see that for the others in the group their fantasy expresses quite a bit about themselves? Take about five minutes for this.

Now close your eyes again and become your animal. Find a posture that he would take and again get into the feel being him. What is your body like? How do you feel? What is your life like? Where are you and what are your surroundings like?

Now imagine that you are in some kind of enclosure that restricts your freedom. Examine this enclosure. Discover what this enclosure is like. How are you enclosed, and what is this enclosure made of? Really investigate it in detail. Touch it and test it, until you really know what it is like. Go around and examine all parts of it. Are there any possible ways to get out? How do you feel in this enclosure? What is outside the enclosure? If you can't see outside your enclosure, imagine what is outside. What does this enclosure keep you away from?

> As a street dog, I have no enclosure. I'm on my own and that's the way
> I like it! No, that's not true; sometimes I pick on smaller animals because

I'm jealous of them. Sometimes I press my nose against the window during holiday seasons and I see little dogs—household dogs with plaid sweaters looking fat and content and I am angry and lonely. "They're stuck," I sometimes say to myself. "Who wants a leash and a master?" But then I think about how I never know what's going to happen the next day. It's hard to have to rely completely on yourself and use your wits every day for survival.

Now imagine that you talk to this enclosure and that the enclosure can talk back to you. What do you say and what does the enclosure answer? Now change roles. Become the enclosure and continue the dialogue with the animal. What do you like as the enclosure? How do you feel? What do you say to the animal? Continue this dialogue for a while. Switch places on your own and play both parts. Carry on this dialogue, be aware of the character and the interaction between the enclosure and the animal. What is going on between the two?

Now become the animal again and continue to explore intensely the enclosure until you find a way out of it. How do you get out of this enclosure? When you do get out, explore what it is like to be outside. How do you feel? What are your surroundings like now? What is your life like, and what do you do? What happens to you? Compare your situation outside the enclosure with your existence inside. Talk to the enclosure again, and see what it answers you. Keep up this dialogue for a while. Now go back inside the enclosure, just for a look around. How do you experience being back inside the enclosure? Do you prefer being inside or outside?

Now slowly say goodbye to the enclosure. Keep your eyes closed, and when you're ready, return to this room and your real body and quietly absorb your experience for a little while. In a minute I'll ask you to open your eyes and share your experience of being this animal in the enclosure with the others in the group. Again, tell your experience in the first person, present tense, as if it were happening now. Okay open your eyes and take some time to express your experience in detail. Again, consider to what extent your experience with this fantasy enclosure expresses something important about your life, and how you're restricted. Take a few minutes to tell each other how you see that your fantasy expresses something about your present existence—your life situation.

Shoe Polish Anonymous

The group is broken up into trios. "Pretend that each trio is a chapter of Shoe Polish Anonymous. Shoe Polish Anonymous is a citywide organization similar to Alcoholics Anonymous. Each of you suffers from the same difficulty, namely, using shoe polish to excess. You are meeting to help each other as much as you can. You each use shoe polish to excess, but in different ways. Your motivations are different and so are the various methods you have tried in the past to overcome your difficulty. Share all of this with the group and really try to help each other. The situation is abnormal, but see if you can stay in the role and take it as seriously as you can."

Rockabye Baby

Sometimes if a patient is very tense and defensive and he requests help in getting over this feeling, the following exercise is relaxing and personally revealing. The patient is told to find an object in the room that seems to symbolize his troubles. He is then asked to imagine what he would like to do with this "bag." Sometimes the group might go outside and help him to bury the object, or he might throw it down the incinerator, or out the window (if it is safe). The group then masses in the middle of the room, picks the person up as high as possible, and gently sways him back and forth. The person is asked to cry out exuberantly—to raise and lower his voice with the motion of the uplifted arms. This exercise is very potent in the way it temporarily relieves acute depressive episodes and cuts right through the superficial defenses that prevent the person from getting his feelings out. Many members cannot remember being held, cradled, or rocked as very young children. People emerge from this experience feeling high, alive, and just wonderful. The rhythm, flow, motion, and gentleness combined to contribute to a sense of peace and elation (Moustakas 1968). Besides providing a relieving symptom change, patients are now able to talk about what was really bothering them without feeling so clogged up.

The Eagle Trip

First, have everybody in the group lie down and go through some kind of relaxation exercise, with their eyes shut. Then you (the leader) talk, shutting your eyes too, to help get in touch with your own unconscious. Let yourself get turned on and let the trip go wherever it wants to.

"Imagine everybody's lying here on the floor, and while they stay there, suddenly time stops. You get up and walk out all alone. And then, after you look around a bit, you look at the sun, and you feel a pull from the sun. You feel you want to go toward the sun. And suddenly you look down and you're covered with feathers. You have feathers and wings. And you realize you're a bird. And you leap up and you start to beat your wings, and you flap them harder and harder, and you begin to rise higher and higher. You're up above the buildings, and you can look down at the trees. And you look toward the sun, and then with very powerful strokes you start to fly higher and higher. And now you set your wings, and you circle round and round and round. As you look down, you see you're now high up over a valley. You look down and you see there are no longer any streets, just a flat valley with a few trees, and you realize that you have gone back in time. You have a feeling that you would like to fly toward the ocean. So you start flying toward the ocean, and your wings are beating, and you can feel the air passing, and there's a surge of power, and you feel the power, and you look far below, and you see the sun on the ocean, the blue ocean. From high above you look down on the beach, and you can see the combers come racing in, and it's all very still, and you set your wings, and you circle round and round and round. And then you feel a pull as though you would like to go toward the sun. You begin to fly steadily along the coast; and you fly and you fly and you fly. As you get further down the coast, you come to some mountains, and you begin to have to rise. You rise higher and higher, and you wonder if you'll be able to make it over the top. The air gets colder and colder, and you can see that the mountains have sharp crags and there's some ice on them. Finally you find a pass, and you coast through. The wind is blowing fast down there, and you just slide down the wind. And then you're out over the desert. And you look down, and there's the desert far below you and you can see the cactus and the sage brush. But steadily you fly, steadily south. As you go further south, you go over another mountain range, and now far below you is a huge broad valley, and you see what looks to you like a huge city, a square city.

And you fly toward it, coming down lower and lower. You can see the city streets and the squares and some place in the center you see a huge sort of pyramid with a flat top on it. You circle. As you get nearer, you look down and there are a lot of people down below. They're standing around, and you realize that they're all dressed up in costumes, and they're looking up. And as they see you, they give a shout, and you can hear it far up in the air. You set your wings, and you circle around the platform, and they are waiting expectantly. Then you land on the top of this pyramid. You look down and everybody is looking at you. As you land, you turn into yourself again. And there's some kind of priest who approaches you, very slowly and very reverently. He says: 'You will have some time here. You will have the time to search out and find the answer to a question for yourself. You should ask yourself the question now, something you want to find out, and you are to go and have an adventure. But I will sound this gong (and he hits it very lightly), and the first time I hit the gong, remember you have to consider coming back. Then I'll give you a little time, and then I'll hit the gong again. Now you must start back. When I hit the gong for the third time, you *must* come back. Now I want you to go on your adventure.'

"Now, the first gong; you remember you must come back. And now the second gong. And now again you hear the final gong, and you start hurrying back. You come to the top of the pyramid and there are the people who have been waiting. And they shout again to you. And you turn into an eagle and you leap off the platform and you start climbing higher and higher and circling, and the people down below are breaking into some kind of a dance, starting some kind of ceremony. Now you turn and start north again, over the desert, over the mountains, and back here, land, and lie down again with the group. Okay, everybody come back, everybody sit up, and now share your trip with us."

Clubs

Mintz (1971) describes how the wit and creativity of a group can often produce wonderful inventions. One such creation, The Loser's Club, stems from a woman who was highly successful as a mother and teacher but who constantly made herself out to be the unluckiest, most inept, most unfortunate member of the group. She emphasized this negative distinction by saying "I am president of the

Loser's Club, Inc." The group picked up on this and any time someone in the group showed a tendency to use kvetching and self-derogation as a means of gaining sympathy, they would be told, "Oh, you just joined the club" or, "The club has a new member." Other popular clubs that have been developed are the Shmuck Club (when people tell about the stupid decisions they've made in their lives for no good reason), the Narcissist's Club (where the group pokes fun at itself and other members for vanity, pompousness, and other evidences of inflated self-importance), the Bitch and Bastard Club, and the Superman Club, etc. By getting patients to laugh at their own defenses and not take themselves too seriously, character structures can be loosened and more flexible courses of action can be adopted.

Art as a Medium for Self-Disclosure

A number of workers have successfully combined art therapy with Gestalt techniques in group settings. Attending the workshops of Elaine Rapp and Janie Rhyne I was very impressed with the new perspectives offered by art experiences. Let me try to convey the flavor of this approach by presenting the format and techniques used by Rhyne:

Right at the start, she had the group lie back, close their eyes, and think about themselves "as they are right now." Gradually she tried to get each person to be aware of where they are, here and now, in this particular room, with this particular group of people. Tried to have them go into what their stomach is feeling, what their bodies feel like, asked them about their breathing.

Then, she gave each participant a great big hunk of clay (25 pounds) and encouraged them to really go at it, using their hands, their muscles, and their shoulders, to get in touch with where they were at the moment and what they were feeling in themselves and how they were expressing this with their bodies. The group sat on the floor and worked with the clay for twenty minutes with the leader encouraging them to say to themselves, "This is me; I am forming myself." Individuals were asked to trust their intuition that what they were doing was right for them—not to think "this is what I should be."

After this exercise, Rhyne called for a volunteer and suggested that the person position himself in the same shape as his clay creation and try to be aware of what he was feeling. The assumption here is that if you can get in touch with and feel your awareness inside of you and then put it outside so that other people can communicate with you, then you're headed in the right direction. Simply presenting the unvarnished you to the group (this is me; I *am*), without explaining, analyzing, or judging, is a very difficult experience. The shapes people assume may be lopsided and convoluted but they frequently lead to feedback from the other members that can be very penetrating and stimulating. It helps the presenter to come out with dimensions of himself that he has always been vaguely aware of, but has never chosen to discuss with anyone else.

Rhyne keeps encouraging participants to find their personal vocabulary for expressing themselves nonverbally. Don't decide what you're going to paint. Just go ahead and do it. Pick a crayon color you like and move it around the paper—scribble, doodle, make happy lines and angry lines. Try out different colors in various shapes. Be aware that they have some personal significance to you. This is your visual language.

While you are drawing, begin making sounds that seem to empress the forms you are making. Don't use real words—only make noises that feel natural to you. Let your sounds flow along with your drawing—don't stop. Now move your body in whatever way you like—try to express through motion what you have drawn, in the sounds you are making. Dance, roll, rock, crawl, stamp, leap, curl up. Express your private sensory language through movement. During the subsequent discussion, notice how your verbal ability is enhanced once you express and become aware of how you are, with your whole self.

Next, Rhyne might distribute chalk and roll out big sheets of newsprint or 4-foot-wide wrapping paper in a roll. Everybody works together for a while. People can sometimes say with lines something they can't say with their mouths or bodies. If the whole group is using the same roll of paper, significant issues crop up; how close do you want to get to others? Do you want to get involved in a mutually shared creation? How do you go about establishing your territoriality? Can you allow interchange or do you draw thick lines to sharply demarcate you versus me?

Rhyne sometimes scatters many pastel crayons on the floor and has each member select those crayons that most reflect his current mood. Members are then instructed to start at one end of a piece of paper and draw whatever comes to them. "Discuss your feelings and production with someone whom you're paired off with. Then select another person, put a piece of paper between the two of you, and each start off from your respective end, looking at each other. Do you find yourself competing, tensing up, rejecting, pursuing, teasing, aggressing?" Keep this up until you feel you have made contact, until you feel that on some level you know each other. Then look at the paper between you. Be aware of its spatial dimensions. Realize that the space you see belongs to both of you. You will both draw on the one sheet at the same time, discovering as you do what you feel in sharing your space with someone else and how you can express your relationship with the other within that space. Using lines, shapes, and colors, you can communicate in many ways. You can insist on being left alone. You can push your partner off the paper. You can support, cross out, cover up, cooperate with, lead, oppose, or follow your partner. When both partners feel that they finished their graphic communicating, ask them to talk with each other, finding out how explicit they were in giving and receiving messages. Change partners and repeat the exercise. See if there are any consistent patterns. Let the entire group assemble and share experiences.

Rhyne employs still another interesting technique, best described as wire twisting. Two heavy, flexible steel rods are stapled to a heavy wood block. The patient is requested to twist the rods into the shape that fits this current feeling state while observed by a partner. Next, the partners reverse roles, all this without interpreting or discussing. Finally, each shapes one rod in interaction with their partner. They are then told to process the experience.

Another technique using art materials is to have the group represent how they feel right now by drawing something—anything—on a large piece of newsprint pastel on the wall, sort of a group collage. "Now who will go first?"

Sometimes I use a similar technique to break through prolonged blocks where verbal interpretations haven't accomplished anything. One woman was rendered stunned and speechless by fellow group members who told her that the problem wasn't the guys she picked—but that she herself felt undeserving of love. They suggested that she picked losers in order to camouflage an even greater hurt, namely a deep inability to receive affection. The woman was mystified, confused, and for thirty minutes, she couldn't work with this material. I handed her a pad and told her to start drawing while she talked. She saw her picture emerging as a spider caught in "his" own web. When I asked her about the choice of masculine gender, she broke into tears. With continued group support it came out that her parents had lost a daughter before she was born, so that she became the "replacement" daughter. She revealed that she never had an identity of her own but was only there to please her parents and to make up for their loss. Her brothers, however, were the prized and fortunate ones. Gradually, she developed the attitude that a woman's major function is to support the needs and ambitions of others. To take something for oneself was selfish.

I've often used this technique when discussion wasn't getting anywhere but a painful block was still present. The doodles or symbols are valuable in providing breakthroughs because they suggest fresh angles of approach and suddenly make the patient come alive again.

A soft way that I've experimented with in generating self-disclosure data in the early sessions is called "The Road of Life Experience." Each participant is asked to place a dot on his paper which represents his birth. Then, without lifting his drawing instrument from the paper, he is to portray a series of critical incidents which he feels are representational of his life. I then ask the group to form dyads so that they may explain their pictures to one another, and later share their discussion with the larger group. Another possibility is that after a brief introduction to heraldry, I can ask the group participants to make up their own coats of arms.

Self-Drawing

Pick out several colors that you would like to use, then take a large piece of paper, place it in front of you, and close your eyes. Get in touch with your body and try to become aware of how you feel inside. Let some visual images come to you that express your inner self.

Now open your eyes and create a drawing that represents yourself with the colors you have chosen. As you draw, notice how you feel. Be aware of the movement of your hands and how the colors appear on the page. Try not to have any specific goals in mind. Let the process take over so that the colors and your hands decide where and how to draw next. Let the lines stop where they want to, go as far as they want to, change directions by themselves, etc. Now make a drawing that represents yourself.

Hold your drawing up so that others can see it and go around the group giving each five minutes to describe this drawing of you. Ask them to do it in the first person as if they were actually describing themselves to another person. For instance, "I'm very complex and muddled; I am very thick around my outside so that it's hard to get in. I have black angry lines that contrast with my happy yellow lines." etc. Also express your awareness of the process of representing yourself and how you felt while this was happening. For instance, "At first I had only the thick black lines but this left me depressed and feeling cut off. I added the yellow to reflect my attempts at optimism and enthusiasm. The two colors mixed together show how mixed up I can get and how turbulent my moods are." Try to pay attention to how you are feeling as you describe your picture to the group.

After the group has gone around, the leader asks them, "What did you discover about yourself and the others as they expressed themselves through their drawings?" Share your observations and discuss them.

A variation of this technique consists of asking each person to choose the three colors that he likes most and the three he dislikes most and tell him to use all these colors in a drawing. Compare the content, the process, and the feelings involved in the use of the disliked colors. What do they represent and what does their use reveal? Another approach would be to ask the patients to draw the parts of themselves they don't like or a feeling that causes them difficulty and then to share and process the experiences with the group.

Group Fountain

Toward the end of treatment the therapist should strive to shift the focus for the patient from heaviness to closeness, and even to play and celebrate (which become greater present-day possibilities for the graduating patient). I begin this exercise by asking everybody to stand up and join hands with the people on either side until a big circle is formed, facing inward. "Now will you close your eyes and for a moment just be aware of the hands you are holding and of the circular chain of hands of which you are a part. . .and feel the warmth in this chain, feel it grow. . .feel the energy pulsing and flowing through the chain, around the circle, from you and through you." A moment later, "Now imagine that you all form a fountain together, a great big fountain in a public square. Become that fountain. If there are movements that fit in, make them. If there are sounds, make them. If things happen that need to be told about, tell about them." At this point we usually have a group of warm people who are creating physically, vocally, and sensitively, a group fantasy. With hands still joined, participants often swoop their arms up and down. The fountain becomes an image of celebration, freedom, sensuality, fun—all in an easygoing, rather wonderful way. The "public place" where the fountain is situated, seems to be taken as a place for openness and community. After five or ten minutes has passed, I say, "Now let your part of the fountain become a part of you, and gradually bring your movements and sounds to a close. Just stay with the fountain feeling for a moment, and know that you will always have that in you." After another moment or so, "Now, open your eyes and talk to whomever you want to, however you want to." Instead of this fantasy trip getting people connected with more difficult feelings (inhibition, judgment, performance, a feeling of being alone) it works in the opposite way—this exercise creates a joyful, pleasurable, closing experience.

One Step at a Time

Jean-Paul Sartre and other existentialists have noted that there is no alternative, no exit, from the realization that man defines his own meaning by his actions and the way he leads his life. He must take ultimate responsibility. Paul Tillich has suggested that existential despair is a result of man's recognition that only he can give meaning to his life and that there's no alternative to this responsibility for self-definition. Resistance is an attempt to obliterate the fundamental despair about which Sartre and Tillich write. In rejecting insights and avoiding self-understanding, the patient expresses his preference for the despair implicit in the statement "I have no choice," over the despair inherent in the recognition that "I have all choices." To the extent to which patients resist, do they try to avoid the knowledge that they have chosen, and having chosen, that they have self-affirmed themselves, even if their choices no longer rest on valid premises? The patient's resistance denotes his unwillingness to acknowledge that he and nobody else has chosen for himself, that he has affirmed himself even if this particular self-affirmation has led to at least partial self-denial, that it has led to his giving up part of himself in order to survive at lease in a crippled form.

Resistance in therapy is then the patient's refusal to admit freedom despite the fact that he has always chosen. Sartre said it well "Man' was condemned to be free." Buber puts it somewhat differently—"Freedom is a cross one must bear." The analysis of resistance is the therapist's attempt to help the patient abandon the despair of no choice and instead accept the despair of all choices. As therapists, we constantly strive to get the patient to live with the knowledge that he alone is ultimately responsible for his life. Daniel Malamud has devised an exercise called, One Step at a Time that is designed to help people discover that, first of all, life is subject to choices; secondly, that by not making a choice, they're letting others make choices for them, and that finally, this is the way life really is— if you make a step, it has consequences, either good or bad, but it's all on the basis of the steps that you take.

I'd like you to stand and distribute yourselves in a haphazard way all over this room. Some face the window, some the far wall, some the doorway, some the other wall. Just scatter all over the room. But once you've settled on a place, stay there!

The name of this game is One Step At A Time. Here are the rules. Each time I ask you to take one step, please do so in any direction you want. But please, only *one* step. It can be a big step or a small one. It can be to your left or to your right, backward or forward, as long as it's just one step at a time.

Each time you take a step, I'd like you to tune in to where you are and how you feel in that new position. Look around and see where you are in relation to the other people here, and where they are in relation to you.

In this game you are going to move through the world slowly and deliberately. Moving one step at a time enables you to take a close look at your moment-to-moment existence.

Another rule: with each step you have the option of making some kind of physical contact with whomever is near you. You can touch the person's fingers, or shoulder, or hug the person, anything that is comfortable and natural for you. This is optional. You don't have to touch anybody, nor do you have to respond to anybody who is touching you.

The main rule is this: please do not talk during this exercise. I cannot emphasize this too much. You will be tempted at various points to exchange small comments. Please resist that temptation. I want to underscore the importance of NOT talking at all during the entire experience.

So, one step at a time in any direction. Each time you take a step, look around, see where you are in relationship to others, and tune in to your feelings. With each step you have the option of touching somebody or responding to somebody else's touch. No talking.

We are now ready to begin. Take your first step. Tune into your feelings about having taken a first step—a step into the unknown. Look around. See how you feel. See who's next to you.

Take your second step now. Each time you take a step you make a choice, and each choice has a consequence. Think about that.

Now take your third step. Each of us has his own pattern of movement in the world. Review your first three steps. Do you see any pattern of yours already unfolding?

Take your next step. There is no way we can get all we want. We have to pick and choose. At each step you take a choice—your choice.

Now take another step. You have a choice as to the direction you take: forward, backward, left, right. You have a choice as to whether or not to make physical contact with someone near you.

Take another step. Look around and see where you are in relation to everybody else, and continue to refrain from any talking.

Before you make your next move, see if you can get in touch with the process that is going on inside you. How your will is working. How your mind in making choices.

All right take another step. Just one step at a time. And now take another step.

We all have our own different ways of avoiding things. Can you become aware of what you have been avoiding so far? Think about this. . . . Now take another step. Are you doing what you really want to do? Or are you doing what you think you ought to do—what you think is expected? . . . Now take another step.

And now take another step. I see that some of you are moving around in the center of the room, and some of you are on the outskirts. Think about that for awhile. Does that mean anything to you personally?

Now take the next step. And another. Everyone is in his own way vulnerable. Do the steps you take reflect this? Think about that.

Okay, take another step. You now have *only five steps left* before the end. Just five. Let that sink in. Think about what you want to do with your remaining five steps.

All right, take the first of your last five steps. Someone once said that we have only ourselves and one another. That may not be much, but that's all there is. Do you believe that?

Take the second of your last five steps. There are only three steps left. Think about that.

Take your next step. With only two steps left, would you think over the various steps you've taken so far? Were there any steps that you took that you can really congratulate yourself about? Can you give yourself warm, generous appreciation for having taken steps on your own behalf?

Take your next to the last step. You have only one step left. Think over what you want to do with it. Do you regret having taken certain steps? Do you regret not having taken certain steps? With one step remaining, can you now forgive youself, really and fully forgive youself, for having done or not done these things that you regret?

Okay, please take your final step. Let yourself experience this last moment. Where you are in relation to the others? Where are the others in relation to you? Where are you in relation to yourself?

All right, that's it.

Three Coins

Group members are requested to bring a nickel, a dime, and a quarter to the next session. No further explanation is given. The following week, the members are told, "Close your eyes and try to get deep in touch with your feelings. . .now feel each coin. Keeping your eyes closed fondle each coin and try to see which one feels most like you. Which coin reminds you of how you feel about yourself right now." The group is instructed to stay in touch with their feelings for a while. Then volunteers are asked for to explain the personal meaning of their own choice. Continue this until everyone has spoken. "Next I want everyone to close their eyes and concentrate on who in this room you would like to give this coin (that represents yourself) to and why. The person to the leader's right starts. The instructions are to give the coin by rising, walking over to the selected person, and placing the coin in his palm. When each person in succession has made his choice, the group is asked to talk about the resulting feelings. Typical themes that emerge have to do with attitudes regarding giving and receiving, self-concept, hidden appreciation, feelings of rejection, apprehension regarding being ignored, jealousy, and competition. One final note: this is a beautiful game to conclude a therapy season with (e.g., just before the group takes a summer vacation). It serves to accentuate the depth of emotion felt and reinforces the bonds of caring that exist within the group.

7

Re-entry Problems

In the short period of its existence, the marathon approach to group therapy has provoked a remarkable amount of interest and controversy. On the one hand, there are many reports of healthy regressions in the service of the ego. Marathon therapists enjoy recounting stories of how their patients worked through early developmental conflicts, dissolved their hated introjects, and eventually reconstituted themselves at higher levels of functioning (Bach 1967, Mintz 1969, Stoller 1968). Most often these anecdotes are filled with strong emotional confrontations, cathartic releases, and the introduction of games, exercises, and role behavior on the therapist's part that challenge the more traditional group approaches severely.

In opposition to these positive testimonials, there has been a tendency to "throw the baby out with the bath water." Many clinicians who have never attended a marathon or run one themselves, and who have certainly not bothered to evaluate the aftereffects of a time-extended group experience objectively, have tended to lump marathons together with nude therapy, encounter groups, and Esalen, and have written the whole thing off as the irresponsible encouragement of acting out (Smith 1970, Spotnitz 1968).

Unfortunately, wasteful preoccupation with such a pseudoissue as "Should there be marathons?" (Let's face it, they're here to stay), tends to obfuscate a basic, more viable question, namely, "What are the aftereffects of marathons?" Surprisingly, aside from a few scattered before-and-after-outcome studies and many extravagant subjective claims and counterclaims, to my knowledge no one has yet considered the effect on the marathon participant when he returns to his regular ongoing therapy group. After all, if the marathon experience is not simply an end in itself but supposedly facilitates future growth and back-home implementation of new-learned roles, then how successful is the marathon member in reshaping his own environment (office, home, marriage, group)? Also, how do the regular group members react when the prodigal son returns? Do they provide a ready outlet for experimenting with new behavior or are they typically resistant to accepting out-of-character behavior? It may be that these questions must be answered separately for each individual. Nevertheless, there are certain consistent, predictable patterns that can be observed. I would like to discuss one such experience in detail and then draw certain conclusions that may prove helpful in making sense out of what may initially appear to be confusing and even incomprehensible behavior.

Seven members who participated in a marathon were drawn from one particular therapy group. During the marathon itself, six of these seven people had bn actively involved, had what they considered to be very meaningful experiences, and came back to their regular group in a state of elation and resolute optimism. A relaxed, harmonious atmosphere began to pervade the group. Everyone seemed to be happy, busy patching up differences, and reminiscing on "How much better things are now than they used to be when we were neurotic." The spirit of spontaneity, playfulness, and pleasure in one another's company lasted for several sessions. The three members of the group who had not been at the marathon and the one member who had but hadn't felt she got very much out of it, tried to keep up with the others. Rather than be considered spoilsports, they jumped on the bandwagon, joined in the mass celebration, and nervously suppressed their underlying irritation.

This spirit of universal harmony and mutual acceptance continued for about a month. Different members commented on how this mood seemed to directly carry over from the final phase of the marathon when a great wave of cohesiveness and comradeship had swept over the participants. Those last few hours were variously commemorated in nostalgic reminiscences of mutual understanding, acceptance, and love. An attempt was made to reenact and perpetuate these rich, paradisical memories in the ongoing group. Two members praised through poetry the wonders of the group, one man brought in cheese and a bottle of champagne to celebrate his liberation, the group organized a social with the spouses, and to top things off, the group surprised me with a birthday party.

The institutionalization of happiness was not just an "in-house" phenomenon. Virtually the entire group began to report marked improvements on the outside. A wishy-washy man entranced the group with a surprising tale of "cockmanship," a secretary made an application for college, someone brought in a sculpting, a downtrodden wife told her husband off for the first time, etc. Anyone who dared to disturb the status quo either by raising external real-life problems or challenging the substance of another member's progress report was neutralized by being ignored, isolated, or cajoled into surrendering his group-alien symptom. The power and need of the group as a total organism to perservere in this flight into health was most apparent in the adamant, blanket resistance evidenced whenever the therapist even mildly tried to point out a discrepancy, question a statement, or label a flagrant sample of behavior as acting out. Practically all interventions were scoffed at as "too analytic;" "introspective, not spontaneous;" "treating us like babies instead of letting us be independent and do our own thing," etc. The myth of homogeneous solidarity and satisfaction with the status quo was demonstrated in many ways.

Joan described a business trip she had gone on with her husband and his boss. "The boss's wife was unfriendly so I snubbed her the entire trip. When she invited me to play golf, I told her there were other things I would rather spend my time doing." Joan then proceeded to relate another incident that took place about a week later where she told off one of her husband's business associates. Joan denied any inference that some displaced hostility toward her husband could be operating. The group applauded her independence and chastised the analyst with declarations such as "Women's Lib would never tolerate your male chauvinism."

During another session, Sam was telling about how his wife had said to him: "I know you don't think I'm so sexy so I'm going to have some affairs and tell you about them so you'll get excited about me like other husbands do about their wives." This story was told in a matter-of-fact way and Sam staunchly defended his wife's statement and agreed that it would probably excite him. The group supported his stand and again attacked the analyst for attributing neurotic motives to this arrangement.

What sense can we make of this peculiar turn of events? To summarize, a group of people seem to genuinely benefit from a marathon experience, they reenter their original group, and turn the sessions into a travesty of mental health through "sweetness and light." They become disenchanted with the therapist and begin to view him as an insincere manipulator, someone who is going to interrupt group progress simply because it's happening independent of his control. During this phase, it is not uncommon for the analyst to be barraged with accusations: "You're a good therapist when we're sick and weak and we need babying. But now that we're strong, you still try to protect us and take responsibility for us. Stop being such a parent. Let us do our thing—stop interfering with our lives." Several respected colleagues have made similar observations and I have personally experienced such happenings in a number of my own marathons.

Let me now try to explain what I believe is the key relationship between the marathon experience and the short-term events that take place afterward, back in the ongoing therapy group. Let us say that a particular marathon left the members feeling exhilarated, euphoric, or at least better. These positive spirits lead to a happy sense of group belonging. The enchantment with the group and with the leader, who is given credit for facilitating the miracle of overnight change, is often short-lived. When members discover their dependence upon one another and correspondingly develop an exaggerated sense of the powers of the leader, the anticipation of the highly saturated, timeless quality of the intense marathon experience being abruptly cut off is terrifying. Members mourn, pine, feel a threat of loss, and experience guilt and ambivalence in relation to objects, external and internal.

It is against the experience of depressive anxiety and guilt that "flight into health" defenses are directed (Riviere 1936). Any significant feelings of dependence or need are obviated, denied, or reversed. Since the aim of the analytic process is to press for insight and reality, we must question the motives behind (1) the denial of psychic reality that is fostered by the indiscriminate encouragement and acceptance of destructive behavior by fellow members and (2) the strong resistance to the emotional experience of having the therapist become a highly valued object.

According to Kleinian theory (Segal 1964) this denial of psychic reality is best accomplished by manic defenses accompanied by the reawakening and strengthening of feelings of omnipotence and particularly of omnipotent control of the object. Referring back to my group situation, the members were in effect attempting to drive the therapist into a dependent position by making it appear that he could function only if the group agreed to be dependent (on him). By placing a negative valence on this "old mode of behavior" and denying strong, very real current ambivalences, the therapist is double-binded. ("Isn't our new-found growth and independence exactly what you've been heading us toward? Then what are you complaining about? Stop all this analysis and let us be.") If the analyst allows himself to be controlled in this way, the group has nothing but contempt for him. If he persists in trying to challenge and interpret, he is kept at bay and ultimately defeated by the collusive denial of the group.

At this point, the reader might well feel even pessimism and despair. Are the group and the therapist hopelessly deadlocked? Were the supposed marathon gains all illusory? Can group members be effectively prevented from their impulse to cushion their separation anxiety by destroying the therapist and his rightful group function? The technical handling of this phase can well mark a turning point in group history by either redirecting the members toward constructive, shared group goals or by further exacerbating rebellious and polarizing tendencies. Fortunately, reparative wishes are at work in most groups. The guilt and despair that are experienced at having lost the love object (the leader) awaken a latent wish to restore and recreate him. Love is brought more sharply into conflict with hate, and is active both in controlling destructiveness and in repairing and restoring damage done. The wish and the capacity for the revival of the good object is the major basis of the ego's sometimes surprising capacity to maintain love and relationships through conflicts and difficulties. Reparative fantasies and activities resolve the group's anxieties. The continued living presence of the therapist and his conveyance of interest and concern make group members more aware of the resilience of external objects and less frightened by their omnipotent fantasy attacks. Moreover, the individual patient's own growth and the restorations that he carries out in relation to other group members with the therapist, brings about an increased trust in his own love, his own capacity to restore internal objects and to retain them as good, even in the face of external frustrations.

If the prospective marathon leader is alert to the possible emergence of these dynamics, he will be better prepared to deal with them effectively. There is nothing wrong with a happy sense of group belongingness but if this eclipses individual identity, it should be clearly seen as a fake attempt to resolve interpersonal problems by denying their reality. The therapist is advised not to side too easily with the "this is a great group; let's not change anything" sentiment. Nor should he be too aggressive in assaulting the group's massive defensive denial during this stage. Rather, the state of affairs should be seen as a necessary subphase in the process of group development, which helps to clear the way for subsequent major forward movements of the whole group (see Bennis and Shephard 1956). The most helpful orientation here would be the interested, involved, but slightly detached, not overly invested observer. Another point that should be taken into consideration is that of homogeneous (most people in the marathon coming from the same therapy group) vs heterogeneous combinations. Future investigation of marathon results should consider the possibility that the massive defenses encountered after the marathon were significantly affected by the clustering of patients with too many overlapping reasons for denying reality. In my own experience, marathon results were more substantial when participants came from different groups because the working-through process subsequent to the marathon met with less resistance.

8

Countertransference Aggression

Early in my career, while I was still attending analytic school, a patient came to see me who, for a time, became the bane of my existence. He rejected every interpretation, constantly complained about the fee ($2 a session), refused to leave when time was up, antagonized fellow group members by his hostility and negativism, and yelled through the walls at my neighbor's pinochle game. Since this man was assigned to me by the analytic school as a suitable candidate for analysis, I felt in a bind. I didn't know how to treat him but if I dropped him, wouldn't that in the eyes of my supervisor reflect on my capabilities as an analyst? (In those days, I was both more omnipotent and more masochistic than I am now.)

After a heavy exposure to the patient of three sessions a week, plus group, over a two-month period, I was beginning to develop stomach symptoms. One day, my doorbell rang during his session. I opened the door and a little old man brushed past me and started walking around my office. The patient was lsing on the couch with his mouth open, flabbergasted. I chased after the man trying to discover who he was, and the whole scene was totally unreal. The man turned out to be a housepainter, and he began to instruct me as to when he was going to paint my office. He was very offensive and arrogant and I was uptight with the patient watching me be humiliated, until I exploded. "Fuck you—get the fuck out of here— you have some hell of a nerve busting in like this—you be here Friday, not Monday, Friday. Now get out of here, and be back at 8 o'clock in the morning." I don't know whether I'm conveying the picture vividly enough, but I really came across as a combination of King Kong and Kirk Douglas. As the painter retreated out the door, I returned to my seat, put my glasses back on, reaised my pen to my pad and said, "Now what were you saying, Joe?"

This episode was significant in that it was the turning point of our work together. Instead of analyzing the symbolic meaning of my outburst and its impact retrospectively, let me simply state that thereafter I became looser, less formally analytic, and more direct and the patient became less provocative, more assertive, and started coming through as more human. Lessing, the eighteenth century German poet and writer, once said, "He who on certain occasions does not lose his sanity, shows that he has none." As analysts, we need not be ashamed to admit that we have tempers or that our threshold for persecutory anxiety is not within human limits. If we temporarily lose our objectivity, hopefully we don't lose it altogether. Only by a healthy splitting that divides his ego into an experiencing, irrational part and a rational, observing one, can the analyst perceive and diagnose the more pathological countertransferential processes. If the analyst has courage and intelligence, he will be able to put the awareness of his overreactions to good use in the course of working through the patient's transference distortions.

For the remainder of this paper, I would like to focus on the vicissitudes of the aggressive countertransferential reaction, as it reveals itself in group therapy. In group treatment every therapeutic problem is intensified. Simply the presence of a variety of persons multiplies the transference manifestations and provocations in both patient and therapist. When we further consider the possibility of lateral sibling transferences, extratherapeutic patient contacts during alternate sessions, and the increased transparency of the therapist, it is remarkable indeed that the prevailing transference can be articulated with any clarity and the boundaries between what is transference and what is countertransference maintained. At this point, let me share with you some suggestive samples of the unconscious participation of the group therapist in the form of aggressive countertransferential reactions that have been raised by my group therapy supervisees.

A woman patient was referred with the presenting problem of a peer relationship with her husband, neglectful attitudes toward her children, and a history of extramarital affairs. She had a brittle personality covered over by a hard, aggressive exterior, was very scattered in her thinking, and very impulsive and explosive in expressing her feelings. After two years of combined treatment, the therapy seemed to be taking hold. The patient developed a warmer, less critical attitude toward the husband, had taken greater responsibility for her children, terminated sexual acting out, and seemed more solid and better integrated. In the midst of this movement toward health, she began to get sexually involved with an acquaintance of the therapist. Her earlier gains began to slip, her resistance to therapy intensified, she began to come late or miss both group and individual sessions, and she rejected any interpretations or advice given to her by either the group members or the therapist. Upon returning to the group after a vacation break, the patient had decompensated to a marked degree, made paranoid accusations about the group plotting against her, and acted in a very erratic and depersonalized way. After about an hour of this, the group was getting restless, unsympathetic, and antagonistic and finally the therapist himself became exasperated: "Quit seeing this guy! Don't you see what it's doing to you? If you're not going to take responsibility for yourself, then why should anybody else?" After getting a blank stare, the therapist went on to say, "If you don't stop now, then get yourself another therapist." Looking back, the therapist's understanding of the situation was that as the patient was getting healthier, she no longer had to isolate sexuality from the therapeutic relationship. On the outside, up to now, her life had been rigidly compartmentalized—at home a husband who was twenty years older and loved her but toward whom she felt nothing sexually, and outside the home numerous sterile, loveless sexual affairs. For the first time in her life, the patient was beginning to constructively fuse love and sex in a single relationship. After an earlier negative transference had been worked through, her feelings toward the therapist were now of a positive sort—warm, secure, with great fondness and affection. She started to have sexual dreams, hesitantly shared sexual fantasies, and underwent a profound change in her feminine identification (lost a great deal of weight, dressed more attractively, spoke more softly, walked with more confidence and self-assurance). As this new self-image accompanied by a more sexualized projection began to emerge, the anxiety and guilt proved to be intolerable. Choosing an acquaintance of the therapist as a sexual substitute served two functions: first, it was a safer, displaced way of expressing forbidden feelings because once again sexuality was manifested in an isolated way. Secondly, it set up a competitive situation where the therapist was put in the position of the jealous father who was vainly trying to repossess his unfaithful daughter. The rage that the therapist finally experienced and his sadistic reproach ("Don't come back unless you get well"), was quite possibly a projection of the analyst's sexual guilt ("I shouldn't be seeing her unless I straighten out my feelings") and his sense of threat that everything that had been accomplished was going to get unraveled.

Racker (1968) in his book *Transference and Countertransference* makes the point that "owing to the prohibition of active phallic impulses in the analytic situation, in which genital behavior is forbidden to the analyst, the analyst's impulses and accompanying feelings easily acquire a passive-phallic character. The unconscious desire may now be that the patient should fall in love with the analyst's penis" (p. 85). The closest substitute for the analyst's genital potency in psychotherapy is his interpretation and his comprehension. By disregarding the analyst's influence, the patient, in effect, renders him insignificant and impotent. The symbolic meaning of being betrayed by a friend, the whole sense of operating from a handicapped position in pursuit of the love object (the patient), and the passive experience of watching something happen beyond his control are all strikingly reminiscent of a primal scene trauma. The analyst's oedipal frustration is expressed through his magical threat: "If you don't return to me and love me the way you used to, I'll pretend you don't exist" (by sending the patient away to another analyst).

Many of the circumstances leading up to the patient's getting involved with the acquaintance of the analyst and her more mature sexual feelings toward the therapist himself were not thoroughly investigated in the group. It is quite likely that the therapist did not actively open up and explore what was disturbing him, out of an exaggerated sense of guilt and helplessness. On the other hand, the patient defended against leveling with the group about combined sexual and affectionate feelings toward the therapist because this would represent a healthier, more advanced, forbidden form of relatedness. The patient's guilt, projected onto the group, made her perceive the other members as bad mothers who would destroy her unless she remained fixated as either the brassy whore or the crumbling, confused, dependent child.

Fortunately, when the therapist overcame his own fear and hesitancy about discussing these possibilities frankly, the patient had enough ego strength to reintegrate herself at a functional level. She returned to treatment, got back into the swing of the therapy, and continued to make steady progress.

A therapist introduced a new patient to an ongoing group in the following way: "Barbara is going to try out our group for a while. Her regular group is disbanding for the summer so at the end of the summer I shall give her a choice of whether she wants to return to the old group or continue in the new one." Halfway through the session, a male patient, Jack, exploded with rage. "What the fuck are you doing, testing us? I don't need a tryout. Get in or get out! Why the hell should I expose myself to you if you have one foot out the door?" When Barbara tried to explain, Jack became even more irate and started to scream and rant. Barbara's further attempt to be conciliatory only seemed to provoke Jack to more extreme accusations ("Get out of here. Nobody here wants you. Fuck off!!"). During this entire episode, the therapist remained passive and made no significant interventions. Barbara hung on for the remainder of the session but she never came back.

At the next session, the therapist lectured Jack about his inability to control himself and his hostility toward women. The rest of the group picked this up and tried to get Jack to explore why Barbara was so threatening to him. Jack became more and more defensive, protested that nobody understood his feelings, and the group fell into a protracted silence. The therapist chose to ameliorate the tension by drawing out another patient.

In supervision, the therapist realized that his way of introducing Barbara had been instrumental in setting her up for Jack's wrath.

Maybe Jack was only expressing the anger that the therapist himself felt but by his ambivalent introduction only indirectly hinted at. The therapist recalled that he had been surprised at Barbara's group deciding to disband for the summer months. When she suggested that she would like to try another group because she wasn't getting so much out of this one (her original group), the therapist must have felt he was dealt a double blow. Instead of facing the possibility of group resistance (acted out through taking a vacation) or Barbara's resistance (acted out through complaining about the first group and suggesting another one), the therapist apparently defended himself against his own hurt and anger by offering Barbara a trial in the second group. The excesses of Jack's reaction was transference all right, but the therapist's transferential anger toward Barbara (for causing him narcissistic injury) was the precipitating ingredient. The therapist now viewed his passivity during the attack as an unconscious way of getting back at Barbara. His moralistic attack on Jack during the subsequent session may have been his way of atoning for the guilt he felt because of his ineptness in handling things.

Another intriguing issue goes as follows: Jack seems to have displaced much of the anger he felt toward the therapist onto Barbara. Jack's inability to express his feelings more directly toward the therapist may well be a function of his (Jack's) father-authority transference. At the same time, however, the therapist's passivity and guilt-provoking attitudes smack of countertransferential problems in the area of aggression. Why didn't he redirect Jack's anger toward himself, where it most likely belonged? If the therapist was threatened by a challenge to his authority and couldn't deal with anger maturely, then we might say that he was at least partially responsible for Jack's inability to channel his own anger more constructively.

A therapist found himself constantly impatient and annoyed at a twenty-three-year-old woman with a hippie life style. The kookie outfits she wore, the "far-out" guys she dated, her lack of goal direction and inability to settle on a career, and her street language all seemed to arouse in the therapist a wish to reform her. When the patient failed to absorb the group's more middle-class values, the therapist virtually cut her off dead. He rationalized his interest in reforming her as being for her own good. "How are you going to get a job looking like that?" It's not responsible to take welfare checks— a strong, healthy girl like you"; "What are you dating these losers for?" "Drugs are an escape. Anybody who takes pot is afraid to face things the way they really are"; "How can you live from day to day? What subjects were you interested in at school? Go back to college"; "Why don't you go to places where you can meet regular guys?" When she resisted his entreaties and benevolent guidance, he stopped listening to her. He would no longer respond when she brought problems up, negated the significance of her feelings by implying that, considering the world in which she lived, none of her experiences could be meaningful, and in general acted as though, until she came around, he would treat her as a nonperson. The patient reacted to this by attempting to shock and provoke the group. The therapist seized on the acting up to justify his stance of "long-suffering parent waiting for wayward daughter to see the error of her ways." The patient and therapist were now locked in a hopeless stalemate. Two months passed and finally the patient announced she was leaving ("Nobody understands me here"). The therapist couldn't let the opportunity pass without saying in a very patronizing way "I'm sorry but I can't help you until you face what you're doing wrong more honestly."

Perhaps the kind of countertransferential aggression most difficult to recognize occurs when the therapist inappropriately pushes for something resembling a "love-in". In this situation, patients are prompted to openly act out their needs, be physical with one another, ask for love, be unconditionally caring and tender. Meanwhile, strong dislikes and hostilities are interpreted away and suppressed like guests who would spoil the party. The all-pervasive climate of forced intimacy and shallow comradeship, coupled with the premature, easy comforting of anyone who is upset, prevents genuine working through of pain and anger. In truth, these are aggressions committed in the name of love.

A research finding by Lieberman and Yalem touches upon a corollary issue. They found, in a comprehensive study, that the greatest number of psychological casualties during encounter sessions were found in those groups where the leader was labeled as charismatic. This kind of therapist is seen by the patients as a desirable, love-dispensing savior. However, the goodies will be handed out only to those who are able to conform to the leader's freewheeling, open style. Those who cannot, get nothing. They are, in effect, aggressed upon and then become what is referred to as "casualties" (they drop out of group, occasionally decompensate and seek help elsewhere, or make suicidal attempts, sometimes successfully).

In conclusion, let me just say that countertransferential reactions are here to stay and that it is even fortunate that we have them. The introjection of the analyst as the good object "free from anxiety and anger" (Heimann 1956), can better be realized if the analyst himself can successfully recognize, dominate, and utilize his countertransference in order to properly understand the transference. I will end by agreeing with Racker's statement that "the danger of exaggerated faith in messages from one's own unconscious is less than the danger of repressing them and denying them any objective value" (p. 171).

9

Group Supervision

The initial stage of supervision is largely devoted to helping the student analyst learn how to report the content of his sessions with the patient properly. This material is not only a means of communicating to the supervisor; it also represents the end result of the student analyst's processing of the psychoanalytic data and permits specific evaluation of his current understanding, sense of timing, and relationship with the patient.

In this paper, I would like to discuss one rather common quality I have observed in training beginning analysts: their tendency to present accounts of their sessions verbatim to the supervisor. Every remembered detail is reported in an unselective manner which largely excludes the student analyst's own train of associative thinking. If the supervisor consistently reinforces this manner of presentation, many important training objectives will be lost. On a more subtle level, the supervisor's willingness to accept uncomplainingly a passive, undiscriminating, blow-by-blow description of a session may serve to obfuscate the hidden relationship between the latent conflicts in the session proper and the student analyst's way of presenting them.

In a supervisory session with three group therapists in training, therapist A was talking about her group in a rather reluctant fashion. "There is nothing terribly interesting to report. For the past three weeks everything has been quiet. No problems—nothing special." After a bit more prodding, she then went on to describe a couples group session where, in successive fashion, three different wives put down their husbands for a lack of involvement, for being too passive, and for not being responsible enough.

Therapist A had been presenting for about fifteen minutes when I found myself growing increasingly withdrawn and restless. I intervened at this point and asked the other members of the supervisory group what they were feeling at that moment. Their reactions being similar to mine, I threw out two questions: Why were we bored? If we were bored, what function did this serve for therapist A?

In answer to question one, the general consensus was that therapist A was showing her resistance toward presenting, by being very obsessive, not focusing on any specific problem, talking in a dull, unenthusiastic manner, not pausing to offer her own feelings while the events she was describing were happening, etc.

Question two was interpreted as therapist A's "conscientiously" grinding out an "authentic" account of what supposedly happened during the session. Her self-righteous attitude was unconsciously conveyed by the diligent reporting (without sparing a word), which put the burden on the supervisory group to focus on the important things. After all, hadn't she done her duty by providing us with such a thorough picture?

The net result was a counterresistance by the rest of the supervisory group and myself. We were being asked to be involved and active in relation to material that therapist A was not really taking responsibility for herself but only seeming to do so. In her defense, therapist A based her reluctance to present on the fact that she was the only one in the supervisory group who currently had an ongoing group, so that while on the one hand she welcomed the opportunity to be special and to get frequent chances to receive supervision, on the other hand she resented having to be the responsible one all the time.

The supervisory group proved to be very helpful by showing therapist A the striking parallel between her associations and those of the patients in her group. Her in-depth, first-person awareness of the dynamics of passive hostility toward feelings of unfair responsibility enabled her to more sensitively appreciate the husband and wife interactions from both sides of the fence (as the "resentful" giver and as the "manipulative" exploiter).

The point that I want to emphasize in this paper is that supervision can be a more meaningful experience if certain presentation rituals are repeatedly explored as potential resistances to learning. Why is one patient focused on more that another? Why does a particular supervisor spend and excessive amount of supervisory time referring to individual patients and neglecting the total group? Why not spend a supervisory hour exploring all those segments of the session which the supervisee hadn't intended to talk about? Asking the supervisee to name the members of his group, whom did he name first? Whom did he name last? Whom did he block on—why? Is there a difference in the therapist's involvement in both the group and in the supervisory experience if he is encouraged to focus on the decision-making processes involved or in his interventions, as they unfold? What role is the therapist structuring for himself and his patients by his remarks? Is he fully aware of the effect on patient expectations of didactic remarks, authoritative "father knows best" statements, seductive "I am more like you than like them" vibrations to adolescent groups, etc.?

To conclude, attending to neglected process dynamics in a supervisory session can be a valuable aid in comprehending the content of the group therapy session proper.

SUPERTRANSFERENCE
IN GROUP SUPERVISION

Everyone seems to agree that the learning of psychoanalysis requires a clear theoretical understanding of unconscious and preconscious tendencies, which will hopefully permit subsequent practical application in treating patients. The supervisor, however, must have command not only of the classical formulations, but also be able to enter into the learning alliance in an empathically communicating manner. He must use himself as a catalyst in the service not of "analyzing" his student but of developing in them those ego functions essential for analyzing. Ekstein and Wallerstein

(1958) see the supervisory process as a "new experience of growth" which is self-limited according to the nature and degree of those irrational attitudes and resistances which operate in either student or teacher. They see this as analagous to the psychotherapeutic situation whereby we work with patients in a mutual endeavor to help them to independence and new insight.

It is the supervisor's responsibility to constantly illuminate the intricate spiral of transactional events which emerge during the supervisory session. Intense unconscious forces can just as well be stirred up in the student by the learning situation as while he is conducting therapy. Emotional responses to the personality and style of the supervisor, to his expectations of the student, to his reality role in relation to the student (evaluation, potential source of referrals), and to his pedagogic interventions, all are an intinsic part of the supervisory experience. The supervisor has the task of recognizing what aspect of a given learning problem originates in reactions to the patient, or whether there are discordant elements in the "here and now" supervisory situation. His ability to grasp the vicissitudes of the learning process, to manage the complex interactions operating within the supervisory relationship, to use his own subjective intuition for objective purposes, and to integrate the roles of therapist and teacher will determine the extent of his effectiveness.

The supervisor, by turning his observing ego on his own experiencing ego as well as on "the case out there" that the student is presenting, is serving as a role model for the student to enable him to recognize how his own motivations affect the analytic process. Isakower (1957) emphasizes the importance of supervision for working through this comprehension to the point where it will provide insightful implementation in practice. When the student begins to experience psychoanalysis as a two-way street, as an interactional process system which encompasses much more than the appropriate utilization of procedures, techniques, and interpretations, then he is really on his way. The construct "process" serves as a backdrop against which clinical phenomena can be viewed in their dynamic, economic, structural, and adaptational perspectives, and become units in a behavioral pattern in which analyst and patient play instrumental roles (Fleming and Benedek 1966).

Leichter (1962, p.5) has recently suggested that the leader should bring himself and his own reactions into the training situation. Utilization of the dynamics which result from this in the training session can "enable student participants and the leader to obtain a deeper understanding of group therapy processes in general, as well as of their own and each other's functioning and patterns of relating in their respective groups." Leichter notes that this supervisory approach (experiential as opposed to dogmatic) had the effect of breaking into the student's parentbound, infantile image of an omnipotent authority figure. To the extent to which this occurred, it helped to reduce each therapist's own omnipotent strivings, and this, in turn, freed their group therapy patients to use their inner resources more creatively in the therapeutic process.

At this time, it might be profitable to concretize some of the points that have been made, by examining the climate and content of a particular supervisory session.

I had just been appointed director of group therapy at a large local agency. One of my functions was to supervise three workers in group therapy. During the first two sessions, I felt there was a definite resistance to my approach. The workers did not seem receptive to the use of current group process for the understanding of their cases, there was a strong reluctance to sharing personal thoughts and feelings, and a general tightness and lack of spontaneity in the air. Feeling the force of these negative reactions, I found myself becoming more didactic and "lectury" than I usually am, thereby cutting off more freewheeling individual participation. I approached the third session with some irritation and apparent counterresistance (I arrived ten minutes late).

Worker A began to present the first session of a mothers' group, where she served as a cotherapist (her partner was not able to come to our meeting because of a conflicting schedule). She described the early part of the session as revolving around themes of despondency and futility. Questions such as, "How long will it be before we see improvement?," "How long do we have to be here?" alternated with frustrating stories by parents overwhelmed by how to deal with their problem children. Worker A said that she tended to take a somewhat passive role in relation to her cotherapist, who met many of the questions with lengthy, literal answers ("Group therapy takes time, maybe two years to work," etc.). She also observed that several of the women seemed to take a more optimistic view of the progress they had made through individual therapy, and the cotherapist interpreted this as an avoidance of their real disappointment in being unable to handle their children better. All of this was reported in a matter-of-fact monotone, with no apparent resentment or strong difference of opinion on the part of the presenter.

After about ten minutes of this, Workers B and C began to press Worker A about whether she wasn't perhaps quite angry at the cotherapist. They challenged her surface placidity and were sceptical regarding her seeming contentment with the passive role. The behavior of Workers B and C was in sharp contrast to the way they had acted in the past. They were much more "off the cuff," spoke more aggressively, showed a greater degree of certainty perceptiveness, and managed to create a sense of aliveness in the room. The only qualifying factor I felt was their need to glance at me, apparently to reassure themselves that they were on the right track.

About this time, I made my first few interventions. I suggested that there seemed to be a number of separation problems operating simultaneously. (1) The patients' surface complaints ("How long do we have to come?") reflected early reactive defenses against dependency on the therapist and other group members. (2) The manifest content of the patients' disappointments in being able to handle their children properly also suggested an overidentification with those children and an inability to see them as separate individuals with their own feelings and preferences. By binding the children to them and then feeling trapped by guilt and anger, the patients had put themselves in a paradoxical straitjacket. (3) By not being assertive in the group, Worker A was subordinating herself to the male cotherapist. Her fear of individuating was rationalized by a pseudodeference to his maleness ("I don't mind his taking over; men are more active and I'm more passive.") I wondered whether she wasn't appeasing her dread of being independent by abdicating masochistically to his superior wisdom while secretly feeling competitive and hateful toward him. (4) The male cotherapist's minimization and perfunctory handling of apparent gross misstatements on the part of the patients encouraged an unnecessary dependency. By focusing on pathology and emphasizing their frustration and disappointments, the cotherapist was widening the gap between himself (health, in control) and them (sick, helpless), and was discouraging the development of genuine autonomy and interdependence.

After some discussion, I drew the group's attention to what was happening in the room (the new freedom of interaction and participation). I wondered whether this didn't represent a constructive way of disengaging from the old passive, frightened, symbiotic-dependent attitude toward me. The furtive glances were interpreted as "I wonder how far we dare go."

Suddenly, Worker A remembered a dream she had prior to the group session. "I was hugging the cotherapist and felt very close to him right after the session. Then I had a feeling of self-disgust." I told Worker A that she had spontaneously hugged me after our last session but that I drew back inside, not trusting what looked like a warm, friendly overture. Worker A's associations to this were, "I guess I'm a very envious, ambitious person, but I don't like to show it. I keep the aggressive side of myself under wraps. I want to look feminine to disarm people. I want to get what wisdom I can from people so I play dumb—sweet, reasonable, and quiet. I think the dream means that I make myself part of people, I blend in with them to steal from them, and then I feel shitty into the bargain."

Now Worker B told about her previous experience as a cotherapist. "We worked for two years without ever discussing the fact that I was black and he was white. I think my speaking up today was my way of showing you (the supervisor) that I didn't want this to happen again. I want to be able to confront you but I guess I'm afraid of you. You know so much."

Worker C began to get restless and distracted. "I can't stand talking about other people when they're not here. You (Workers A and B) aren't being fair critizing them when they're not here." I interrupted at this moment and paraphrased what was being said in separation terms ("We shouldn't be separate people who can talk and act as we please"). The ghost of the others—the parents—always has to be hanging over us."). In response to this, Workers A, B, and C commented on the fact that it was not so much that they felt guilty about discussing an absent member, but that they felt an impassable gap in approaching him when he was present. There was a consensus that Mr. X was "hard to talk to." (But if we can't talk straight to colleagues, how can we talk to patients or expect them to talk to us?)

Now the conversation began to drift away from the business at hand. The previous Tuesday, these same workers had both timidly and provocatively (by asking at the last moment) approached the administration about getting time off for anti-Vietnam demonstrations on Moratorium day.

We should really unionize here but there's too much dissension. We can't get together, we're not organized or militant enough." I began to interpret this content in terms of our original case discussion. The issue as I saw it was what conditions have to operate in order for children (workers) to feel strong enough to deal sensibly with parental authority (administration). Is it possible to ask for what you want and say what you feel without manipulating, ingratiating, or feeling self-righteously exploited? These comments led Worker A to wonder out loud if she could differ publicly with her cotherapist, even (God forbid) in front of the group. Workers B and C chimed in at this point and said they were going to take a chance with me right now. "What you have to say is good but you sometimes sound as though if we don't accept it, we're no good— stupid maybe. I wonder whether we didn't stay quiet to punish you and make you feel stupid." I responded by saying there were certain times when "I felt very much alone, as if I was making a speech to an empty house." As an aside, I mentioned that it didn't feel that way today. "As a matter of fact I'm feeling a lot of contact today, like I'm really being myself and it feels good." Workers A, B, and C now began to share in-group secrets with me. It turned out that I had been given as a sop to them. "The administration here has a traditional analytic approach. They don't want group therapy, they only give it lip service. They brought you in to shut us up. Their intake policies are ridiculous as far as group therapy is concerned. They eliminate nine-tenths of the patients and see group as a place to cut down on the waiting list or get rid of unwanted patients." I related these comments to the silent war that existed between us during the first two sessions, and I also questioned whether this didn't have significant implications for understanding some of Worker A's problems in dealing with her group more effectively. Apparently I was seen as an extension of the workers' helplessness and futility, coming around to stimulate interest in group, while the truth was, from their point of view, I was foiled from the beginning. I now saw the worker's passive resistance as a suspicious (but somewhat realistic) refusal to bite at something fresh because beneath it all they knew that there was no chance of success. The facts about the administration policies I hadn't known about, but I was aware of having succeeded a rather prominent group therapist, as director of group therapy at this agency. I suppose I had a fear of not being able to live up to his reputation and thereby disappointing the workers. My insecurity must have conveyed itself in the form of trying to control, giving aggressive, enlightening, rock'm-sock'm interpretations, and generally trying to compete with an ego ideal that I couldn't possibly match. My ambivalent attempt to fuse with this personified ideal (my predecessor) found life in my unsuccessful attempts to get the supervisory group to merge with me, to follow my style, to submit themselves to my pronouncements, and thereby validate my worth and my identity. The supervisory session ended with a short didactic discussion of the conflict between wanting to lose oneself in the protective omnipotence of another compared to the loneliness of a positive, independent stand.

Throughout this chapter, I have tried to explore and illustrate the dynamics of the supervisory experience, in terms not so much of the content particulars as on the subtle shifts in the interpersonal meanings of communication processes. Birdwhistell (1959, p. 104) has gone so far as to suggest that "an individual does not communicate; he engages in or becomes part of communication. He may move, or make words.... but he does not communicate. He may see, he may hear, smell, taste, or feel—but he does not communicate. In other words he does not originate communication; he participates in it." In a similar fashion, supervision is not a simple linear mode of student presentation followed by supervisor's intervention, leading to further student presentation or pause for questioning of what the supervisor meant. Supervision is a system that is only to be comprehended on a transactional level. Future research in this area would do well to investigate just how the student analyst projects his countertransference onto the supervisory group, and how the induced reactions in the listeners (the supervisory group) can be used to recapture in very vivid fashion the atmosphere surrounding the analyst and the patient in session together. The answer to such questions would clarify some of the existing theoretical confusion regarding internalizations, identifications, and introjections. This approach of participating leadership and the free use of the process emerging in the supervisory session help to dispel the omnipotent parental transference image and seem to lead to increased empathy, responsiveness, perceptivity, and intuition in trainees.

Conclusion

In conclusion, let me summarize the following points that have been made throughout this book:

Alternative techniques can have value to a group if they're used appropriately, have relevance, and meet the ongoing therapeutic needs of each individual.

On the other hand, these new methodologies can become very convenient vehicles for resistance against tolerating and dealing with anxiety. If we fulfill patients' wishes for immediate gratification by reaching for gimmicks that provide "quickie" solutions, then working through is not accomplished and conflict is circumvented.

In light of the universal transference wish for a magical, nurturant mother, the therapist should be aware of the dynamic meaning that is often hidden behind a patient's request for the introduction of new techniques (e.g., "My friend's group is using Gestalt; can we try it here?" "Do you know any encounter games? I hear they get down to the gut level. Our group is too intellectual and boring").

In the use of these newer modalities, the conscientious therapist must guard against two major countertransferential tendencies:

1. In order to maintain the image of the "good mother," the therapist may be tempted to be very active, exciting, giving,

innovative, and protective. His liberal employment of new techniques is designed to demonstrate his nurturant qualities, to reduce group and individual tension, anxiety, and discontent, and to head off any patient's thoughts that the "grass might be greener" in another group.

2. In order to avoid the image of the "bad mother," the therapist may feel compelled to control, dominate, and regulate. His presence and participation tend to overshadow the promising of patient-to-patient involvement. This need to be "the master hand" inhibits spontaneity and fosters dependency. The analysis of group process is severely curtailed because the out-of-proportion therapist input contaminates the natural flow of interactions.

Despite the potential drawbacks of structured group procedures, it is the author's final estimate that significant benefit can be derived by the measured use of them. The true value of these promising innovations awaits further experimentation and research.

Appendix
On Being in Group:
Principles and Procedures

What is Group Psychotherapy?

The process by which individual difficulties in living are observed and understood within a milieu involving interaction with other individuals. This process includes the mutual study by therapist and group members of all phenomenon emerging in the group. Typical of such material are dissociative reactions; tendencies toward alienation, isolation and exclusion; pairing and multiple alignments; disjunctive transactions between self and others; transferential responses, blocks in expressing emotions, insensitivity to feelings and needs of others, the emergence in transactional behavior in the here and now of unconscious and preconscious sexual and aggressive fantasy content, attribution of non-tolerated innercontents from self to others (that's you not me etc.); and repetitions of nonadaptive past response patterns within the group.

Why a Group?

Often the experience of stereophonic (multiple) feedback and consensual validation of feelings, of insights, is far more supportive,

260 ACTIVE TECHNIQUES AND GROUP PSYCHOTHERAPY

real, and growth producing than in the one-to-one relationship of individual treatment. In addition, some of the necessary working through in therapy can only take place in a reconstructed peer group atmosphere. In effect, the group acts as a new socializing force leading to more 'present' as opposed to anachronistic values and standards, to a realignment of expectations regarding self and others. Also, the reaction provided by multiple contact in a group is often more profound and more integrative than in a one-to-one setting where it is either my head-or-yours.

How Does a Group Work?

A group depends on several factors: the presence of a supportive atmosphere for self-exposure, a variety of members with a range of life experience to be shared, the development of common goals toward which the group moves, and in addition, a sense of cohesiveness or unification in purpose and motivation, the participation of a trained leader, the agreement of all in the group to adhere to the conventions, goals, and underlying philosophy of investigative psychotherapy.

What Are the Goals of Group Therapy?

Group therapy seeks to foster personal growth by acquiring insight into hitherto unconscious and selectively inattended operations, to test here-and-now reality against previously unexposed fantasy about self and others, to learn new modalities of establishing closeness, separateness and straightness in dealings with others, and in addition, to broaden the scope of inquiry into transference and interpersonal behavior beyond that of individual treatment.

What Sort of Commitment Do I Have to Make to Join the Group?

All the members are asked to commit themselves to a minimum period of eleven months. Whenever possible, no admissions will be made except at the onset of the treatment year (September to July). Moreover, no new admissions will be made without discussion by the group. And persons terminating are asked to discuss the issue with the group before crystallizing this decision.

Can I Be In a Group Without Being in Individual Treatment?

Yes, if the group therapist feels that individual therapy is not indicated. However, no one will be accepted into a group without having had a course of individual treatment and without adequate screening. In addition, if the therapist should decide that further individual treatment is indicated, he may request that the individual in question obtain it. Referral to another private therapist or to a clinic will then be made. In the event that the member does not elect further individual work, and the issue is not resolved, the therapist has the prerogative of discharging the individual from the group.

What is a Group Therapist?

A group therapist is a trained mental health professional, usually either a licensed psychiatrist-physician, licensed clinical psychologist or certified psychiatric social worker. In addition to the prescribed training in these disciplines, a group therapist must meet the qualifications of the American Group Psychotherapy Association. This means completion of seminars, supervision, and personal group therapy. In large urban centers, the majority of group therapists are also trained psychoanalysts. While ancillary personnel (psychiatric nurses, social psychologists, special education teachers) may do group therapy, they may do so only under supervision of a qualified professional. Many others do attempt group therapy but this is unethical. New York State is currently formulating legislation to enforce the ethical code outlined above.

Is the Therapist a Part of the Group?

Yes, but his or her function is different from that of other members. He is a participant observer who is not present to resolve his or her own personal difficulties in living. Thus, on the basis of clinical judgment the therapist may elect to reveal feelings or other relevant personal content but may also elect not to do so on the basis of clinical formulations. This is similar to the present convention practiced in individual treatment. The therapist is present for the group and not vice versa. The therapist's main functions are to provide support, to clarify and to interpret process or content, to act as a leader in locomoting the group toward its goals, and to facilitate the group's development of its cohesiveness. As the leader, the therapist sets the conventions and structure of the group, although these may be opened to discussion with the entire group.

Are There Any Explicit Conventions to Which Members of the Group Must Adhere?

Yes, a group cannot function without an atmosphere of absolute confidentiality. Without this it becomes impossible for trust— already a salient issue in any interpersonal situation—to be established or maintained. This means that *no* communication about the group or its members is permitted outside the session, by any member to another member, or to a third party. This includes *all* of the group contents—even the names or occupations of its members. Absolutely no discussion of any kind is allowed. Violation of this rule will result in immediate discharge from the group, by the leader.

A second convention pertains to outside contact other than that described above. It is considered unduly restrictive to prohibit contact among members outside of the group. However, several considerations should be borne in mind. The group is not a social situation. The purpose of the group is not to form friendships. In fact, such outside contact often hinders progress both in the group and in individual sessions. Members who undertake such contact should be aware that they *may* be expressing unconscious material actually belonging to the treatment situation. They should recognize the risks incumbent in such contact, and be fully prepared to scrutinize this contact with the group. It is known that outside contact dilutes the material usually brought into the group. Actually, contact is often employed unconsciously to funnel content *out* of the group. Thus, at the minimum, members are asked to bring into the group the interactions which occur on the outside. Moreover, the following is a rigid rule of the group: no sexual contact between any members of the group is permitted. Violation of this rule will result in immediate discharge from the group, just as will violation of the confidence rule.

What is the Policy Regarding Fees?

The fee for group therapy is $60 per month. Statements are usually rendered at the end of the month or beginning of the following month. All statements are due within thirty days except by explicit arrangement with the therapist. Failure to meet this obligation will result in termination from the group.

References

Abraham, J. (1949). *Mental Health in Nursing*. Washington, D.C.: Catholic University Press.

Adler, A. (1927). *Understanding Human Nature*. New York: Greenberg.

Akaret, R. (1972). *Not By Words Alone*. New York: Peter Wyden.

Assagioli, R. (1965). *Psychosynthesis: A Manual of Principles and Techniques*. New York: Hobbs, Dorman.

Bach, G. (1954). *Intensive Group Psychotherapy*. New York: Ronald.

————(1967). Marathon group dynamics: dimensions of helpfulness. *Psychological Reports* 20:1147-1158.

Bennis, W. and Shephard, H. (1956). A theory of group development. *Human Relations* 9:415-437.

————(1964). Patterns and and Vicissitudes in T-Group Development. In *T-Group Theory and Laboratory Method,* ed. L. Bradford, J. Gibb, and K. Benne, pp. 80-135. New York: Wiley.

Bion, W. (1961). *Experience in Group*. New York: Basic Books.

Birdwhistell, R. (1959). Contributions of linguistic-kinesic studies to the understanding of schizophrenia. In *Schizophrenia: An Integrated Approach*, ed. Alfred Auerback, pp. 99-123. New York: Ronald.

Blatner, H. (1973). *Psychodrama, Role-Playing, and Action Methods*. Belmont, California: Privately published.

Buber, M. (1970). *I and Thou*. New York: Scribner.

Campbell, P., and Dunnette, M. (1968). Effectiveness of T-group experience in managerial training and development. *Psychology Bulletin* 70:73-104.

Cartwright, D. (1951). Achieving change in people: some applications of group dynamic thought. *Human Relations* 4: 381-392.

Clark, J. (1967). Toward a theory and practice of religious experience. In *Challenges of Humanistic Psychology,* ed. J. F. T. Bugental, pp. 253-258. New York: McGraw-Hill.

Coffey, H. (1952). Socio and psychological group process: interventive concepts. *Journal of Sociological Issues* 8:65-74.

Coler, J. (1973). Unpublished personal correspondence with the author.

Corsini, R. (1957). *Methods of Group Psychotherapy.* Chicago: William James Press.

————— (1966). *Role-Playing in Psychology.* Chicago: Moline.

Culbert, S. (1970). Accelerated laboratory learning through a phase progression model for trainer interaction. *Journal of Applied Behavioral Science* 6:21-38.

DeSoille, L. (1965). *The Directed Daydream.* New York: Psychosynthesis Research Foundation.

Dickoff, H., and Lakin, M. (1963). Patient's views of group psychotherapy: retrospections and introspections. *International Journal of Group Psychotherapy* 13:6173.

Elkstein, R., and Wallerstein, R. (1958). *The Teaching and Learning of Psychotherapy.* New York: Basic Books.

Elliot, J. (1971). *Circle Voicing.* Group Leaders Workshop, 1.

Ellis, A. (1958). Rational psychotherapy. *Journal of General Psychology* 59:35-49.

Erikson, E. (1959). *Identity and the Life Cycle.* New York: International Universities Press.

Fagen, J., and Shepherd, I. (1970). *Gestalt Therapy Now.* Palo Alto, California: Science and Behavior Books.

Fairbairn, W. (1952). *Psychoanalytic Studies of the Personality.* London: Tavistock.

Fleming, J., and Benedek, T. (1966). *Psychoanalytic Supervision.* New York: Grune and Stratton.

Foulkes, S. (1969). Meeting of the group analytic society. *Group Analysis* 1:15-23.

Gendlin, E. (1969a). The experiential response. *Psychotherapy* 5:28-37.

————— (1969b). Focusing. *Psychotherapy* 6:4-15.

Gibb, J. (1964a). Climate for trust formation. In *T-Group Theory and Laboratory Method,* eds. L. P. Bradford, J. R. Gibb, and K. D. Benne, pp. 279-309. New York: Wiley.

—— (1964b). The present status of T-Group Theory. In *T-Group Theory and Laboratory Method,* eds. L. P. Bradford, J. R. Gibb, and K. D. Benne, pp. 279-309. New York: Wiley.

Guntrip, H. (1968). *Schizoid Phenomena, Object Relations and the Self.* New York: International Universities Press.

Heimann, P. (1956). Dynamics of transference interpretations. *International Journal of Psychoanalysis* 37:48-61.

Isakower, O. (1957). Problems of supervision. Report to the Curriculum Committee of the New York Psychoanalytic Institute. Unpublished.

Joel, W., and Shapiro, D. (1950). Some principles and procedures for group psychotherapy. *Journal of Psychology* 29:77-88.

Kadis, A. (1962). Failures in group therapy. Paper presented at AGPA conference.

Kernberg, O. (1966). Structural derivates of object relationships. *International Journal of Psycho-Analysis,* 47:236-253.

King, C. (1959). Activity group therapy with a schizophrenic boy—follow-up two years later. *International Journal of Psychotherapy* 9:184-194.

Kingsley, L. (1968). A preliminary report of a test for evaluation and prognosis in group psychotherapy. *Group Psychoanalysis and Process* 1:71-84.

Kohut, H. (1971). *The Analysis of the Self.* New York: International University Press.

Leichter, E. (1962). Utilization of group process in the training and supervision of group therapists in a social agency setting. Paper presented at AGPA Conference.

Leopold, H. (1957). Selection of patients for group psychotherapy. *American Journal of Psychotherapy* 11:634-637.

Leuner, H. (1966). *The Use of Initiated Symbol Projection in Psychotherapy.* New York: Psychosynthesis Foundation.

Levitsky, H., and Perls, F. (1969). *The Theory and Technique of Gestalt Therapy.* Lafayette, California: Real People Press.

Lieberman, M., and Yalom, I. (1971). A study of encounter group casualties. *Archives of General Psychiatry* 54:116-123.

Liff, Z. (1970). The group encounter movement and group psychotherapy. *AGPA Newsletter,* pp. 14-16.

Luft, J. (1963). *The Johari Window in Group Processes.* Palo Alto, California: National Press.

Malamud, D., and Machover, S. (1965). *Toward Self-Understanding: Group Techniques in Self-Confrontation.* Chicago, Illinois: Charles C Thomas.

Martin, E., and Hill, W. (1951). Toward a theory of group development: six phases of therapy group development. *International Journal of Group Psychotherapy* 7:20-30.

Mill, C., and Ritvo, M. (1969). Potentialities and pitfalls of nonverbal techniques. *Human Relations Training News* 13:4.

Mintz, E. (1969). Touch and the psychoanalytic tradition. *Psychoanalytic Review* 56:3.

―――― (1971). *Marathon Groups, Reality and Symbol.* New York: Appleton-Century-Crofts.

Moreno, J. (1956). Psychodrama. In *Contemporary Psychotherapists Examine Themselves*, ed. W. Wolff. Springfield, Illinois: Charles C Thomas.

Mosak, H. (1958). Early recollections as a projective technique. *Journal of Projective Technique* 22:303-331.

Moustakas, C. (1968). *Individuality and Encounter: A Brief Journey into Loneliness and Encounter Groups.* Cambridge, Mass: Howard Doyle.

Mullan, H., and Rosenbaum, M. (1962). *Group Psychotherapy.* New York: Free Press of Glencoe.

Neto, P. (1970). Group analytic commentary. *Group Analysis* 3:171-174.

Olivera, W. (1968). The analyst in the group analytic situation. *Group Psychoanalysis and Process* 1:85-99

Otto, H., and Mann, J. (1968). *Ways of Growth.* New York: Grossman.

Papp, P., Silverstein, O., and Carter, E. (1973). Family sculpting in preventive work and "well families." *Family Process* 12:197-212.

Parker, S. (1958). Leadership patterns in a psychiatric ward. *Human Relations* 11:287-301.

Perls, F. (1969). *Gestalt Therapy Verbatim.* Lafayette, California: Real People Press.

Rabin, H. (1970). Selection procedures in group psychotherapy. *International Journal of Group Psychotherapy* 20:135-145.

Racker, H. (1968). *Transference and Countertransference.* New York: International Universities Press.

Rhyne, J. (1969). Art therapy. *Group Leaders Workshop* 5:1-8.

Rhyne, J., and Vich, M. (1967). Psychological growth and the use of art materials: small group experiments with adults. *Journal of Humanistic Psychology* 1:163-170.

Riviere, J. (1936). A contribution to the analysis of the negative therapeutic reaction. *International Journal of Psycho-Analysis* 17:304-316.

Roffenbuck, A. (1971). Your mother's face/father's face. *Group Leaders Workshop* 9:1.

Rogers, C. (1951). *Client-Centered Therapy.* Boston: Houghton Mifflin.

Schutz, W. (1967). *Joy.* New York: Grove Press.

Segal, H. (1964). *Introduction to the Work of Melanie Klein.* London: Heinemann.

Simkin, J. (1968). *An Introduction to the Theory of Gestalt Therapy.* Cleveland: Gestalt Institute of Cleveland.

Shellow, R., Ward, J., and Rubenfeld, S. (1958). Group therapy and the institutionalized delinquent. *International Journal of Group Psychotherapy* 8:265-275.

Smith, R. (1970). Encounter therapies. *International Journal of Group Psychotherapy* 20:192-209.

Spotnitz, H. (1968). Discussion. *International Journal of Group Psychotherapy* 28:236-239.

Stevens, J. (1971). *Awareness*. Moab, Utah: Real People Press.

Stoller, F. H. (1968). Accelerated interaction. *International Journal of Group Psychotherapy* 18:220-235.

Stoute, A. (1950). Implementation of group interpersonal relationships through psychotherapy. *Journal of Psychology* 30:145-156.

Sturm, I. (1965). The behavioristic aspect of psychodrama. *Group Psychotherapy* 18:50-64.

Sullivan, H. (1953). *Interpersonal Theory of Psychiatry*. New York: Norton.

Taylor, F. (1958). The therapeutic factors in group analytic treatment. *Journal of Mental Science* 96:976-999.

Thorpe, J., and Smith, B. (1953). Phases in group development in treatment of drug addicts. *International Journal of Group Psychotherapy* 3:66-78.

Truax, C., and Carkhuff, R. (1967) *Toward Effective Counselling and Psychotherapy: Training and Practice*. Chicago: Aldine.

Welch, G. (1973). Core connections. *Group Leaders Workshop* 14:48-52.

Wells, E. (1953). *What to Name the Baby: A Treasury of Names*. Garden City: Garden City Books.

Whitaker, D., and Lieberman, M. (1964). *Psychotherapy Through the Group Process*. New York: Atherton Press.

Winnicott, D. (1965). *The Maturational Processes and the Facilitating Environment*. New York: International Universities Press.

Wolf, A. (1949). The psychoanalysis of groups. *American Journal of Psychotherapy* 3:525-541.

Yalom, I. (1970). *The Theory and Practice of Group Psychotherapy*. New York: Basic Books.

Ziferstein, I., and Grotjahn, M. (1956). Group dynamics of acting out in analytic group psychotherapy. *International Journal of Group Psychotherapy* 7:77-85.

Index